THE WAY TO THE KINGDOM

Being

DEFINITE AND SIMPLE INSTRUCTIONS FOR SELF-
TRAINING AND DISCIPLINE, ENABLING THE
EARNEST DISCIPLE TO FIND THE KINGDOM
OF GOD AND HIS RIGHTEOUSNESS

By the Writer of

THE IMPERSONAL LIFE, THE TEACHER,
WEALTH, BROTHERHOOD, THE WAY
OUT, THE WAY BEYOND

Joseph Benner

Martino Publishing
Mansfield Centre, CT
2010

Martino Publishing
P.O. Box 373,
Mansfield Centre, CT 06250 USA

www.martinopublishing.com

ISBN 1-57898-981-7

© *2010 Martino Publishing*

Cover design by T. Matarazzo

Printed in the United States of America On 100% Acid-Free Paper

THE WAY TO THE KINGDOM

Being

DEFINITE AND SIMPLE INSTRUCTIONS FOR SELF-
TRAINING AND DISCIPLINE, ENABLING THE
EARNEST DISCIPLE TO FIND THE KINGDOM
OF GOD AND HIS RIGHTEOUSNESS

By the Writer of

THE IMPERSONAL LIFE, THE TEACHER,
WEALTH, BROTHERHOOD, THE WAY
OUT, THE WAY BEYOND

Joseph Benner

Sun Pub. Co.
Akron, Ohio
1932

CONTENTS

CONTENTS

THE WAY TO THE KINGDOM

CHAPTER 1

"Seek Ye First the Kingdom"

THESE words are addressed to those who are seeking the way into the Kingdom of God—the Kingdom where a Great Love and Wisdom, the serving and the inspiring of others, and the utter forgetfulness of self, are the natural life of everyone who dwells therein.

If you who read have reached that stage on your journey through life where the world without can offer you nothing that will stay your efforts to find that Kingdom, and you welcome any directions that will clearly point you there, then you are ready for these words, and they will be to you a quickening power that will hasten you on your way and perhaps will enable you speedily to reach the goal.

One traveling in a new country is always better able to make his way if provided with maps and information about the conditions to be met and the requirements to be observed along the route. Therefore, we will first try to map out for you the various stages of the journey into the Kingdom, and to tell you of some of the conditions through which you will pass, and what will be required if you expect to reach your journey's end without mishap or undue delay.

This naturally is no new knowledge being offered you, but is what has been learned and tabulated from the experience of many who have passed over this route—the one over which we would direct you, and which is the narrow and only way that leads straight into the Kingdom.

All may essay the journey into that far country. Indeed, many have started more or less consciously on it, but are now loitering on the way, enticed by the myriad allurements of the senses, the emotions, or the intellect, and by yielding to the appeals of the self to halt and enjoy. Only the few, the very few so far, the *earnest and determined ones,* and for whom these words are intended, are definitely consecrated to winning the goal. These it is our purpose to help reach it quickly, and to inspire them to help recall the loiterers to their objective and speed them on their way; for it is vitally important at this time that every soul seeking the light but whose human self is wandering in darkness, be led back upon the path.

If you are one of the earnest ones, you will recognize much of what follows as part of your own past experience. Others, it will help to understand the meaning of that through which they are passing. This journey into the Kingdom, sometimes called "The Path," is symbolized in the allegory of the Prodigal Son, who wasted his substance in riotous living and, when he had spent all and could nowhere get anything to eat, remembered that the hired servants in his father's home had plenty of bread and to spare; and he awoke to who and what he was, and rose up and said, "I will go to my father and will say unto him, 'Father, I have sinned against heaven and in thy sight; make me as one of thy hired servants.' "

The Prodigal's journey back to his father's home was not as speedy as the allegory seems to depict. Jesus mentioned none of the vicissitudes of the way; He only wanted to show that the Father is always waiting and can see us coming afar off, and will lovingly welcome us and shower upon us all the good things of life when we come back consciously into His home and love.

This journey, in reality, is a long one, covering a greater or less period of years, oftentimes several lifetimes, depending upon the nature and soul status of the individual. The early stage of the journey is evidenced by a spiritual awakening similar to that of the Prodigal Son, followed by an intense and eager thirst for knowledge of the realities of life; a turning away from former sense attractions and obeying an insistent urge from within to seek Truth wherever it can be found. In this stage the urge is largely unconscious to the seeker, especially as to its meaning and purpose; only the insistent desire *to know* being felt and that desire has to be satisfied.

Gradually, through the deeper knowledge of the meaning of life gained as a result of the cumulative force of this urge, something unfolds in the con-

sciousness. It can be likened to the life within the
stalk, concentrating, as it were, upon the building
and forming of the bud, pushing out, expanding,
swelling itself, becoming big with that which is unfolding, evolving from itself. It can also be likened
to the conception and growth of the child in the
womb of the mother, and approaching the birthing
time.

For that which is felt by the seeker is indeed a
birthing—it is the stirring of the Christ-child within,
the life that has concentrated in your part of the
human stalk now grown to the stage where it can
unfold its true nature—your Love nature, and can
come forth and blossom in your life as a compelling
desire to help others and especially to give to them
of the truths you have found.

Such is the sure outcome of such seeking—for
those who are not seeking merely for self but to use
the knowledge gained for the good that may be done
with it. The Christ-child is born in the heart, the
bud opens into the blossom, and the fragrance and
beauty of the life within shows and proves itself to
all who are near.

This is the first stage of the journey back to the
Father's house. It is called the stage of the Aspirant
or the Neophyte. It is necessarily a long and very
gradual stage, starting with some definite experience—perhaps a physical healing by a Metaphysi-
cian, the death of one very dear, or some extreme
mental suffering—which are the birth-pangs preceding the awakening of the Spiritual nature. With

such there is born the urge to know for one's self, and after many years of following this urge it develops into a final push which results in an expansion of consciousness and opens up a new world, one of which previously the seeker had been wholly unaware, although it had always been present awaiting his recognition.

There were many soul experiences leading up to this point, many steps along the Path, many vicissitudes and trials, and much mental suffering over leaving behind worn-out joys and useless habits and possessions acquired in the old state of consciousness. This may have resulted in decided changes in outer conditions and things; wealth gained by selfish, ruthless methods; health always before natural and unconsidered,—these now taken away, and their lack a constant source of concern. All or many of the old states of mind given place to new ones, thus prepared the way for the new birth.

From all this seeking, most students think that what was gained was merely some knowledge of life's realities. But the gaining of any Truth avails little unless the living of that Truth and the building of it into soul consciousness has become the supreme desire of the Aspirant. When such a desire has been awakened, the soul dedicates itself to living a life of Truth, or consecrates itself to God or Christ in fervent prayer and supplication, after which sooner or later the birth takes place.

At the time the Aspirant most likely will not be aware of what is happening, but he will soon realize an increase of inspiration; a coming in touch with others who will open up new and higher fields of study; a clearer grasping of essential truths, and a discarding of the unimportant; and he will realize God and Christ in some intangible way as being much closer, more real, more approachable and loving. For They have in very truth heard his supplication, have accepted his dedication, and are taking him at his word. He has now deliberately consecrated himself to the Higher Life and has set his feet definitely on the Path. The finding of the Kingdom has become the goal, even if he may not be fully conscious of it in his brain mind.

After this new birth, this dedication, the Aspirant enters the second stage of the journey—he now becomes a Disciple *on probation*. In other words, he is given his chance to prove whether he is worthy and qualified to enter the Kingdom.

Our Immediate Purpose

As our goal is the finding of the Kingdom, the aim and purpose of those back of this Work is to help and encourage all earnest seekers by providing the necessary instructions for self-discipline and training that will enable them to attain *spiritual enlightenment individually*. The Master within the heart of each Aspirant has called him to come within and follow Him. To all who follow and obey, His Knowledge, Love and Power are ever available and will be given freely to those who no longer seek anything for self, but only to help and serve their fellow men.

Spiritual enlightenment can be gained only upon the straight and narrow path that leads to the Kingdom. Therefore the seeking of the Kingdom must be made the *first* thing in your life; that sets your feet firmly upon the path. It is not impossible to find the Kingdom, no matter how long or how unsuccessfully you have sought in the past. All that it takes is earnest and determined effort under the guidance that will be given. But it must be the *first* and the *supreme* desire of your heart. No other desire can supersede it. You must want it more than any other thing in life. When that desire *has become supreme,* it will not be long, for all the Brothers in the Kingdom nearest you will be with you in your search, helping, inspiring, and strengthening you in every possible way.

THE KINGDOM

We will try to give you a glimpse of what the Kingdom will mean to you when you find it—not what you will find there, but how you may know when you have found it.

We all know that Jesus found it, for He tells of it with the authority of one who knows. We speak of Him as Jesus, the Christ. The Christ, or the Christos, is a title given to one who has reached a certain Spiritual unfoldment. It means "The Anointed One." We know from certain statements of Jesus that most of His teaching was done while in the Christ Consciousness. Whenever He used the words, "*I am,*" in the peculiar way He did, such as, "*I am the Way, the Truth, and the Life. No*

*man cometh unto the Father but by Me." "I am
the vine," "I am the door,"* etc., we know it was not
from the human mind that Jesus spoke, but from
the Holy Spirit within Him, or from His Christ
Consciousness. We are told that when Jesus was
baptized in the River Jordan, the Holy Spirit descended upon Him as a dove and abode with Him.

All these experiences will come to every seeker of
the Kingdom sooner or later. After the Christ-child
born in the Aspirant is grown to maturity of Discipleship during the testing and proving period of
the Probationary stage, and has come to the Jordan
state (beyond which lies the "Promised Land") he
is ready for baptism and to begin his lifework as an
Accepted Disciple. Then will be given him the
baptism of the Holy Spirit, during which the Spirit
of God, which means God's Consciousness, will descend and enter in and abide with the Disciple.
This Spirit is the Christos, and the Disciple becomes
the "Anointed One." Jesus was the "first fruit" of
them that slept.

Now the Christ Consciousness or the baptism of
the Holy Spirit must come to all before they can
enter the Kingdom. In fact, the Christ Consciousness gives the right of admission to the Kingdom,
and is the Consciousness of everyone who abides in
the Kingdom. And what is the nature of that Consciousness? It is *Divine Love* which must be born
in the heart of every seeker, must be nourished and
thrive and grow until it becomes the very life of
the Disciple. When in ripened maturity, after many

given opportunities have proven that Love is the *nature* of his soul and is not of the mind only, the Disciple is permitted to enter into the joy of His Lord, the Christ, and to abide with Him in the Kingdom of His Father's Consciousness.

All this may be beyond the present comprehension of some who read, but if something deep within impels you to seek out its real meaning, telling you that it is for you fully to know and to possess, then it is earnestly hoped you will obey, and nothing will be permitted to stop you until you have made His Consciousness your consciousness.

INNER WORK

By the foregoing you will perceive that this must be an *inner work* and, of necessity, an individual work; for no one can do it for you or can help you, other than to point out the way and explain the experiences through which you pass—if you cannot get their meaning *direct*. For remember, there is always One who is ready and waiting to explain and teach you all things—your own Higher Self, the I AM, the Christ of you, dwelling within your heart, in the Kingdom there.

We take it that all of you who read and are deeply interested are more or less acquainted with His Presence within you. If not, as we are going to speak much of Him from now on, we urge that you begin to learn to know Him intimately, if you wish fully to appreciate and profit by what is contained in these lessons. To that end we suggest a careful study of *"The Impersonal Life,"* for the consciousness from which its words were written is His Consciousness, which is also in you—is the Light which lighteth you, and from which consciousness each one of you may speak and teach your own self.

As a part of our work we purpose to bring out the *inner meaning* of certain teachings already given. All must admit that enough teachings have been given and are available to all who are ready for them. Comparatively few, however, are able to get more than an intellectual understanding of them as yet. It is only by opening up the *inner* meaning to the mind that the Spirit within is *quickened.*

All earnest ones, as they grow and unfold spiritually, through study and meditation, will receive guidance and instruction from their Higher Self in symbolic dreams and visions. They should keep a diary of such, writing down every spiritual experience, as they will prove of great value to the one receiving them when correctly interpreted. They will, in fact, aid in determining the stage on The Path of the soul to whom they are given. Assistance in the interpretation of such experiences will be gladly given on request.

The Plan

This being an Inner Work, no outer organization is necessary. As individuals come into the enlightenment that awaits, they will naturally enter into the realization of who they are and of what they are a part. That realization will show them that they are in very fact disciples of the Master, and that Master is even Christ, the Higher Self of them and of their brothers, and they will *know* that they are an integral part of the GREAT BROTHERHOOD of the Spirit of which He is the Supreme Head and Life. This finding and knowing the *real* Brotherhood of the Spirit that exists within and back of the personalities of their fellows is finding the Christ in His Kingdom, and this realization will prove to be a Haven of Refuge in which, while abiding in it, no outer force or circumstance can reach or affect them. Only when in this Haven can one know and be sure of the Master's Voice and can be led, taught, guarded and cared for by Him when necessary.

Our part is to help quicken all truly earnest ones into finding and entering this Haven of Refuge —the actual consciousness of the Kingdom of God and His righteousness, and to enlist them in His Service. This will link and bind them in *Spirit*, making them one in Christ. The only outer linking will be after the inner pattern. Wherever possible, Aspirants will form naturally into Groups for meditation and service. Each Group will thus be a Chalice serving as a cup or reservoir into which will be poured all the Love and Wisdom of the Master and of THE GREAT BROTHERHOOD, and which will flow—as water flows through a faucet turned on—to each Aspirant for use in Service as they consciously connect up with THE BROTHERHOOD of which they are a part.

The quickening of our younger brothers is our sole purpose in this book, and the carrying of the

Light of the Christ to all seekers wandering in the darkness of separation is our chief endeavor. But let none of us forget that we of ourselves can do nothing. Only as we give ourselves over wholly to the Father's will, being concerned only that we are letting Him lead and speak through us, permitting no thoughts to enter our minds that are not His thoughts, can we do His work as He intends it to be done.

Many have been expecting and longing to be given some real work, not realizing they have already been given it in the past; but because it was not something definite in the way of healing or helping others, and was instead a work of preparation, a learning to discipline and control the mind and the emotions so as to enable the Aspirant to enter the desire and mental planes of consciousness as master of self when necessary to go thence, they think they have accomplished nothing, and long for tasks for which they are not yet fitted.

It is all a part of the injunction, "Seek ye *first* the Kingdom, etc," for you cannot find the Kingdom until you are able to control those forces of your emotional and mental nature that heretofore had their way with you almost unopposed. If and when you are able to command, "Be *Still*, and know I Aм," and be instantly obeyed on all planes of consciousness, then and then only will you be able to do the work that will be given you; for then only can you work in the Consciousness and with the Power of Christ—the Master within.

There is a real work—much real work to do, and never doubt, when you have once proven your ability to do it and to subject your self and your whole nature to the Master's will, and when they have become an impersonal instrument which He can use, you will be given so much to do that there will be little time left to think of self and its concerns.

DEFINITE WORK

Daily meditation is the first and most important requisite of the Aspirant. No real progress can be made without it. To help prepare and start you on the right kind of meditation, study carefully and use often the Meditation No. 1, to be found in the appendix. In it is condensed the essence of Jesus' teaching, and there is nothing that will help you more to find the Loving Christ and His Kingdom within than its illuminating words.

This Work has in it no place for laggards or for the mentally lazy. It is only for those who are imbued with an unquenchable determination and a fiery zeal to find the Master and the Kingdom.

Many think they can contrive no regular time to meditate, but in bed after retiring or early in the morning are times always available if really sought, and are often most satisfactory. There will be no danger of falling asleep when the mind learns to obey you. Again, while doing simple tasks around the home or in the office or factory, real meditation can be done and most profitably. It is really possible at such times, as you will find, to "be in the world but not of it," for you can go in thought wherever you will, while your hands are busy at their regular work.

Instead of worrying about it, simply put it up to the Higher Self, stating that you earnestly desire the time and opportunity to do regular meditating, and if He sees you *really mean it and want it,* you will find it will be arranged for you in a most natural manner—if you leave it in His hands and trust it all to Him.

Therefore rouse yourself to action. The Kingdom is not for those who still crave for or are held by the allurements of the world, the flesh, or the devil—self. The time has come when all such must be left behind, if you would lift your heart and mind to Christ. When you have found—*earned*—Him, then you will join with the other Brothers of the Kingdom in helping those who will be sent to you also to find Him and THE BROTHERHOOD, of which you will then be a conscious integral part.

While meditating, an effort should always be made in the I AM consciousness to *command* the forces of the mind, the emotions, and the physical senses to be still and *know* that *You*—the *God of you*—speaks and *must be obeyed.*

Sooner or later, after persistent effort, you will realize that *you are that Consciousness,* and that these forces are listening to and obeying you. Then, *in that Consciousness,* you can continue speaking as in *"The Impersonal Life,"* and your mind will receive and accept what comes as from the God of you, and you will *know Who you are.*

CHAPTER 2

"THE LIGHT WHICH LIGHTETH EVERY MAN"

A THOUGHT FOR CHRISTMAS

IT IS fitting at the Christmas season, when all Christians are celebrating the birth of the Christ, that those traveling the journey to the Kingdom should strive to realize fully what that birth has meant and now means to each one who experienced it.

Therefore try to recall that experience in your life—when you first felt the quickening of the Christ-child (Love) in the womb of your heart, when it began to stir actively there, not only making you very conscious of its presence, but compelling you to cherish, serve, and worship it; until finally, when undergoing some deep, soul-stirring experience, the day of delivery came, and there was born from within a new consciousness—a yearning to love and bless and to help everyone to come into that new world of understanding you had entered, and which now is the all-compelling spirit of your life.

You will remember that this experience came when you were shepherding your thoughts during the night period, when all seemed most dark and you were sustained only by the faith born of your long seeking. It was then that a glow of wonderful light flooded your night of waiting, and a song as of angels filled your consciousness. In deepest humility you sought to know the meaning of it all, and you soon found there was cradled in your heart a tender, beautiful, all-compelling love, that from then on filled and possessed you, and gradually grew in power until it influenced and inspired much of your thinking, speech, and actions.

Surely at the Christmas season we should remember the birth of the Christ-child, especially now that we know that It is the actual love of our Father-God—His Holy Spirit, growing, thriving, working in our hearts, seeking to merge our whole nature—body, mind and soul—with His Nature, that He may without hindrance live His life in us, do His will in us, and be His Christ-self in us.

Ah, dear ones, let us not only remember, but let us open our hearts wide that He, the Blessed One, may come forth and possess us and do with us as He wills. May we dedicate ourselves wholly to Him, letting His Love be our life, and our bodies and brain minds His perfect means of expression.

It is true that some who read may deem the above but words, it having no real meaning for them, the Christ-child not yet having been quickened in their hearts. To such we would say with Jesus, *"Verily, verily I say unto thee, except a man be born again, he cannot see the Kingdom of God."* Like Nicodemus, they may be masters of Israel and have great occult knowledge of the law and of the inner worlds, but unless they are born of the water of

Divine Inspiration and of the spirit of Christ-Love, they can never find and enter the Kingdom.

In the preceding chapter, Aspirants were reminded of that point reached on the Path where they had more or less consciously renounced the old life and were quickened into a new consciousness; the Christ-child had been born in their hearts; the Prodigal had started on his return journey to his Father's house; the dedication of the Aspirant to the higher life had been registered and he had become a Disciple on Probation.

It was at this point that you actually started out to seek the Kingdom of God and His righteousness. Whether you were aware of it or not in your brain consciousness, your soul had unfolded to the stage where it saw its Father's house afar off; and now it no longer can find rest until it reaches home and can abide there forever.

Along with the birth of the love-nature there awakens the desire to serve selflessly, and from then on according to the extent that Love is permitted to grow and lead, will the Disciple gradually become aware of a voice within which speaks whenever it gets the attention of the conscious mind. It will be no audible voice, and there may be no actually heard words, but nevertheless something speaks within and the Disciple will hear and understand. He will also note that when he heeds and obeys a blessing in some form follows, but when he fails to obey the hints or "leadings" given, failure, trouble and often suffering result. Thus the Disciple gradually learns of his higher and inner nature, and that it is unmistakably related to Love; more and more he finds himself turning within and seeking to know more of this inner self and he strives to let it guide and direct him in all things.

As he thus definitely gives his allegiance to Love and to his better self, he is made aware of qualities in his lower nature rising unexpectedly to prominence and displaying elements of selfishness and baseness that surprise and startle him. For the lower self that had held a dominating part so long in his life is not yielding without a battle—in fact it is fighting for its very existence.

It is then you begin to realize that the Path upon which you have entered is not an easy one. The fact is, in the conquering of the lower self, you are assuming a task that will test you to the limit of your strength and endurance. But you will gradually discover that from the same source that comes the Voice will also come the strength needed to conquer and to sustain you along the way. Also you will learn that loving and selfless service releases the strength and gives the wisdom to meet every test, for while serving you are enlisted in the Cause of Brotherhood and in such work the Great Brotherhood of the Spirit always supplies all the wisdom and the strength needed to accomplish it.

For you who are truly seeking the Kingdom, the time has come to hear certain truths, to see if your Higher Self deems you ready to receive and accept

* Read in connection with the foregoing the first two chapters of "Brotherhood."

these truths and to make them a part of your soul consciousness. If so they will bring to you an illumination of understanding that will quicken your soul, free your mind from what has been holding you back perhaps for many lifetimes, and will consequently now permit you speedily to proceed on your journey.

But if you are not yet ready to accept these truths it is well, for your Higher Self has certain necessary experiences in store for you, from which He will be enabled later to teach you to accept them and to want to follow us on our way to the Kingdom.

Consider first the real meaning of these words spoken to His Disciples by the Christ of Jesus— *"I am the Way, the Truth, and the Life; no man cometh unto the Father but by Me."*

Can the *Divinity* within any man be reached by any but the Christ Way? These words of our Master tell us definitely, *No.*

Many of you who read may have come along the route of Theosophy, Rosicrucianism, Spiritualism, and other *occult* movements, and according to your study and understanding of what they teach you have an intellectual grasp of much knowledge of the constitution of man and of the Universe, of the laws of matter, and of the hidden side of life, which should be a great aid to you in governing your life and actions—up to a certain point. These. movements help man very considerably to know himself

and thereby enable him to gain mastery over qualities and elements in his nature whose influence before was not understood. Such knowledge should
dispose him to deal more kindly and justly with his
fellows who are of like nature. But does that always result in those who have all the knowledge
that these movements teach?

Those who gave this knowledge to the world
through these different movements are said to be
Masters of Wisdom, Adepts, Initiates, or at least
very learned Teachers. Unquestionably some of
them are of vast knowledge and powers, those who
have far outstripped ordinary humanity—Supermen
—our elder brothers, judging from what they taught
and what they know. It is their due that we honor,
revere and be grateful to them for all they have
taught us, and we certainly should strive to use the
knowledge gained wisely and for the good of all.

But who was the real teacher who pointed out in
the teachings that which you were to accept and
which to pass by? Who helped you to apply the
truths in the teaching to the experiences of life
through which you were led? And who guided and
chided and cautioned, and always held before your
mind's eye the ideal toward which your face has
ever been turned? Was there not One *within* you
who did all this, and Who has a purpose for you
and a part for you to play—when you are through
seeking without for what the world and its teachers
have to offer and you are ready to turn within and
get fully acquainted with *Him,* and are willing to

wait upon Him and to sit at His feet and to be consciously taught by Him?

We say to you *who have been "born again,"* you
within whom the Christ has been born—you Disciples on Probation, that One is your Master—even
the Christ-Self of you, Who has more knowledge
and power than any initiate, adept or master who
has not received the anointing of the Holy Spirit—
who has not yet been Christed. For such are but
"masters of Israel," like Nicodemus. They are great
souls, even as John the Baptist was great, of whom
Jesus said:

*"This is he of whom it was written, behold I send my
messenger before thy face, which shall prepare thy way
before thee.*

*"For I say unto you, among them that are born of
woman, there hath not risen a greater than John the
Baptist; but he that is least in the Kingdom of God is
greater than he."*—Matthew 11:10–11.

Just as John the Baptist lost his head, so may
even one of great knowledge lose his head (mentally) unless he has wedded wisdom with Love.

Such Masters who inaugurate new movements for
the enlightenment of men in our modern days are
as the Prophets of Old Testament times. They may
be considered as the lower part of the pyramid.
They represent the great body of human knowledge,
or the Law, and *"The Law is the schoolmaster to
bring us to Christ."* Jesus Christ is the capstone of
the pyramid. But it often happens that He is *"the
stone that the Builders rejected, the same that is*

become the head of the corner."   The capstone itself
being a perfect pyramid, Christ thus is the Apex,
the Zenith, the Essence of all that lies beneath.

It shall be even as Jesus said: *"He that falleth
on this stone* (stumbles against this truth—fails to
see Christ, not merely as the Master and Teacher,
but as the God-Self of every man) *shall be broken
to pieces; but on whomsoever it shall fall* (or who
shall fail to accept or admit this truth) *it will scatter
as dust."*   For Christ is the actual life of humanity
—The Light that lighteth every man, consequently
they who repudiate Him, and consider and teach
that He is only a Master among other Masters, remain in darkness and wander far from their Father's
house.

Theosophy, Rosicrucianism, and other similar
movements brought to the modern world the vision
of Brotherhood.   And for what purpose?   It is
claimed, to awaken men to their real mission on
earth and to prepare them for HIM WHO IS TO
COME,—for the Christ who promised to come and
redeem His own.

But can you not see that not until He has been
born in our hearts, has grown and thrived, and become matured in our lives, can He appear to our
consciousness and can make Himself known as *He
Is*—"The Light which shineth in the darkness" of
our human minds, and which He will illumine so
we may know that our minds are really His Mind,
are God's Mind shining within us.

Ah, dear comrades on this journey through life, all the vast past—all the many eons through which humanity has struggled—has been an evolving, a growing, a preparing and fitting of us for this very day and age we have now reached. The Christian Era was the final stage of our training. God, our Father, Who is responsible for *all*, Himself sent His Holy Spirit, the Christ, down to earth, taking on a human form, purposely to prepare us by direct teaching and example what was necessary for us to find our way back to His Home and to enter again into His Eternal Kingdom. Therefore Christ— *Christ within us* is our highest Teacher, and the sole Authority for every man—for He is *"the Light which lighteth every man that cometh into the world."*

There is much said in the different occult teachings of two paths to God—the path of the occultist, and the path of the mystic, or the way of the head and the way of the heart. Yet all great teachers say that the way to Divinity is the way of Love; and surely the way of Love is the way of the heart. But the Love that leads to God is not the intellectual concept of love that occultists speak of, but is God's Love *in the heart*—the Christ Consciousness there—which cannot be simulated, and which all those in whom Christ has been born and lives *know and show forth*, and they can never be deceived by a substitute.

Gautama brought the teaching of Divine Wisdom and Compassion to develop and prepare the mind of humanity to comprehend God's Love. And even as Gautama came first and brought Wisdom, so Jesus followed and brought us Divine Love to join with Wisdom and give us Understanding, thus completing the Divine Union in Christ of the twain that in the beginning were originally one.

We might say Gautama was the manifested Mind of God and Jesus the manifested Heart of God, God having evolved the mind of humanity to the point where it was now ready to know Him in the fullness of His Nature; so He showed Himself to us in the person of Jesus—His Beloved Son—the Fruit of His Divine Love—the First-fruit of them that slept.

If you are able to receive it, you will soon have done with all intellectual teachings, and you will be interested only in those brought to you by the Loving One within that He may point out to you the laws and truths He wishes you to know, thus recalling to you the knowledge gained in the long, long past. For if you can realize it, it was through many past, long forgotten lives, extending over vast eons of time, that He brought you to your present state of unfoldment; and therefore in your soul there is much knowledge at present hidden from your brain mind that soon He will uncover to you.

But before that can be, a far more important matter confronts you—the finding and *knowing* of Him, your True Self—the *Christ within you,* so that He can reveal to you these and all things, when you *need* to know them. Throughout this eon He has spoken from the heart of every awakened soul—

*"Seek ye first the Kingdom of God and His Right-
eousness, and all things else will be added unto you."*

Christ has been the Great Mystery of all ages.
Once you comprehend *Him* you can know All, for
all mysteries lead to Him, and He is the solution of
all. All the Prophets of old foretold His Coming.
The story of Moses and the children of Israel; the
story of Abraham, Isaac, and Jacob; the story of
Adam and Eve in the Garden of Eden,—all are
parables telling of Him—the Lord Christ, to prepare us for His Coming. Likewise the ancient re-
ligions of India, Egypt, Chaldea, and Atlantis ever
held forth to the humanity of their days the sacred
Mystery of the One we know as Christ. Verily He
is the First and the Last, the Beginning and the
End of all things.

*"In the beginning was the Word, and the Word was
with God, and the Word was God. The same was in the
beginning with God.*

*"All things were made by Him (the Word); and with-
out Him was not anything made that was made.*

*"In Him was life, and the life was the light of men.
And the light shineth in the darkness, and the darkness
comprehendeth it not."*

Read and meditate on the above and with it the
remainder of the first chapter of John, especially up
to the 19th verse.

MEDITATION

With many meditation seems to be quite a problem. Some deem it a task and approach it with
hesitancy and some reluctance, because of strain in

previous attempts, or of not getting any apparent results.

Others think they cannot find the time for regular meditation. It is not so difficult to find the time; meditation can be made part of a well ordered life as easily as can any other factor. System, that manifestation of the harmony and rhythm of the universe in the affairs of men, will provide the time and the way, if given the opportunity by your earnestly desiring it.

True meditation is the simplest and most natural thing in the world, because it is but a retiring into the quiet of the soul, a letting go in the mind of all outer things and relapsing into a peace and a rest in which the Spirit can come forth and speak to the mind. If you only know it, many times a day do you meditate—when your mind dwells upon things in which the personal self is interested. When that part of you is really concerned about a thing, your mind automatically obeys and dwells upon and ponders over that thing until its interest is appeased (worrying, being anxious, grieving, and such are all negative, *unconscious* meditation).

Thus you can see that meditation is natural and in no way difficult. It only appears difficult because *the human mind,* which has been accustomed to having its own way and to thinking of only the personal things in which it is interested, rebels against restraint, particularly when required to think of impersonal and abstract things that *you* are interested in and wish light upon (purposeful thinking is positive and *conscious* meditation). We will try to indicate more clearly what we mean.

In *"The Impersonal Life"* you are shown that it is really God who is living in your body and is your Real Self, and that you are of no importance whatsoever, either to yourself or to the world at large, until you recognize this great truth in a more or less conscious and intelligent way. This of course is not easy to grasp by a mind that considers you and itself separate and apart from God.

Now consider that the life that grew you and is *living* you is the same life that is growing the grass, the flowers, the trees, the animals and all humanity, and is so wise and powerful a life that despite every obstacle it develops all to the maturity of that which it is their destiny to be. Did you or anyone of these others have any conscious part in the direction of or actual process of such growing? You know that you did not, and you know that this life and intelligence and will doing it all is God—Who is All in all.

Now try to realize that this life that is growing you, this mind that is intelligently directing all, and this will whose power is accomplishing all, is actually God and cannot be you or anyone else. Try to perceive the great truth of this by imagining how it must be.

To do this you must lift your mind away from this page and meditate upon what has been stated, and if you are greatly interested, you will find your attention fixed upon this life within you, *imagining it as God* living in your body, a very wise and loving Consciousness filling and possessing it, moving it and causing it to do what He wants it to do. And it will gradually dawn upon you that the part of you that is considering all this *is only your mind*, and then in a wondrously illuminating way it may flash into your consciousness that therefore you are not at all what you before thought was the you living in your body, but that it is a much bigger and more wonderful you—*that it is God! that God is the Real You!!* and that the other you is but a part of His Mind—a center of His Consciousness that before had thought itself separate from Him.

If you have truly followed this and actually caused your mind to consider and do everything suggested, some illumination must have resulted, for the God of you would surely respond to a heart earnestly desiring to know Him.

The above would be real meditation, and real *inner* work, as you will by this time have realized.

All meditation is nothing more nor less than a pondering over or reflecting upon any subject to which you direct your mind's attention. The reason we urge the use of meditation is two-fold: that you can cultivate the power and ability to require your mind to consider thoroughly any subject you wish it to understand fully, realizing that as you hold the subject firmly before your mind's eye, light will pour in, enabling you to see it from many angles. Also that your mind may gradually learn *who* you are—learn of your inner self—and that it, the mind, is your child, your instrument that you are teaching, training and disciplining so that it will serve you selflessly and efficiently.

Until you have disciplined your mind, you cannot control your thoughts, and as by being able to control your thoughts you can control your emotions, you can then bring your body into harmony; for its health is largely controlled by the emotions or feelings harbored in the heart.

When you become more or less master of your mind and dedicate it to the service of the Christ— your God-Self, your *real* work begins; for all such earnest ones are accepted and put to that work for which they have been fitted and prepared.

But not until the mind is thoroughly under control can *real* work be given. *Real* work awaits, but it will be mental work—in the Silence and at night, when the brain minds of those who seek and need help are still, so their souls can hear and accept. *Such Real Work will be given when you are ready.*

Groups

Wherever it is possible we urge that groups be formed for study and service, for our Master has promised *"Where two or three are gathered together in My Name, there am I in the midst of them."*

Aspirants who put service first, and in whom the personality has been submerged, always accomplish

more and unfold more rapidly while working and
studying in a group, for there they quickly become
aware of the one Power and Presence and individually feel the results in their daily meditation
and work.

It is suggested that all who feel so led watch
for others of their acquaintance who they think
may be ready for these teachings—those who are
not seeking for self, but who are longing to serve
the Master within in some definite way. The first
lesson, *"Seek Ye First the Kingdom,"* will be sent
to any of such, if their names are forwarded to the
publisher.

In groups real ways of service will open up to all
in due season—when the unfoldment awaiting is
able to manifest. This does not imply that only in
groups can one unfold in consciousness so that the
Master can accomplish His Will through you, but
only that in them He can make known His Presence
more easily as He indicates above.

Many are so situated that meeting with others
regularly is difficult and often impossible. Such
will be shown that their present opportunity for
service is in the very condition where they are now
placed, but all such should be just that much more
faithful in their regular communion with Him
through meditation.

CHAPTER 3

"I Am the Way, the Truth and the Life"

WE HAVE arrived at that place, in our pointing out what is to be met by a traveler on the path to the Kingdom, where the Voice of Love has become the recognized and accepted Guide.

If you will remember, the traveler has become a Disciple on Probation—the Prodigal is now on his way back to his Father's house. After a long period of trials and testing, he has proved that nothing can entice or stop him from his determination to reach the goal. Finally there comes the supreme test—for this period; in some deep soul experience he is required to make a heart-rending choice, between a long cherished ideal and a plain duty, perhaps. And if duty wins, and it will win—if he turns in prayer for help to this sure Guide within—his Christ-Self, then he enters a new and brighter stage of the journey. For his dedication has proven to be a *soul* consecration—not merely one of the mind and the heart, and he is now accepted as and has become a *real* Disciple.

From this on he grows more and more conscious of definite guidance from within; the Voice speaks more clearly and insistently; the love in his heart becomes more pronounced and will not be denied. Gradually he learns, by centering his attention deep *within*, that there a wonderfully wise and loving

Self exists, one that is ever ready to teach, help and
strengthen, when asked; and the Voice there, which
says with unmistakable authority—*"I am the Way,
the Truth, and the Life; no man cometh unto the
Father but by Me,"* is the Voice of his Christ-Self,
ever speaking from out the heart—when the mind
is stilled so that it can be heard.

Then it is that the Disciple begins definitely to
realize that he is not his human mind with its concerns that has to be stilled and be made to listen,
but that in some mystical yet natural way he is a
part of and can actually enter into the consciousness of that Christ-Self within, and can at will command the mind to be still and can *compel* it to
obey.

And it dawns upon him that while in this consciousness *He is the Master,* but when without in
the brain consciousness he is only the Disciple. And
then he realizes that by opening his heart and letting Love pour out he can at will enter into and
be that Love, and that in that Love consciousness
He and Christ are One; that he is conscious, even
as Christ Jesus was conscious, that *He* is the Way
—the *only* Way, the *only* Truth and the *only* Life;
that the brain mind is but the self consciousness
which He is teaching, training and disciplining to
be His perfect instrument of expression.

And the Disciple learns, as the brain mind lets
go, stands aside and watches what happens, that all
that is ever necessary, when the Disciple is called
upon to teach or help anyone, is to open the mouth

and begin to speak and the words are given him to say; or to start to do anything—no matter what—and a wise and loving power puts forth from within and enables him to do it. Likewise if he wishes to know anything, he needs only to ask and then to get quiet and absorb the wisdom that pours in and floods his consciousness.

Thus the brain mind slowly and surely is taught its part and place, which is to look up to, wait upon and serve You, abiding now in the consciousness of your Christ-Self. When in *that* consciousness, verily You *are* the Master, and the brain mind—that which is now reading these words and trying to understand them—has become the humble and loving Disciple, or hopes—longs to be such.

If you can conceive of what all this means, you can understand that gradually, as the Disciple—the human mind—more and more lets the Master work through him, the Master's Consciousness truly becomes his consciousness, so that the Master is actually living His life in him, doing His will in him, and being His Self in him. As a result of this the human mind as the Disciple is now in a position where the Master is able through it to do the Work He came here to do, and for which all these many years He has been fitting and perfecting the Disciple. They now work as one, in perfect harmony with all the other Brothers of the Kingdom, serving the Great Cause of Brotherhood under the leadership of our Supreme Lord and Master, Jesus Christ.

We cannot point you further on the way, for this

is as far as the human mind can enter in consciousness at this time.

Read the above many times. Ponder and meditate over the words as they are written. Something very wonderful may result for you. If not now, you will at least know what awaits, if you faithfully follow with us and obey the suggestions given.

From the above you can learn that real Disciples may always be known by the work they are doing, by the unquestioned good accomplished, by their self-sacrificing service to humanity. They live only to serve—their every thought and interest is for others; for are they not now integral parts of that Great Brotherhood of Servers Who abide in Christ and obey only Him?

The Christ-Self—the Master within—thus is revealed to those who are worthy to know Him—and to become His Disciples. All others know Him but as a wondrously kind and helpful friend, who is ever seeking to do good to others, to anticipate their needs and to assist them in a loving way whenever and wherever possible.

Understanding all this, you will note that few as yet have become accepted and therefore are actual Disciples. A goodly number are Disciples on Probation. But there are many who are still Aspirants, but who, we hope from the quickening received by earnestly following the suggestions given in these pages, will in time consciously reach the Disciple stage. For this work is, and these articles are written principally, for Disciples. Those whose hearts felt and responded to the call, *"Seek ye first the Kingdom,"* actually obeyed the command of their souls—no matter if their intellects reasoned them away later. All such are Disciples in their soul natures, and they remembered and tried to have their personalities also understand. Our part is fully to awaken such and to uncover to their brain minds what they in their souls inherently are, so that they may journey back to their Father's house—the Christ Consciousness—and learn there of the Work awaiting them as souls.

All those who definitely feel the appeal of these words, and deem such as possible for them, may know that they are destined for Discipleship in this life. May the souls of all who read and who before did not fully understand, be so inspired by the truth herein revealed that the Blessed One—the Master within—may this very hour call them forth to follow and serve Him the rest of their days.

I Am the Way

In the preceding chapter we sought to convey a very great truth, which has become wholly necessary for every one to know who seeks to enter the Kingdom of God. In fact this truth must be faced and fully acknowledged—must be built into the soul consciousness, before one can ever proceed very far on the journey to the Kingdom.

This truth is that *within* you is the Light which lighteth every man that cometh into the world—

that *that* Light is the Christ of God, which shines ever brighter and brighter in the darkness of man's mortal mind as it unfolds in consciousness through the ages and in time turns away from the half-light of human knowledge and experience in a soul demand for an understanding of the true Light which alone will satisfy. That Light is the Holy Spirit that shines deep within every man. It speaks from the heart of every earnest seeker, and with no uncertain voice says, *"I am the Way, the Truth and the Life; no man cometh unto the Father but by me."*

Why will men not listen, even those who yearn for the fullness of life, that they may know the truth and be shown the way? Because they have not yet unfolded to the blossoming stage—the bud of their souls has not yet matured. The Love-life within has not yet become strong enough to force the covering of self to let go and open so that the sunlight of the Spirit may unite with the light of the soul, and draw forth the fragrance and beauty of the life within.

If that is so, then man has nothing to do with this unfolding process, you say. Yes, that is really true. No *man* can actually hasten the process. No one can truly help another—except by pointing out to the human mind the meaning of that through which a soul is passing, thus causing the mind to quiet down, thereby permitting the life within to develop the petals of the soul to maturity—the time of blossoming. It is the self-seeking mind that seemingly interferes and holds back growth, yet all the time the mind is serving the purpose of providing a strong protective sheath, absorbing from without the little light that it can gain from human teachings—just enough to protect it while the Love-life within builds up the soul qualities needed for its perfect expression when the blossoming and fruiting seasons arrive.

Many very earnest seekers cannot yet accept that which we have been to such pains to explain. They are still so engrossed in acquiring what they call knowledge, and think that so wholly necessary that they may belittle the importance of what has been stated. But that is the John the Baptist stage. Even as he came to announce and to prepare the world for Jesus the Christ (read carefully John 1:6–27), so must the mind be prepared by a true and full intellectual understanding of the meaning of Christ *within* as Love, before the Holy Spirit can descend and quicken the heart and the Christ-Self can stand forth *in the consciousness* and minister in the Father's Name unto all who believe. Those who still think of Christ as embodied only in Jesus and cannot feel and know Him within their own hearts, may be masters of wisdom, adepts in the use of the law, but if they have not the consciousness of Christ as the Love of God in their hearts, they are but as sounding brass and tinkling cymbals.

Not long ago there was published in the newspapers the story of a recently discovered 13th century Latin manuscript found in the Chapter Library of Hereford Cathedral in England. From its style it is believed to be a portion of the Gospel of St. Peter, which was in use among Christians in the Second Century. Hear what the Three Wise Men spake unto Joseph, the father of the babe Jesus whom They came to worship.

"Do not thou, then, look upon us as ignorant men; but know thou of us that He to whom thou art appointed as foster-father, He is the God of gods and Lord of all lords, and King over all princes and powers, the God of angels and of the righteous. It is He that shall rebuke all kings and rule all nations with the rod of His name, for unto Him belongeth majesty and empire, and He shall break the sting of death and scatter the power of hell.

"Him shall kings serve, and all tribes of the earth shall adore Him and Him shall every tongue confess saying: Thou art Christ Jesus, our deliverer and our Saviour, for thou art God, even the power and the brightness of the eternal Father."

Read carefully again the preceding paragraph and you will realize that while embodied in Jesus— even as a babe—was very God Himself, and that Jesus as Christ is now ruling in Spirit as the God of gods and Lord of all lords, etc., yet it could not possibly be Jesus, the man, whom kings shall serve, and all tribes of the earth shall adore and every tongue confess, our deliverer and saviour—but that it is Jesus, the Christ or Holy Spirit of God, Who is *the brightness of the eternal Father* IN EVERY MAN which will deliver and save.

Let all who still feel the urge to seek from human teachers and masters learn all that such have to

offer, and it may perhaps cause them to hear the
voice of the loving Teacher within, pointing out
what these others and their teachings *are not* and
cannot teach. Repeated experiences of such nature,
with their fruits of disillusionment and discouragement, will inevitably bring the Aspirant to the place
where that Voice within can be heard. When that
happens the change begins, the heart, through the
distress and unhappiness caused, is quickened, and
the Master abiding there more and more makes His
Presence felt. The mind begins to take note, listens
and ponders over what comes through to the consciousness, and in time the Light—the Holy Spirit—
illumines it, and the Disciple is born.

You, who are seeking "occult" teaching and
training, may perhaps be surprised when told that
within these pages are contained more *true* occult
or inner teachings than dozens of such books afford.
For these, if persistently followed, will bring results
that will cause joy unspeakable to the spiritually
unfolding soul, instead of suffering and dismay,
which often result from the practice of the teachings in such books.

Personality

On our journey to the Kingdom you will learn
that you cannot go far with your eyes and mind
fixed on the personalities of your fellow travelers.
For always will you see in them things that will
hold you back. In some mysterious yet very true
way you will be shown by the loving Guide within
qualities in them that are but reflections of quali-

ties still existing in your own self. This is so because on this journey *Love* leads, and if the human mind and its thoughts are permitted to be distracted by appearances, and are not centered upon seeing the Light within your companions—their Christ-Selves—you will be thus shown every thing within yourself that prevents the unfolding of the inner sight and hearing, and you will stay out in the shadows, wondering why you cannot progress as your soul longs to do.

It is hard for many to believe that what they see in others is because of what still exists in themselves. But that is only because they are still more interested in judging others than in listening to the Loving One within, Who always seeks to draw their thoughts to Himself, that He may open their hearts so they may feel there His love, and thus may see with His eyes the souls of their fellows, shining in the darkness of mortal consciousness, ever seeking to be free, even as their own souls long to be free.

The way to the Kingdom is *within*—where personalities do not exist. On that journey therefore they *must* be left behind. No one may expect to drag personality along and get very far. For the earnest ones—the true Disciples of Christ—have speeded on ahead unhampered by the load others are attempting to carry.

The Disciple is one who has been a Prodigal Son, one who has traveled in a far country and has wasted his substance in wrong living. But he has gained much experience thereby, and with it much knowledge of what the world does not and cannot supply. For with that knowledge has come an understanding heart and a compassion for his fellow men whom he sees wasting their substance and who are still engrossed in the things he now knows to be of no value. And therefore, because of his own former weaknesses, he makes allowance for the weaknesses of his brothers who do not understand. So he does not judge and condemn as he formerly was wont to do, but somehow sees right through the personality the souls of others who are wandering in the darkness of his own former state, seeking everywhere without for the Light that all the time is shining deep in the midst of them, and they do not know it.

It is thus that the Disciple's inner eyes are opened; compassion and understanding lift the veil of self and enable him to see through into the souls of his fellows, and thus to know his oneness with them.

A Disciple learns early not to deal with men and women, but with souls. Gradually he becomes more concerned with the *effect upon himself* than with what others say and do to him. He seeks earnestly to learn what weakness or inharmony in himself drew forth such unkind words or harmful acts that hurt and caused his soul disquiet or trouble. By thus noting such and asking the Loving One within to point out the cause, he gradually learns to avoid and eliminate all such weaknesses and tendencies.

Likewise in dealing with others it is not so much

what the personality says or does, as what the soul is and seeks to be that interests him.   Knowing that intrinsically their Higher Selves are one in Christ and that therefore their purpose is one—that they may come forth and express their real nature, often the conscious Disciple will enter into a secret conspiracy with the Higher Self of the other to foil the other's personality in its every attempt to exercise its lower nature.   Such are occasions for real inner growth and unfoldment.

If you would be a Disciple and would feel the joy of entering into such a conspiracy, seek through the eyes of love to see the soul of your brother; for in it you will see the Beloved One, your Christ-Self— the Light which lighteth every man—and He will show you how to foil the selfish, thoughtless self of both you and your brother.

MEDITATION

There are probably some who are impatient at what they think to be the slowness of their progress and who wish to be put to work, evidently not recognizing that very definite work has already been given them to do in the two preceding chapters.

Such may not be the work they are looking for— it may seem to them too simple, even unnecessary, not yet glimpsing that the work they later will be called upon to do is mental work and of an extremely difficult kind—to those who have not learned to concentrate and to control their thoughts, to shut them off at will and to direct them upon any desired subject.

All such must learn that to be of real service to the Master within they must be able to hear His Voice when He speaks, and that cannot be until they have learned to become quiet and to turn their thoughts within for the definite purpose of finding and getting acquainted with Him. That is plain enough, is it not?

We wish to help every earnest seeker to accomplish this, but before that is possible mind-control *must* be attained. This is only stating in another way what has been told several times already, and it will be repeated again and again until all realize the necessity of regular and systematic meditation —for the twofold purpose of training and discipling the mind until it becomes a perfect instrument for the Master's use, and of learning to find and to know Him. In doing this you will soon realize that you are fulfilling the wishes of your Higher Self— by His approval shown in the results attained, and you will surely learn *Who* is the Master. Also you will learn thereby why this is not inconsistent with what was said above about no one being able actually to hasten the process of Spiritual growth.

The Meditation Exercises

For this purpose alone are the definite exercises given you in the Meditation No. 2, which will be found in the appendix. They are for the use of those only who are no longer seeking anything for self, but that they may fit themselves perfectly for the Master's use. Such are candidates for Discipleship, and such are always provided with the help

necessary. Should the powers gained be used selfishly, those so misusing them will learn through
sorrow and much suffering that the Light within
has become obscured and spiritual darkness hides
the way. Let all heed these words.

In trying to grasp the wonderful meaning of your
being a center of God's Consciousness, "see" yourself as an *idea* in His Mind, that idea being your
Christ-Self—His beloved Son—formed in the
Father's image and likeness. The *Real* You *is* such
an idea, a loved concept of your Father's Mind,
and therefore it is ever *within* that Mind and is
always open to receive or perceive *everything else*
in that Mind.

If you can "see" the Sun as the outer symbol to
your human mind of your Father in Heaven, and
can realize It as the Source of all Life, Power and
Light, it will help you to glimpse that Great Mind
within you; for your human mind *is* a center of *that*
Mind, which radiates to every Center of Itself
everything that It is, even as the sun shines and
provides all life, power and light to all in its universe.

Ponder and marvel over this wondrous Truth.
This will help you to see yourself as a center of
Light, Love and Power, always receiving from the
Eternal Source within you the radiant God quali-
ties which they symbolize to your human mind.
This being true, all that you need to do is to KNOW
this, and by so knowing you actually connect up
your consciousness with your Father's Conscious-

ness, and thus let any quality you can clearly visualize pour into you and *shine;* for where God's qualities are they will shine forth and express themselves.

Remember, these instructions are for those who wish to fit themselves for self-less service under the direction of the Christ within. While we call them instructions, yet they are in reality only suggestions that will call forth the *actual* instructions and guidance from the One within Who is the only authority and teacher for you. He will either approve and amplify or modify what is suggested, or will restrain you until He intends you to follow them, or others better adapted for you.

By that time, with the training received in hearing and knowing His Voice, you will know that He alone is your Teacher, and that He can teach you everything.

The Importance of Daily Study

These articles are not intended or expected to be interesting or easy reading for the average mind. In fact they are not addressed to the mind, but to the soul. Of course they will have to be received through the mind, but the student will find at first it may be a distinct effort to compel the mind to read carefully enough so that it can be shown the meaning hidden back of the words.

When the soul perceives this, it will become deeply interested and will search carefully for the intended meaning and will require the mind to con-

centrate upon the reading so that it likewise will
understand.

This will be a good time to try to note the difference between the mind and the soul. Watch the
reactions of the mind to what was stated above,
while re-reading to catch its significance, then see
if you can tell when the soul is leading and when
the mind. This knowledge is necessary in order
later to know when the Master speaks.

Later there will be given a clear definition and
explanation of what is the soul and its relation to
the mind. In the meantime and in order to prepare
the mind so that it can understand, try to grasp as
well as you can the distinction between the two and
to become acquainted with your own soul.

Do not forget that this is *inner* work, and until
you are able to follow us and do what is told you
cannot get very far in your journey *inward* to the
Kingdom.

Therefore study earnestly all that is said in each
article. Every thought in them is chosen to assist
you in finding the Master within, that *He* may help
and guide you on your journey. Merely reading
them over once or twice will get you nowhere.
That, of course, will be the result if they make no
appeal to you. If so, this Work is not for you. But
if they do appeal, and they make you long to be
worthy of all they hold forth as possible, you may
be sure, if you faithfully do your part as suggested,
real joy of accomplishment awaits.

Consequently we cannot stress too strongly the importance of reading an article at least once every day during the month, preferably just before your meditation hour. If you do this, earnestly seeking the full Truth of each thought expressed, new meanings will unfold with every reading, and often actual illumination will result.

For you are seeking the greatest goal possible for your soul, and all the Brothers of the Kingdom are lovingly waiting to help and to send you all the Light needed—when it is earnestly sought—to quicken mind and heart so that you can become one with Them in Their Christ consciousness and understanding.

CHAPTER 4

"I Am the Door"

WE HAVE shown the three stages reached by those whose feet are definitely set upon the Path that leads back to the Father's House—the stages of the Aspirant, the Disciple on Probation, and the Accepted Disciple. We have tried to show each traveler the stage he or she has attained, so that they may understand the meaning and purpose of the experiences through which they are now passing, and also of those which await in the stages ahead.

All who have accompanied us thus far and who have earnestly studied and meditated upon all that has been said cannot fail to realize that this is a mental journey we are traveling, and that we are headed *inward*—for is not the Kingdom of Heaven *within* us? Also all such are beginning to see why we have been so insistent upon those accompanying us taking the suggested daily exercises in meditation and mind control. For it will be utterly impossible to continue with us until the mental faculties have been trained along the lines indicated, so that they will obey you and permit you to direct and use them to any desired end.

This journey, naturally being an inward one, will lead us deep within the mind, or rather within the consciousness that fills and really is what is called mind. But do not become concerned about it yet—those of you who have not made much progress in thought-control, for we are only trying to prepare you—to get you to understand what is necessary, and that it is not at all a difficult journey—when you are properly equipped for it. You are already provided with the required equipment,—you have all your mental faculties, you have an earnest desire to go, a will awaiting your command to direct and put the faculties to work, and plain and simple exercises that you are asked to follow. Therefore, if you are really in earnest and the seeking of the Kingdom *is* FIRST in your heart and mind—why not get busy now, and let nothing interfere with your gaining perfect control of your mental faculties and thus becoming fully equipped for this all-important journey.

Under the subject of *Meditation* it was stated, "All must learn that to be of real service to the Master within they must first be able to hear His Voice when He speaks, and that cannot be until they have learned to become quiet and to turn their thoughts within for the definite purpose of finding and getting acquainted with Him."

Many think it most difficult and vouchsafed only to the favored few to hear the Voice of the Master —the Higher Self, but when we say that practically everyone who reads these words hears His Voice many times a day and is being guided and directed by Him almost all the time, you will see that it

really only needs that you get better acquainted
with Him to enable you to know when He speaks,
and to permit you to work with Him and to follow
where He directs. It is our wish and aim to make
you so well acquainted with Him that you may
always know when *He* speaks, and when it is the
voice of self that you hear.

First, try to recall the times during the day when
you see yourself doing something foolish or wrong
—not what you would have done had you first taken
counsel with yourself; or when you find yourself
saying something that hurts another, that arouses
anger, or that is not true, which you would not have
said had you exercised control of yourself.

You will note, if you read again the preceding
sentence carefully, that *you see yourself* doing and
saying things. We will repeat it in a little different
form—to see if you can learn why: "You see your
self doing something foolish or wrong—not what
it would have done had it first taken counsel with
you; or you find your self saying something that
hurts another, that arouses anger, or that is not
true, which would not have been said had you
exercised control of that self."

Here apparently are two selves—at first they
may seem to be one—yet a careful reading discloses
a distinct difference; there is one that sees and
knows, and another that is seen and does not know;
one that can control the other, yet at times lets
the other have its own way—evidently for a purpose.

By studying the activities of your mind and the tendencies of your nature you will discover that there is a part of you that is willful and wholly selfish and which, if not restrained, gets you into much trouble; also that there is another part— one that is all mind, which knows all about and can restrain the other part—the emotional side of your nature, when it wills to do so, but which it seldom does, until it has learned by experience the wisdom of so doing. Now this part—the mind that learns by experience—more and more becomes conscious of a quiet Voice within pointing out the lessons of such experiences and continually suggesting, cautioning, chiding, denying, accusing, shaming, and gradually getting the mind to listen to and heed it. This continues every day for years, until the mind is taught much knowledge—especially the results of listening and obeying.

If you can now see this part—your mind that is learning to listen and obey and also learning to restrain and control the other part, the animal and selfish side of your nature—as the Disciple, the John Smith part of you; and the Voice speaking from within the depths of the soul as that of the Master, the *Real* You—the Spirit of God, the Christ-Self of you,—you will begin to glimpse a great but a very simple truth. Pause here and try to get the full significance of what has been stated in the last five paragraphs.

Again, at times you find yourself sitting back— outside of your human self as it were—viewing the

John Smith part of you in all its petty meannesses
and selfishness—its shortcomings, faults and weaknesses, pointing them out to your mind so that it
sees them clearly through your eyes and becomes
heartily sick and ashamed of itself for permitting
such things to be, and determines definitely to overcome and eliminate all such from your nature for
the good of all concerned.

Please note carefully that in this case your consciousness was back with that of the Master—that
it was practically one with His consciousness, and
you were seeing with His eyes and with His understanding. In fact the Disciple was temporarily in
the consciousness of the Master—showing how simple a matter it is for the loving and obedient
Disciple to enter actually into the Master's Consciousness.

We have given you these two proofs that it is
not difficult to hear the Voice of the Master and
that a Disciple hears it many times a day. Indeed
that which thinks, which decides, which directs you
as a Disciple in every activity of mind, speech or
body, is the Master—is *You*, the Christ of you—
the one and only Self, telling your brain mind what
You want it, your instrument, to think, say or do.
You who are living in this body, built it with its
physical brain and five senses for *Your* use, and are
now teaching, training and fitting its brain and
mind so that it will be fully conscious of *You* and
will acknowledge *You* as its Master and will lov-

ingly and obediently compel its body likewise to wait upon and serve only *You*.

We know that many will find it difficult to follow closely the thought of the above, but we earnestly urge that you stay with it, meditating upon its every word, until the meaning becomes clear, and you will surely be rewarded by the consciousness of having made a great truth your very own for all time; and it will unfailingly help you later to enter the Consciousness of the Master *at will*.

But let no one think one may enter this Consciousness when anything of self, desiring it for the use of self, is in evidence. For as we have so definitely shown, no one can get very far on this journey to the Kingdom when self and personality still are prominent; and this Consciousness comes only to one who has dedicated and is requiring self to serve the Loving One within. In fact, it is only such who ever become *His* Disciple.

By this time you will have realized that these words are especially written for Disciples and that they only can fully understand and appreciate the value of what is stated. This does not mean, however, that those to whom it has a strong appeal, but who feel that they are not yet worthy to be Disciples, are not receiving the benefit intended. For in very truth such are potential Disciples, and these words that make such strong appeal will quicken the soul and accomplish just the expansion of consciousness necessary to permit the Master within to make His presence more definitely felt.

"I Am the Only Way"

In the third chapter we tried to show that the
I AM—the Christ Consciousness—is the *only* way
unto the Father, the only Truth and the only Life;
that until the Disciple recognizes and accepts the
Christ within as the Higher Self and Divine Master
he has not yet found the Way, cannot really know
Truth, and consequently the perfect God Life of
him cannot express and enable him to be his Real
Self. Until then the brain mind—the Disciple—still
thinks itself separate from You—the Master—and
naturally, therefore, separate from its Source—the
One Mind of God, its Father. You in your Christ
nature *know* that You and the Father are One—
even as Jesus knew; hence You are trying to teach
your brain mind by the words above and by those
that follow to realize that only by knowing its *Oneness with You,* can it come into Oneness with the
Mind of the Father.

"I am the Way—the only way you can travel—
either without or within; for only by using *My*
power can you *be,* can you *express,* can you *do,* can
you *go.* Hence only by finding and knowing *Me*
as your true and *only* self, can you ever find the
Kingdom.

"I am the Truth. There would be no *knowing*
in you if it were not for *Me in you.* For am I not
the Interpreter—the only Teacher of Truth—the
only Knower—for you?

"I am the Life. There would be no life in your
body if I were not dwelling in it—for I am the Life

that *lives* it. I am the Life of God that flows into, centers in you, expresses you, and Is you.

"Therefore you must seek and find Me, that you may *know* and *become* I AM—for only by entering in and *being* Me, can you come into the Consciousness of the Father, Who is One with Me."

Jesus in so many ways proved for our benefit that the Christ of Him *knew*, and He was all the time teaching His Disciples by demonstration and Truth statements, trying to convey to them the above great truths—even as we are trying to convey them to you. For this consciousness—this KNOWING—is absolutely essential, not only before you can enter the Kingdom, but before you can become a real Disciple—a real servant of the Master.

Is your soul yearning to heal, to teach, to work in the Cause of Brotherhood? Then you know now what should be your first accomplishment. When that is attained you will be able to enter at will into the Consciousness of the One Mind— will be able to connect your mind with It as easily as pressing the electric button turns on the light, or as turning on the faucet causes the water to pour out. This you will prove and demonstrate for yourself in healing, teaching and serving, with the attainment of that KNOWING—for that will make all easy.

Is it worth working for? Then meditate daily upon what has been given, faithfully practicing the exercises, for they will surely bring that KNOWING to the soul that earnestly and persistently seeks it.

I Am the Door

"I am the door; by Me, if any man enters in, he shall be saved, and shall go in and out, and find pasture.

"Verily, verily, I say unto you. I am the door of the sheep. He that entereth not by the door into the sheepfold, but climbeth up some other way, the same is a thief and a robber.

"But he that entereth in by the door is the shepherd of the sheep."—John 10:9, 7, 1–2.

He—the I Am—the Divine Self of us—thus shows us that He *is* the door—the *only* door into the Kingdom. Man must become His Disciple—must become the loving shepherd of his thoughts, feelings, motives—dedicating them all to Him, shepherding them ever toward the heavenly pasture— if he would save them, and he, himself, be saved. Once having found his Divine Self—the Christ— and having entered into His Consciousness, he can go in and out at will, and will find that everything needed is always available for use in His service. For having found Him and entered into His Consciousness he becomes One with Him—and thinks only His thoughts, speaks only His words, and does only His will.

He who climbeth up through pure will-power, uninspired by Love; or by great intellectual knowledge, unwedded to Love; or by magical rites claimed to be a short cut; the same thereby is a thief and a robber—no matter how wonderful the things he teaches, the mysteries he reveals, or the seeming miracles he performs. For now you know that the true knowledge, the mysteries of the Spirit, the power to perform real miracles, come only from and are used only by the Christ-Self, Who abides in and works only from the Kingdom.

In the days to come—in the near future—there will appear many seemingly great teachers, revealers of the mysteries, and performers of miracles. Our beloved Master, Himself, told us:

"If any man shall say unto you, Lo here is Christ, or there; believe it not.

"For there shall arise false Christs, and false prophets, and shall shew great signs and wonders; insomuch that, if it were possible, they shall deceive the very elect."—Matthew 24:23–24. (Read the whole Chapter and become acquainted with it, for we shall refer to it again.)

Our work is to awaken the elect—and all those who can be saved—to call them forth from out their darkened sleep of self into the light of true understanding, and thereby into the service of the Christ *within*—their beloved Master; so that when these false Christs *without* appear, they may know them instantly for what they are—thieves and robbers. (Read all of the 10th Chapter of John.)

All of these wonderful words of truth that Jesus spoke nineteen hundred years ago are so simple and so grandly true that they are easily provable today, and are well known by every Disciple. For does He not speak them to us daily from within in His efforts to win us utterly to Him?

So that our hearts yearn with a strong yearning to have everyone who reads come quickly into the great Joy of His Presence that every Disciple feels. He waits within with longing, open arms, calling you to Him. Can you not hear His loving Voice appealing to you deep within your heart? Surely you are learning to know that Voice and to feel there His Presence—in His Love that surges outward for recognition.

THE PRAYER

In the appendix is a Prayer or Invocation for the assisting of Aspirants to enter into the consciousness of the Higher Self—the Christ within. Try to realize in voicing this Prayer that in *that* consciousness the Father can actually be known in Spirit, as well as can our blessed Master, Christ Jesus, and all of our other Brothers in Christ. For in that consciousness, which is truly the Father's Consciousness—His Kingdom, all are One—there is *no* separation.

The only way into the consciousness of the Higher Self—the Christ within—is through the door of the heart. By opening wide our hearts we let out our Father's love, which quickens and spiritualizes our minds, and enables us to feel and recognize His Presence within as our Christ-Self; when His love actually becomes our love, enabling us to see with His eyes and to know with His understanding what He wishes us to know.

We then have the right to ask Him to cleanse us of all consciousness of the separate self, so that our Christ-Self may live His life in us, do His will in us, and be in very truth His self in us.

And when we go about thereafter in His consciousness, He can give us of His wisdom to light and direct our way, so that we may make no more missteps; may be empowered by His will to abide in the consciousness of His ever Presence, so that His Words may abide in us; and may feel His dear Love always within and active in our hearts, so that our Spiritual eyes may remain open and we may see His beloved Self looking from out the eyes of every soul we meet.

Let everyone seek to get the full meaning of the above, so that this Prayer may be to you all that is intended. Make no mistake, it will surely repay the effort made to comprehend fully what you are asking. For it is the soul prayer of every true Disciple of Christ. Once it has become *your* soul's longing, do not enter the inner realms at night in sleep without repeating it in deep earnestness, no more than you start the day without similarly repeating the Lord's Prayer.

One Method of Healing

We will now suggest an application of the power of concentration gained by the exercises given in the two Meditations, which will be found in the appendix.

Read carefully the first part of the small Meditation, trying to get the full meaning of what is stated about the consciousness of the One Mind circulating freely to every center of that Mind. Then try to realize that every cell in every organ or in any part of the body is a center of consciousness of that Mind, and therefore is a center for the expression of the One Life—God's Life; that that Life, being God's Life, will grow and heal and make perfect any expression of Itself—that it will naturally and automatically do this, because It knows no disease —it knows only Life.

This it does in the bodies of men, animals, vegetation and even minerals, as almost everyone knows. That is why, when there is a cut, a bruise, or an injury of any kind to any one of these bodies, that Life immediately begins to repair, restore and heal—if left alone and if not interfered with by the human mind with its fears, anxieties and misbeliefs—and will quickly make it whole as before.

It stands to reason that It should do this in any part of the human body—where alone It is ever interfered with—if the brain mind which controls the consciousness of the cells there fully co-operates with this Life, by simply *knowing* Its power and impressing upon the consciousness of the cells the same knowing—instead of the usual fears and states of panic when a serious injury occurs or a disease is discovered.

The practical way of proving this is—first to know the truth just stated. Then to "see" or visualize this Life, directed by your will, pushing right through the darkness of the consciousness of the cells of the injured or diseased part—for remember, your consciousness, when it knows truth as God knows it, *is His Consciousness;* and wherever His Consciousness is, His Life must be and operate— bringing Light and Life and once more Oneness of consciousness and therefore of health, harmony and wholeness to these cells, driving out all darkness of ignorance, misconception and wrong thinking that may have been instilled there by your human beliefs, and starting nature's healing processes immediately to work again.

For you must realize that this Life is Spirit—is purest Light and Love; and being the inner essence of all Life, it instantly penetrates to the center of all consciousness—easily into the darkness of the consciousness of cells created by human misconceptions of what is life—when directed by the will of one who knows the truth above stated, and quickly dispels all sense of pain, inharmony or disease— aye, just as easily as carrying a bright light into a dark room causes the darkness instantly to disappear.

Read the above over many times, each time trying to get its full meaning before trying to prove it. Then do not attempt to prove it until urged by a Loving Power within to respond to a call for help from one who suffers. Then with a prayer for that Power to come forth and use you as It wills to drive out the darkness from the suffering one, obey whatever you are led to say and to do.

This brings up the question of when is it legitimate to use this healing knowledge and the power it gives. Do you think that you are wise enough to know what another soul needs, or if its Higher Self wants you to heal it of a disease brought upon it as a result of disobedience or of breaking a definite law? Of course few are wise enough for that. Then until you are, it were best not to attempt to use this knowledge and power only under certain well-defined conditions—which we will make clear.

Above we plainly state that one should not attempt to prove it "until urged by a Loving Power within in response to a call for help from one who suffers." That means that one must *know* when that Loving Power speaks—that one must become thoroughly acquainted with It, and learn to work with and for *It*.

You can now see why we are trying to help you get acquainted with that Power—the Loving Christ within; so that you can let *Him* come forth and use you as *He* wills "to drive out the darkness from the minds of the suffering ones," by bringing to them the Light of His knowing *from within themselves*.

When you are fully conscious that *He* knows *all*, and therefore deep within is watching over, caring for, and in complete charge of all, you will leave it all in *His* hands in supremest confidence, always ready however to fly at His command to do what He wishes you to do, knowing that as He starts the healing current through you there can be only one result and then probably you will be given actually to see it manifest.

CHAPTER 5

"I Am the Resurrection and the Life"

An Easter Thought

ALL nature is feeling the approach of a new Easter day, the day of Resurrection—a commemoration of the rising from the tomb of our dear Lord and Master, Christ Jesus, and a promise of that annual rebirth or coming back into manifestation of the life that was dead and buried in the dark and cold of Winter—that ever-recurring and necessary period when the soul of things retires deep within to its source for rest and assimilation and a renewal of power for additional experience.

We ask you to realize with us that all humanity is a part of nature—is as much a part as are the trees, the flowers, the grass and the fruit of the vegetable kingdom; and while seemingly we do not die yearly and give up our bodies—our outer vestments—as do many of the members of that kingdom, yet in reality, in the indrawing of the life so evident there, man, being a part of nature, must be similarly affected and at least in his feeling or emotional nature, must in very truth enter the dark, cold, dreary state of Winter along with all that of which he is a part, and his soul together with the universal soul go back to its heavenly home and there renew and restore itself with the life of God

63

and prepare to come forth with greater vigor and intention to express that life.

All can see that life out-breathes itself during the Spring season, fills all nature full of itself in the fruitage and harvest season, and then begins to in-draw itself during the Fall, until in the cold and bleakness of Winter it is wholly invisible and un-manifest.

Why should man not be as much affected by this out-breathing and in-breathing as any other part of nature; and if he is unconscious of such change going on within himself, is it not because it is so common and natural a change that his attention has never been called to it?

Perhaps this will account for the discouragement, the depression, the despair, the seeming uselessness of living, experienced by so many sensitive ones during the Winter months; and it may cause all who read to take a deeper interest in that mysterious life working in their bodies, preparing to unfold it-self in the springtime into a new and higher phase of expression.

Perhaps it will blossom forth—in unison with the flowers of the fields and the Easter lilies, the songs of mating birds and the joy of all nature at being able to express life freely once more—in some of those who feel the thrill of life's renewal—its re-birth within themselves.

Perhaps one here and there may even unfold the wondrous life of the Master within, having been called and chosen by Him and quickened so that the inner world will become as the outer, and that they may see as He sees and know as He knows.

For at each Spring Equinox all candidates for initiation into the Higher Consciousness are brought to their Spiritual Teachers who await to see if they are prepared to enter upon the Easter Feast of Realization, and to take their places in the Hall of Learning, that wonderful palace of Truth within the ethereal realms where all followers of Christ are bidden to come and all are helped to enter by their Teachers.

This being the renewing and restoring period when life pushes itself forth into larger moulds for wider expression, naturally gives opportunity for all those who have co-operated with it and who seek no longer to interfere. Such are approaching discipleship, and at Easter time may blossom forth, even as the pure white Easter lilies, fitting symbols of those who have attained their full growth.

While we are dealing with and helping to prepare disciples for this great ordeal, do not forget that all is leading up to that far greater initiation—"the Crucifixion" of the lower nature—the death of the self in preparation for its resurrection from the tomb of matter as the glorified Christ-Self.

Try to realize fully that this life that all nature is feeling so big within itself is the life of God—that which Is and grows all things that have form and life; and there is nothing really dead, for that which Is cannot but be alive. And this life of God in manifestation is actually His Love, which is both the cause and reason of all being. And His Love as we know is His Holy Spirit—His beloved Son— the Christ, sent into the world to redeem it and to lift it once more back into Oneness with His Consciousness.

Therefore the yearly crucifixion and resurrection we see and feel in nature are but to recall to us and definitely to show us what our great Exemplar and Master taught by His Life and words—that if we would follow Him we must go through the same crucifixion of self to win the resurrection of Christ —must express in our life the fullness of His life *within* us, which is the life of God, our Father, unfolding us to the same fruitage He manifested in Jesus.

I Am the Resurrection and the Life

"I am the resurrection and the life; he that believeth in me, though he were dead, yet shall he live.

"And whosoever liveth and believeth in me shall never die. Believest thou this?" John 11:25.

In the above words and in the whole of the 11th Chapter of John is plainly pictured a mighty truth. We would that we could convey to all who read the absolute verity of Christ's statement in the above lines and that He says these very words constantly to every true disciple.

"I am the resurrection. I am the life. He that liveth and believeth in Me shall never die."

Conceive if you can that this life that is in you— that *is living you,* is very Christ, Himself. You know that it is not *your* life, that you cannot control it; but instead you have to obey it, for it always has its way with you, makes of you and does with you what it wills. You have not yet learned that it is a loving life, for most of the past you have spent in opposing it, in rebelling against it, and in trying to thwart its purpose for you. But where have you gotten and what have you accomplished? For all that you did was only that which life had you do in order first to teach you that you of yourself can do nothing, and then that you might gradually come to realize that this life had benevolent intentions for you and was actually inciting you to such rebellion and opposition, in order to build for itself a strong, capable personality and an intelligent brain mind which later it could use to fulfill its real purpose—the one it created you for in the first place.

It has now brought you to your present stage of consciousness. With our help you are beginning to recognize it as a really wonderful life, for you are learning that the only harmony, the only happiness that comes to you is when you co-operate with it and accept it for what it is—the only true, wise, powerful, helpful part of you—and acknowledge it as the Master—aye, as the blessed Christ within.

Thus does He, the I AM of every man, the Life that lives him, teach man's brain mind to come to Him. He brings to that mind everything it thinks it wants, lets it want everything it can see, lets it try to get all of it for self, lets it grow strong in wanting and struggling and getting. Then when strong enough He takes all away and allows it to suffer and thus burn away the selfishness acquired in such struggles, leaving only the strength and other soul qualities gained for the purpose He intended them to be used.

Then follows the teaching of the mind to know the difference between His will and self's desires—between His voice and the voice of self when they each speak.

So in time the brain mind—the disciple—learns through striving and failure and suffering to know that He, the Christ within, *is* the resurrection and the life and that just as he believes this and lives in that consciousness he *knows* that death does not exist and has no reality for him.

THE PATH

By this time most of you who read actually know that there is a Path, one on which some of you have been traveling for some time, while most are just setting out upon it. We have tried to point out much of what you may expect to meet upon this Path and to explain the meaning and the why of that through which you have been passing. But in order that you may have other authority than ours, we cannot do better than quote the words of that great disciple, H. P. Blavatsky, who brought to the Western world the first definite explanation of the meaning and purpose of "The Path."

"There is a road, steep and thorny, beset with perils of every kind—but yet a road; and it leads to the Heart

of the Universe. I can tell you how to find Those who will show you the secret gateway that leads inwards only, and closes behind the neophyte for evermore. There is no danger that dauntless courage cannot conquer. There is no trial that spotless purity cannot pass through. There is no difficulty that strong intellect cannot surmount. For those who win onwards, there is reward past all telling—the power to bless and save humanity. For those who fail there are other lives in which success may come."

From this you may learn that this road we are traveling to the Kingdom is not for weaklings, for those who doubt if they can accomplish it or who are unwilling to do the necessary work; nor is it for those to whom the reaching of the goal has not become the supreme desire and purpose of their lives.

We have started inwards toward a country traveled consciously by but few, but which we hope all will learn to know and become thoroughly acquainted with in a general way before we have traveled very far therein. We mean the country of the mind, and in the previous chapter we pointed out what was the necessary equipment to help you pass through it intelligently, quickly and easily. To prepare you for this journey we have repeatedly sought to show that those who did not strive faithfully and determinedly to discipline and control their mental faculties would find themselves shortly dropping out, because of not being able to keep pace with their better equipped comrades.

All this is said, and so often repeated, not to discourage anyone. but with the hope that it will inspire all aspirants not to let anything in their own natures or in the conditions surrounding them prevent their continuing the journey,—for their souls intend that they accompany us, the proof being that their hearts sanctioned it when responding to the call of *"Seek Ye First The Kingdom."*

So can you not see that what alone will prevent will be the lower animal-self prevailing upon the mind with such specious arguments as: it will be too hard work, will take too much of your time, and you know you are not ready for it anyway. For those minds which listen to and *heed* such temptations, it were indeed best that they drop out. But for those who set their teeth together, when hearing and recognizing such testings, and grow all the more determined to embrace this opportunity and never to turn back, a "reward past all telling" awaits—"the power to save and bless humanity."

All such we now ask to turn to the last article in the booklet *Brotherhood,* entitled "The Kingdom of Heaven," and to read and study it thoroughly during the month until you fully understand the different realms of consciousness through which it is necessary to pass on our journey within the "heart" to the Kingdom. This understanding is vitally necessary in order that all may become well acquainted intellectually with the inner planes of being, so that when you enter them consciously or in dreams or visions you will comprehend the significance of all that you see, and it will not be as if entering a strange country.

Healing

Would you heal yourself quickly and perfectly of every inharmony of body, mind and affairs? Then follow *faithfully* and *continuously* the suggestions given below, and such health and harmony will be yours:

Realize that it is actually *God*—I Am—Who is living in this body you call your body, Who is walking around in it, doing in it what you do, and causing your brain mind to think and your mouth to say what you think and say.

For have you any life, any power, any mind, any intelligence of your own apart from His life, His will, His mind?

Think! Are you anything at all but that He is in what you call you? Is He not *all* that there is *of* you and *in* you? For you *know* he is *All in all!*

Grasp the full significance of this great truth, and it will enable you with our help to see and be that which we have said already you Are—whole and perfect as all expressions of God are whole and perfect.

We have just shown you a very wonderful truth. But what are you going to do with it? Many truths have you "learned" with your *brain mind* in the past—but of what use are they to you? In fact your brain mind is stuffed with such truths and you are soul-sick because seemingly you cannot make any practical use of them—as can the few exceptional souls that you know who have used them.

Above we said if you would grasp the full significance of what had been told, *with our help* you could see and be that which you already are. For without help seemingly you will do nothing.

Therefore, we tell you to realize *this very moment* that it is not you, *but God,* living in your body.

Stop! Hold your mind to that one thought—hold it to the exclusion of every other thing; for it is the one great reality of your being. Hold it until it fills your consciousness—until it *is* your consciousness.

Every movement that you make, realize that He is doing it. Every word that you speak, let Him say it. Every thought that comes, let Him handle it, point out its meaning and purpose, and direct its use.

Just *know* that God and God alone will do all— Is *doing all;* He must be doing it—for He is ALL in ALL—there is no one else.

Hold to that! Do not let any of the old thoughts —those of self and separateness approach. Hold fast to the truth—no matter what comes. *Hold* to it. Be faithful—let there be no slightest wavering.

Just know that *He is doing it*—that *He* is the "I" of you—the *only* "I"—the only *self.* Let go of your mind—of your self, of all sense of responsibility— and just rest in the consciousness that *He* is doing it all—that His Love which is His Life *must* express Him, must be I Am in you.

We have told you now *how*. We have given you the help promised. That is all we can do. *You* must do the rest—you must now *use* this knowledge so freely given—if you would be free.

All that your soul is seeking awaits your *accepting* and *using*. Oh, dear one, we have led you back to your Father's house—back to God. Awake! Open your eyes! See! *Know! Act!*—Now!!

* * * * *

All who practice faithfully the above suggestions will receive a blessing beyond their present comprehension and for which they will be so grateful that they will want all their friends who are ready to enjoy the same blessing. For therein is shown the way to the highest and therefore the most effective Spiritual Healing.

This will help also. Go about your daily work imagining—actually *feeling* God's life in you, freeing you, vitalizing you, permeating to the center of every cell and atom of your body, driving out all former separative consciousness—as light drives out darkness—and then possessing—*being* you, and expressing and radiating from you as health, vitality, power, love. See this—*feel* it actually taking place. Go about in that consciousness.

If there is pain, inharmony, or disease in any part of the body, just *know* that *God's* life, *His* consciousness, *His* love is there—not what you had previously thought was there. Just *know* this truth —and watch the pain, inharmony or disease disappear.

Spiritual Growth

We receive many letters from students who tell of long years of seeking in different Movements and Teachings, that in this Work they have finally found what they missed in all others—the loving impersonal teaching of the Christ; and given so clearly and simply that all may understand, and which their own Higher Selves had been trying to tell them, but which, because of the purely intellectual concepts with which their minds had been filled, they had not been able to understand clearly and therefore to translate into tangible form for meditation and putting to actual use.

Does this not prove that no teaching coming from without is for you unless it thus confirms what you already half-consciously know within? If so, do not let anything else intrigue you and get you involved in it because of its mystery or its tone of authority. There is only one Teacher for you, and it is on His authority alone we would have you rely. Hence by listening to and following only those teachings that turn you always within to Him for His approval— when in doubt—will you gradually but surely learn to know His Voice and His Will for you with certainty—as you determinedly strive to give over to Him all your old ideas and desires so that they no longer interfere.

On the other hand, others write us that they "enjoy" the teachings, but they cannot find much time to study and meditate and do the exercises suggested. These undoubtedly feel in their hearts that there is much of real value awaiting them—when they can compel their minds to take advantage of the opportunity thus afforded. But will they ever do that? Such evidently are not yet ready—are not really in earnest about finding the Kingdom; there is too much without that is still interesting and holding them back from their soul's desire.

We mention these things in order to let you see the different stages on the Path of the various seekers. Some of you who read, perhaps, may recognize yourselves among those mentioned. But know that everyone goes through all these stages, and eventually arrives at the deeply-in-earnest stage of discipleship.

Many wonder what is Spiritual growth—wherein is it different from the so-called intellectual apprehension of truth; and also what causes such growth. That is rather hard to understand, for the greatest growth is not when the personality is striving the hardest, but when it is suffering the most. Even as all vegetation grows fastest during the night time, so in the dark and troublous periods of life the soul grows faster—because during these periods the mind turns inward and comes closer to the spiritual forces moving and controlling the soul, and thereby unconsciously co-operates with them, instead of, as in the bright, smooth-sailing periods, hindering them by selfishly choosing only the pleasant paths of life.

When one has learned truly to co-operate with life and nature, a definite and highly important point on the Path has been reached. But before reaching that place many hard lessons have to be learned.

ONE MUST PAY FOR WISDOM

One of the most important lessons to be learned is that life requires one to pay for every lesson it teaches. It plays no favorites and no one can gain wisdom without paying dearly for it. We are speaking of soul knowledge—which alone is wisdom —not of the intellectual knowledge that one can get from books and from teachers. Such wisdom comes only from hard, persistent effort, forced by a determination to gain it no matter what the cost. Such are the efforts of all real disciples. They gain wisdom—for they gladly pay the price.

Strange to say, however, there are many who yearn to serve and to become disciples—even think to find the Kingdom, who seek and accept instructions such as found herein, which their hearts tell them are filled with deep wisdom; yet back in their minds they hope they may not be called upon to pay—either in money, which is the least and easiest thing they can pay, or in the sustained effort of definite mental work, which they certainly not only will be asked but will be constantly pressed to pay —if they continue on their quest with us.

In Spiritual matters as one receives so must one give—one cannot get anything for nothing, but must pay one way or another. A constant receiving without giving is like a pitcher that has become full—no more fresh water can be added until some has been poured out. Yet some wonder why they have gotten nowhere after years of seeking and studying. It is chiefly because they do not give out and apply what they have learned—are always wanting to get and are never interested in giving or using what they have received.

We have gone to these pains to point out the Law in order to show that we have now reached the place where every aspirant should determine for himself if he is really prepared to travel further on this journey. We mean that if curiosity or just casual interest has caused you to stay with us this far, there should be a definite study made of yourself to see if you are willing to pay the full price of discipleship, and if you are sure you truly belong in this, the Master's Work.

All who do *belong* in this Cause understand the importance of this requirement, and gladly show that they do—for at heart they are His disciples and their souls compel them to respond—even if their minds do not yet fully recognize what it all means. It is by such response that we learn to know our Brothers—those whom He has called to follow Him, who hear His loving Voice within and never hesitate and are always eager to obey.

With these we are always in close touch.

CHAPTER 6

"If Ye Abide in Me!"

BY THIS time all who have been journeying with us have become more or less aware of the loving guidance they are receiving *from within,* and are gradually becoming more acquainted with The One who is not only their Guide, Teacher and Master, but who is the Source of all their life, strength and health.

All such have learned from the preceding chapters and from the books suggested for collateral study what constitutes a disciple, and we trust all are determinedly striving to become wholly empty and clean of self so as to be deemed worthy to be accepted as such by their Divine Master and to be given definite work to do. Those who have been accepted or who are approaching that stage understand what we mean by such work, and also comprehend the deep significance of the words of our Beloved Master when He says: *"If ye abide in me and let my words abide in you, ye shall ask what ye will and it shall be done unto you."*

In order to help others to perceive this significance, we will study the inner meaning of the wonderful words of the Master beginning the 15th Chapter of John:

"I am the vine, and my Father is the husbandman. Every branch in me that beareth not fruit He taketh

*away; and every branch that beareth fruit He purgeth
it, that it may bring forth more fruit."*

First realize and always keep in mind, whenever
Jesus spoke in the first person, using the words "I
am" and similar terms, that it was not he, the mortal man, but the Christ or Holy Spirit within him
that spoke. Realizing this, then in very truth the
Christ or Holy Spirit is in the nature of a vine
whose branches are in every human heart, even as
It is also a light that in many "shineth in the darkness and the darkness comprehendeth it not."

Likewise we know that the Father, like an expert
husbandman, when a branch does not blossom or
bear any fruit, cuts it off, takes it away and burns
it. On the other hand every branch that produces
fruit such a husbandman trims close, lets it bleed,
and thus purges it, in order that it may draw to
itself the special renewing force of the life in the
vine, which makes it grow more freely and thereby
bring forth fruit more abundantly.

Can you not now see why the disciple receives
so much trimming and is brought under so many
purging influences, until all former selfish human
traits are finally bled away from him?

*"Now ye are clean through the word I have spoken
unto you."*

From this purging process the disciple gradually
learns to feel and know the presence and influence
of the Master—the loving Christ within, to hear
His Voice and to receive daily teachings from Him,

so that he becomes clean and empty of self and seeks only to heed and obey every word of the Master.

"Abide in me, and I in you. As the branch cannot bear fruit of itself, except it abide in the vine; no more can ye, except ye abide in me."

The disciple thus learns to abide in the consciousness of the Master, and in so doing the Master actually abides in and works through him; for he has learned through hard experience that he of himself can do nothing, and except as he enters and abides in the consciousness of the Master within him, he is as a branch cut off.

"I am the vine, ye are the branches. He that abideth in me and I in him, the same bringeth forth much fruit; for without Me ye can do nothing."

This is now become very plain, showing that the I Am, the Divine Self, who alone is the expression of the Life of the Father, is the conscious partaker and producer of the fruit of His Love—is the Vine whose roots are in God—and ever seeks to produce through His disciples, the branches, but cannot until the branches recognize their identity with the Vine, and thus abide in Its life and let Its life abide in and flow freely through them. Only then can that life blossom and bring forth its fruit plentifully.

"If a man abide not in me, he is cast forth as a branch, and is withered; and men gather them and cast them into the fire and they are burned."

He who recognizes not his identity with the Vine —the Christ *within* him, and thus is unable to re-

ceive of the Divine Life of the Father, naturally
becomes as a dead branch and withers away spiritually.   Of course it is because he is still attracted
by and yields to the lures of the world, the flesh
and the devil.   Such the men of the world gather
to themselves and lead into the fires of sensation,
until all desire is burned away from them.   And
that often takes many lifetimes.

*"If ye abide in me, and my words abide in you, ye
shall ask what ye will, and it shall be done unto you."*

Now you can understand what will be the results
of abiding and of not abiding.   One who abides in
and waits upon the Lord within, naturally is in His
consciousness, and asks only to be given the wisdom
and strength necessary to do the things required
of him.

*"Herein is my Father glorified, that ye bear much
fruit; so shall ye be my disciples."*

As you thus learn to abide in the Master's consciousness—which means in His Love, and you let
His Love abide in and direct you in all your ways,
in very truth is the Father—the Source of all love,
of life itself—glorified, and you are caused to bear
much fruit.   Naturally all such are beloved disciples.

*"As the Father hath loved me, so have I loved you;
continue ye in my love."*

As the Father pours into the I Am, the Christ
within, His Holy Love—the fullness of His Life,
so will the disciple feel and receive of the Master's
Love and Life.   And the disciple, once partaking

of that Love and Life in its fullness, will surely continue in It.

And then the Master tells us *how* to continue in It—how to fit ourselves so as to receive and express the fullness of His Life and Love so that His Joy may become our joy and that it may be complete.

"If ye keep my commandments, ye shall abide in my love; even as I have kept my Father's commandments and abide in his love.

"These things I have spoken unto you that my joy might remain in you, and that your joy might be full."

Heed and ponder long over all these wonderful words, all the time trying to feel that the Loving One within your heart is speaking them to *you*, His disciple.   Before very long, as you determinedly seek to realize His Presence there, you will *know* that He is ever speaking them from out a great Love, and your joy will indeed be full in that knowing.

Occultism

We hear much these days about occultism and its teachings, offered by many movements, cults, societies, orders and fraternities that have attracted and are still attracting thousands of earnest seekers; attracting them not only because they are holding out the opportunity of gaining in their teachings knowledge of the hidden side of life and of the laws that govern them, as well as of gaining the powers such knowledge gives, but that in them may be found definite instructions for self training and discipline that all such seekers feel they need.

Many of you who read have had experience with some of such movements, some of you gaining real knowledge that now is proving of much benefit; and others getting a little knowledge and much disappointment and disillusionment, because of finding that the personalities of the leaders and teachers of such movements failed to live up to their own teachings and principles.

But out of it all most have learned much of what these do *not* teach and practice—the true inner teachings of Christ. Outer knowledge they all teach —as much as they have to give—with more or less clarity, or they could not attract and hold, their followers; but the earnest ones soon find that intellectual knowledge alone does not satisfy. Their souls call for something more.

Those who have come through such occult movements and have studied earnestly what they taught and have faithfully practiced what was required, have profited much and have had a real and necessary preparation for that which is now being offered them in these teachings. They are the ones who instantly recognize the value of the self-discipline and training provided in the meditation and healing exercises. They will find such much easier to practice than will those who have never previously had definite instructions in meditation and mind control.

We wish to say here that what is called "New Thought" as taught in Christian Science, Unity, Divine Science and the various "Truth" movements, has brought to the western peoples a form of occultism truly fitting the needs of minds developed in the intense commercial activities of the modern world, in that it is preparing these minds to understand the higher and later needs that will appear when the soul has unfolded to the stage of potential discipleship. During the past twenty-five years such preparation has proceeded rapidly, and at the present time many are being called and chosen who have become able to hear the Master's Voice in their hearts.

Because of the odium and disrepute into which "occultism" has fallen in the minds of many New Thought students who do not understand its real meaning—a disrepute of the same effect as that in which "New Thought" has fallen in many churches, we feel it wise to explain that as we use it occultism means simply a study into the hidden or inner phases of life and things—those which are not cognizable by the five senses; while New Thought is any philosophical system of thinking that differs from the orthodox theology of the churches.

We intend that students of the inner and hidden laws of life shall find in these articles what they have been seeking, for we are endeavoring to instruct them in such practical yet simple laws—easily proven by the mental exercises suggested, when faithfully followed—that will equip them with both knowledge and power for any task in life —no matter how great.

In the Home

We have had numerous inquiries from deeply-in-earnest housewives who are rearing families and are surrounded by duties, precluding their finding much time for systematic study and meditation or even for meeting regularly with others, whose hearts respond to all that these articles contain, and who yearn and ask for greater opportunities to serve.

To such we say, the work the Master has chosen for you is right in your home by your own fireside. In fact there is no greater schooling in patience, charity, tongue-control, and watching over one's thoughts, than in the home among those dearest to you. If you can find greater opportunities for self-discipline and for forgetting self in compelling self to wait upon and do only what the Loving One within wants you to do for those He has committed to your care, we wonder where they are. Most housewives in this Work know that, but if you find self rebelling and ambitious to do greater work —know that you can render Him no higher service now; for *here* is your work—here where *He* has put you to serve, and also to gain those qualities you lack, and which when gained will fit you for that which will then follow naturally—as night follows the day. But He will arrange all that—will have it all waiting for you when you are ready for it—and not before.

In fact, your present work—and this applies to everyone, housewife or other worker—is *just where you are today.* For there the One Who

Knows—your Highest Self—has placed you to learn the lessons you *must* learn, and where you can best learn what you need to know to gain the soul qualities lacking and absolutely necessary for the greater service that awaits.

This applies also to those of you who are now more or less active in some church or movement that has helped you to come into your present consciousness. For remember, you as a disciple are no longer seeking to get, but to give and to serve; and surely among those you know and who know you is the best place to demonstrate the love and the understanding of the truths you are gaining from your meditation and study.

And surely those nearest you and who know of such study are justified in expecting you to prove that you are getting real benefit from the time and effort expended. There are none so ready to judge —and condemn—as those who are not themselves awakened or called by the Master to serve, and who therefore see only with the cold, calculating eyes of the world, but who nevertheless will understand and appreciate a real demonstration of the Christ-life when it is actually shown them.

Therefore, disciples must keenly realize the importance of making their lives—and not their words merely—prove, not to the world so much as to their own better selves, whom they serve.

In the church or the movement which enlisted your previous interest lie many opportunities of sowing the seed of the true Christ teaching, for there the soil is fertile, if fallow, and only needs cultivation, proper watering and sufficient sunshine to cause that which is in the seed to spring up into real life expression. Hence much can be done there—if the Master is permitted to lead and speak through you to those He wishes to reach and call forth.

As disciples learn to wait upon Him and allow Him thus to use them, they will soon see that it makes no difference where they are—for He in them always places them where He can accomplish the most with the limitations and weaknesses of the human nature still existing in their personalities.

PRACTICAL WORK

There is no finer "occult" training for man or woman than what we now suggest—if faithfully practiced until you are master of all those thoughts and emotions which formerly played such havoc in your life.

Each morning after awakening and when in full possession of your faculties, prepare yourself by an earnest saying of the Lord's prayer, in which you seek to put your soul's desire. Then try to "see" yourself actually doing the day's work that lies ahead of you in some such way as the following:

First, try to realize who you are—a Son of God, in truth very God, Himself—for you know that the mind in you is His Mind—that your life, your will, your intelligence, your power to say or do any-

thing are not yours but God's. Try to realize this
Life or Power or Mind in you that is God as motivating and using you all through the day. But
see clearly that the only way to Know it *is* God is
to let Love thus use you. If you let Love rule and
motivate every thought, word and act you *will* know
it is God before you go very far, for a mystical
assurance will come from the results that manifest
which will absolutely convince you.

Then "see" yourself rising from your bed in this
consciousness, bathing, dressing and meeting the
family in it, talking to them in it and to all whom
you contact during the day, ever feeling that tender,
wonderful Love in your heart inspiring and directing your every conscious act. Try to feel yourself
resting in, merging into, *becoming* that Love, so
that you see only through Its eyes, hear only with
Its ears, and know thereby that Love is the essence,
the substance, the animating cause and purpose of
all being and expression.

Seeing or imagining in this way, motivated by
an intense desire to have what is imagined become
a manifest reality, is an explanation of the success
of all so-called "demonstrations." Realizing this
you are now ready to rise and actually do what you
have just visioned yourself doing. And with a silent
prayer to the Loving One within—your God-self,
begin your day's activities.

The proof of your "seeing" will quickly evidence
itself. According to the clearness with which you
previously imagined the details of your actions and

of your contacts with others, will you have prepared and fortified yourself for the tests you will
meet.   For there will be many tests, or rather
opportunities to utilize and grow accustomed to this
new consciousness—this Love to which you have
given yourself.

So if you are greeted with words that irritate or
hurt from the first of your dear ones whom you
meet this morning, don't be discouraged if momen-
tarily you are pulled from that Love consciousness
and you retort in the old way.   That is to show
you what it means when you decide to abide in
that consciousness, and that you have to be keenly
on the alert every moment if you would not slip
away from it again.

And there will be many slips, perhaps, the first
day, and the next, and the next.   But that is natural
and to be expected, for the Love consciousness is to
be won only by acquiring true spiritual strength and
thus keeping the self wholly under control.   For
it is the self that becomes irritated or impatient,
or is hurt or grows angry, and thus tries to retain
its domination over your mind and to continue
its selfish life in you.

But you have determined that this shall not be,
and so if you persist and prove to self that *you* are
now the master, it will gradually fall in line and
begin to obey and serve you.   And you who have
now learned to abide and work in Love will discover that you are connected with a strength and
a power and likewise with a great wisdom which,

whenever there is need, you have only to call upon, and all things will be made known to you or be done for you—even the subduing of the self and getting it to recognize the Divine Power which you are.

So our final word in this connection is—do not become discouraged or feel remorse, or ever allow your mind to brood over any seeming failures, for they are only temporary and are really necessary— to show you what you still lack and what must be persisted in until you conquer. Besides it is not *you* who grow discouraged or feel remorse—it is only your human mind, which still thinks itself separate from you and is therefore still more or less dominated by the self it has created. You—the Real You—are Love—are the God-self, who knows no weakness, no lack or limitation of any kind.

A Serious Problem

Many approaching discipleship find themselves confronted with a problem that tests their faith to the limit.

They have become more or less conscious of inner guidance. They feel that a Wisdom and a Power is directing their lives and that their personalities are quite as puppets moved by a Force that often seems ruthless and in no way interested in their material welfare. For if some great bereavement has not been brought upon them, either their health has failed and is seemingly being purposely withheld, or all means of financial support have been taken away; so that they are nearing the end of their personal resources, and they are being forced to turn within to God for help.

And in such extremity seemingly they are finding Him, for if He takes them at their word, accepts their dedication and begins to cleanse them of all things that are preventing their making the seeking of His Kingdom first in their hearts and lives and thus keeping them separate in consciousness from Him, they must expect to have their selfish personalities humbled to the dust, and should rejoice with great rejoicing, for they are actually being prepared and made worthy for real discipleship and for the work under the Master's direction they so crave to do.

As was said before, many are facing such problems. If it is one of bereavement, and one has poured all one's love upon a human personality— no matter how dear and deserving—to such extent that the Loving One within is scarcely recognized or considered, because of the heart being wholly centered upon the loved one without,—it sometimes becomes necessary to call that loved one away from such a selfish love which unknowingly binds the soul and prevents it from following its own destiny. In the sorrow and loneliness that follows the Loving One within can then gradually make His presence felt and His voice heard.

Many who have lost health and have sought everywhere from human physicians for the consciousness of physical harmony and wholeness they formerly enjoyed, know that it was only through such seeking and such failure to find that they instead found God—the only physician who can truly and perfectly heal them.

But those who have lost all physical means of support and have turned to God as their guide and sustenance, and who are now looking to and depending upon Him as their sole support, have a different and a difficult problem, because of the exercise of a faith and trust it calls for that tests them to the very limit of endurance. It is because money and income had grown to be of supreme importance in their lives and had influenced all their thoughts and motives, that now both are taken away it is extremely hard—almost impossible—to let God actually be their support and sustenance.

We know that many who are facing that problem will eagerly welcome any suggestions that will help them to let go and let God actually and completely take charge. All such realize intellectually the necessity of doing just what the Master says below:

"Therefore take no thought, saying, What shall we eat? Or What shall we drink? Or, Wherewithal shall we be clothed?

"For your heavenly Father knoweth that ye have need of all these things.

"But seek ye first the Kingdom of God, and His righteousness; and all these things shall be added unto you.

"Take therefore no thought for the morrow, for the

morrow shall take thought for the things of itself, Suffi-cient unto the day is the evil thereof."
—Matthew 6:31–34.

(Read also 24–31, the preceding verses, to note what leads up to the above.)

Therefore they are faithfully and sincerely striving to "take no thought" either of what they shall eat or drink or wear, or of the future, believing that tomorrow all these will be taken care of.

And they are letting tomorrow take care of all, and perhaps also letting their families be without sufficient food or clothing or go through much mental agony in their fear of what is to become of them.

For so often the family have not the faith that the aspirant has in God, and they think the aspirant should do something and may condemn him and say many harsh and unkind things that try the faith of the aspirant exceedingly.

Now just what should one do in such straits? Is one ever justified in causing others to suffer for a faith that they do not understand and with which perhaps they have no patience? Let us see.

Is not your first duty to those for whom you have assumed the responsibility of feeding and clothing and providing a home? If there is a wife or children or parent dependent upon you, must you not provide for them—if you are mentally and physically able? Dare you compel them to endure hard-

ship just because of your faith in God's promise that
He will provide—and you do nothing but sit at
home meditating and praying and waiting for a
job to come to you or for some one to come as God's
representative and help you? Think! Would that
be fair, or as God intends for you?

Then why does the Master say we should take
no thought for the morrow?

But note that He also adds, *"for the morrow shall
take thought for the things of itself."* Which means,
does it not, that when tomorrow comes we will have
plenty to do in obeying what we are shown to do
then. For think you the Loving One within has no
work for you to do, and is not intending to tell you
what it is and just how to do it—when you are
ready and willing to hear it by putting all ideas
out of your mind that led you to think that you
need do nothing—that God will provide and take
care of you and the family also?

God *will* provide, but He provides you with ideas,
inspirations, leadings, every one of which you must
follow regardless of where they lead or what results
—if you truly seek to do His Will. In order to see
if you are really willing to give up your own will
and ideas, He may bring to you an opportunity to
do some menial work with scarcely enough pay to
make both ends meet. If you refuse to accept this,
deeming yourself worthy of something much better,
He then lets you abide a while longer in darkness.
For had you thought of those dependent on you
rather than of yourself, and had been willing to do

anything that would bring food and money and relieve the strain for them—which surely would be much better than sitting still, doing nothing—He would soon have brought to you an opportunity for work of a higher type and more pay, which in turn would lead to something much better—as you proved your ability to give of the best you had to the task allotted you.

This last applies only to those whose faith had weakened—by letting all kinds of fears, worries, and negative thoughts creep in and undermine it, although they were striving desperately to hold on. For there is a faith that nothing can cause to falter, but *it* is a positive KNOWING that the Father will provide. It is only such knowing that makes the mind an open, clean channel into and through which can pour the good which the Father intends to out-manifest.

Did you ever realize that every idea, every thought and impression that claim your attention are from God, or that He lets them come to you for His own purpose? And do you realize that no man ever became successful in any line of endeavor who did not draw all his ideas, inspiration, power and ability to accomplish, *from within himself*— from his God-Self—the Source of all good?

For remember, God is living in your body—is your Real and Only Self, and is putting you—the little you with its human ideas—through this present experience in order to teach you a great lesson —that *He* is your Supply, the Giver of *all*, and that *all is good.* And until you are able to give up all *desires for self,* all ideas of self, and are willing and glad to do anything that *He* wills, and to do it by putting in it your whole heart and soul in a desire to please Him, you have not yet proven that you are free of self and worthy of the real work and the accompanying compensation He has waiting for you.

When you can get your brain mind to realize that God *is* the Real You, and is actually living in your body and waiting for your mind's full recognition of Him and co-operation with Him, by giving over to Him complete charge and direction of all your thoughts, speech and actions,—not until then can He bring about the adjustment in your life and affairs that will enable Him to express through you the perfect harmony and abundance of all good things that is your divine right and which He intended for you from the beginning.

CHAPTER 7

"I Have Chosen You!"

MANY—very, very many—are still at that place in the unfoldment of consciousness where they are wondering, "What is the purpose of our being here?" "Why, if there is a loving God, has He made men as they are—some so wise or good or powerful, and others so ignorant, evil or weak; has given so much to the few and so little to the many?" "What is it all about, anyway?"

Such are those who have not yet awakened—who have not yet felt any strong, compelling urge to find the answer to such questions; they are still in the wondering stage, and are not enough interested to do more than accept what they have learned from church or school, or such books or lectures they have happened to read or hear, with no ability or inclination to do any deliberate thinking for themselves.

But when they find themselves wondering more and more frequently, and after awhile—maybe years later, usually preceded by some soul-stirring experience such as was described in the first chapter—they are impelled definitely to seek an explanation of the purpose of life,—then you may know that something is happening within, that their minds have been awakened, caused by the soul deep within the human consciousness being quickened and now getting ready to express itself. This quickening is like the first stirring of the child in the womb of its mother, and a coming forth in due season may be looked for as the natural result.

We are trying, as before, to show that this is a growth—that the first outer effect to be noted is the awakening of the mind, manifesting as a compelling desire to know the reason and purpose of life. It is the awakened ones that we are trying to reach. They alone are ready for what these articles contain—with the sole exception of the "elect," those who came into this life with the full knowledge in their souls of all that we have to say, but who, through a combination of circumstances due to early orthodox education and perhaps later to false teachings and detrimental environment, have never had presented to their outer minds pure truth in such simple form or with such sure appeal.

We have found it is such to whom *"The Impersonal Life"* comes as a "revelation from heaven"— a revealing of what they already knew in their soul consciousness; and from that moment they are "awake" and *know* that what we are offering them is just the spiritual food they need and which they have long been seeking.

To all such possible—the elect and the awakened ones—we are sending this call of the Master. It is to tell them how to find and to know Him, how to learn to know His loving voice within their hearts, so that they may receive direct from Him their own guidance and teaching; also that they may join with all other disciples in the now most important service of awakening and calling to Him all those that He is able to reach through them.

This is but preliminary to the much higher work each will soon be called upon to do—if they have become prepared and are capable of doing such work. All that has been suggested to you in these articles—all the mental discipline and the meditation work—is part of such preparation. Those who have not found the time or felt the significance of our exhortations and have done nothing more than read over the articles one or two times, will wonder why and perhaps be very sorry when they find that they are unable to help even themselves, not to speak of others, when the dark days come and the Master needs and calls for every possible worker and helper.

All who have eyes to see and who understand the sinister import of the dark conditions now holding humanity enslaved and bound, with no sign of relief but only plain evidence of greater darkness ahead, know the vital necessity of getting the word to all of the chosen ones as quickly as possible. Therefore all who wish to help now should ever bear this in mind and follow every urge from within that they receive to that end.

To all such we now bring the Master's own words, in the 15th Chapter of John:

"This is my commandment, That ye love one another as I have loved you.

"Greater love hath no man than this, that a man lay down his life for his friends."

Surely, dear ones, we want to be His friends, we who are seeking to be His disciples; and all that we need to do is that which *He within us* commands us to do. If you are a disciple you *know* that you must love one another—for He within you *compels* you to do that; and if He requires it, you know that you would lay down your life for your friends. Listen now to what such love leads:

"Ye are my friends, if ye do whatsoever I command you."

"Henceforth I call you not servants, for the servant knoweth not what his Lord doeth: but I have called you friends; for all things I have heard of my Father I have made known unto you."

Do you realize what this means? It is a definite promise that by obeying His commandments we become not servants any more but His *friends,* which means that we are privileged to abide in His Consciousness and thereby to know all things that He knows. Just think of it! But this comes only when He sees that we not only obey Him but no longer have any thought for or of self, but so great a love for Him that we seek to serve Him in all of our friends and brothers. Listen!

"Ye have not chosen me, but I have chosen you, and ordained you, that you should go and bring forth fruit, and that your fruit should remain; that whatsoever ye shall ask of the Father in my name, he may give it you."

Can anything be plainer? If He has called you into this His Work, and you acknowledge it as His

Work and have truly dedicated yourself to Him—your Highest Self, and seek only to serve and obey Him,—then you are ready for the ordaining. Nay, if in your heart and soul you want it more than anything else, you may know that He *has* ordained you; and all that remains is for you to *realize* this and go forth and bring in the fruit to which He will lead you. Believe this then and go forth confidently, taking no thought of how or what you shall speak, for as you let Him speak through you He will awaken and call forth these new brothers (the fruit), and they will then surely remain. Which means that whatsoever you ask in His name, or from His Love in your heart, will the Father grant.

It is for this that He has chosen you and has long been preparing you—you who love your fellows as He loves you. Our part is but to *convince you* of this, so that *you in turn may convince others* and lead them to Him.

MAMMON

We wonder how many realize what a mighty power Mammon has become in the world—in fact that he seemingly rules the world.

If you do not realize it as yet, consider what follows, and then perhaps you will agree that there are very few indeed who are not under Mammon's sway, who do not fear him, and who are wholly free from his power.

First look around among your friends and note how money, or the possession of it, means everything to them. Without it they are "looked down upon" by those who have it. With plenty of it, especially if they spend it freely, they are "good fellows." Those with a superabundance of it are "looked up to" with more or less awe by those who have less or little, while others bow and cater to them, deem them a great success, and generally consider them as having reached an exalted place in the world.

Can you admit that the possession of money, to-day, in the eyes of the world, does not mean more to the vast majority of people than the possession of any other thing? Which means that practically everyone acknowledges Mammon as their lord and master, yields to his demands, and thereby gives money absolute power over them.

Do you think this is stating it too strongly? Then answer to yourself these questions:

Are you who read truly free from its power? Think! Has it no hold whatever on you? Are you not in the least afraid of losing your job, your social or financial standing, or your investments? Or should you lose all, have you not the slightest fear for yourself and of your power to regain what is lost?

Are you sure in your social relations with others that their possession of wealth or lack of it has no effect or influence whatever on your attitude to-wards them—that the beggar and the banker are alike your brothers?

Are you sure, in your business dealings with others that the prospect of profit or loss in no way influences your statements or causes you not to listen to a desire to help them, when you want to sell them something?

Can you truly say that money means nothing to you, that the possession or lack of it in the eyes of your friends has no place in your thoughts, and that you could be a tramp or a millionaire with equal disregard of Mammon's power to cause you to deviate one iota from your loving service to the Lord Christ within?

If you can answer "yes" to these questions, then have you truly reached the stage of discipleship, and are ready for or are now really doing the work of the Master, for you have passed a supreme test and are worthy of doing the work you came here to do.

This article is written in the full understanding of the insidious power Mammon has acquired over practically every seeker of the Kingdom, a power that very few are aware of, and which it is our duty to show up clearly, so that each may know for him or herself and deal with it definitely from now on.

This power has so instilled itself into the consciousness of nearly everyone that it is most difficult to free one's mind from it sufficiently to see the hold it has obtained upon our thoughts and lives. If we will only admit it, it influences unconsciously most of our motives, desires, aims and actions, and it ever drives us onward with the whip of fear so that we cannot reason calmly and see that self is being wholly misled by a false god to the forgetfulness of the Loving One within, who promises if we seek *first* His Kingdom and His Righteousness *all* things else will be added.

Therefore we say to you, search deeply into your mind and heart and make sure that you have not unconsciously been worshipping Mammon, obeying his mandates and living under his rule, rather than God's.

This applies as much to those to whom the need of money is perhaps at this moment paramount in their thoughts, as to those who have an abundance of it and who are living in an atmosphere of wealth.

Money of itself, of course, is no more than a medium by which we exchange one commodity for another, and is therefore neither good nor evil. But a selfishness that seeks more than one's share of it or more than one needs and can use, is undeniably evil, for that deprives others of their just share or needs. Such a selfishness, however, has become so common that it is not considered to be selfishness any more. It is deemed to be a normal process of nature—a "survival of the fittest," when from the foregoing it is plainly seen as perverted nature.

Therefore many millions of souls are living in a perverted state, entirely under the dominion of a self-created power, existing, maintaining itself and fast gaining a stranglehold upon its creators, solely because they do not realize whom and what they are serving—their own selfish wills.

Mammon is thus seen to be crystallized selfishness —nay, entitized selfishness, because money has no power unless it is gathered together in the hands of a few who purposely deprive many others of their rightful share in order to maintain their power and to further their own evil ends. We will not go further into this phase of the subject at this time, but for fuller light upon it refer to you the article on "The Enemy" in the booklet *"Brotherhood."*

One thing each seeker of the Kingdom must clearly determine here and now—the influence that Mammon has had over him in the past, and that this influence must be eliminated from mind and heart henceforth and forever.

This means that from this moment his allegiance is to God alone and that he will look to Him only as his support and his supply, and will have full and utter faith in His promise of what will result if he makes the seeking of Him and His Righteousness first in his life.

But realize that much will come to test this faith, and outer circumstances may grow very dark and friends and loved ones may condemn and consider you gone daft. But know that when everything is darkest, and it would seem that God and all else have deserted you, the time of deliverance draws very near. For there is no truer saying than that it is always darkest just before dawn.

Those who have the booklet *"Wealth"* should read it again in the light of the foregoing. It will prove most illuminating, and you will find its pages filled with inspiration and helpfulness.

HUSBAND AND WIFE

We wish you now to think with us on a subject that is very close to some of you—especially to those who are married, and which perhaps is of more importance to such than any other subject we could consider.

It happens that many seekers after truth, many aspirants—aye, many even who are approaching discipleship, are traveling alone in their search, unaccompanied by husband or wife, who seemingly are unsympathetic with—if they are not actually antagonistic to—their aspirations and efforts to follow and serve the Master.

We wish to recall to you some of the deep truths stated in the chapter on "Soul Mates" in *"The Impersonal Life,"* or rather to restate them in different words. After which we suggest the rereading and studying of the whole chapter.

First, do not think for one moment that it was an accident or a mistake that you are wedded to the one who is now legally your husband or wife. For the I AM, the Higher Self, the Knower, Lover, and Doer within you—and within all—never makes a mistake. Then there must have been a deep purpose in your coming into such special relationship with this other soul, must there not?

Next, remember that this other soul is an Angel from Heaven, even as are you—an attribute of God, a Divine Being—confined in a human body and looking out through the barred cage of its personality. The human mind in that body knows not why it is here in this particular condition and environment, but the soul—if it is awakened—knows, and with the help of the Higher Self often tries to tell the human mind. Some of you who are approaching discipleship have been able to give to your minds glimpses of the purpose of such relationship. You are those who will understand what follows.

Can you not see that two souls never come together intimately in any family or other relationship who do not in a way belong together? That is, they either complement or fit in with one another in such a way as to bring about or fulfill certain necessary conditions that will develop and round out their characters and bring wisdom to their souls, so that harmony may eventually express in their outer lives.

Ponder over that a bit, and you will realize that it must be true—you who are learning the law of Love and Harmony. And then perhaps it may occur to you that the principal reason for the one coming to you as husband or wife in this life is to help each of you to learn your lessons, which evidently you failed to learn in the past, and this time to strive more determinedly to conquer those qualities or weaknesses in you which the other seems uncannily able constantly to bring to the surface—each thus under the direction of the Higher Self actually teaching the other.

Of course, if you are still quite selfish and headstrong, and refuse to face yourself and see only those qualities in the other which show up your own weaknesses so glaringly, and you rebel against it all and seek to remain apart from the other, it only postpones the happiness and peace your human mind seeks and which your soul longs for and keeps urging you toward.

On the other hand where human love is still very strong—and selfish, and unwilling to allow the other the freedom of life and thought which you insist upon having for yourself, and you try to force that other to think and see as you love to do,—you will have to learn through much suffering and unhappiness that the strongest demand of the soul is for perfect freedom, and that one who would bind another soul can expect not love, but rebellion, deceit and constant antagonism, if not smothered hatred.

This, however, hardly applies to one on The Path. Such a one gets inner glimpses of the caged soul of the other, and strives hard to conquer those old claims of the selfish personality and even to help the other to awaken to that which is holding him or her back from what their soul is seeking. To such human love is gradually lifted up into divine love, and while the other, if anything, is more greatly loved than ever, despite all weaknesses, yet it is with a love that unites with that of the Higher

Self of the other, as it were, in a great yearning to bring the other consciously into a true understanding of the purpose of their coming together and consequently into the same joy of the Lord that the knowing one feels.

Some of you are beginning to see that as a disciple of Jesus Christ the only thing now to do is to face this task that is closest to you, whether it is with husband, wife, child, parent or other relation of a family, friendship or business nature, and to take it out of the hands of the personal self and to give it over wholly to the Loving One within, determined to let Him inspire and direct every thought, word and act from this time on. For you now realize what a mess you have made of it, and that He and His Love alone can bring to you and to the other the understanding, the consideration for others, and the self-control that will unfold and broaden your souls and enable you to learn the lessons that you had to come together to teach each other, and thus to help your Higher Selves to bring about that oneness of consciousness that must be in serving Christ.

The principal aim of this Work is to bring awakened souls to Christ. Naturally such souls cannot find and enter the Kingdom with such a task unfinished. You will keenly realize this later—if not now. Therefore, it is necessary to get busy. With the Master's help many of the mistakes of the past can be quickly undone and remedied by those who truly seek to bring every department of their life into harmony with His Life.

Try to realize what a wondrous thing it would be if your husband or wife were working side by side with you in the Master's Cause, each of you equally in earnest and determined to find the Kingdom—you who think this now improbable, if not utterly impossible.

Do you know that there are many such couples in this Work? And there will be many more, for one of our chief endeavors is to join husband and wife in spirit or in the consciousness of the divine purpose of their coming together in this close relationship—where they can truly learn with each other's help to master the lower self, and then to work as one in loving service under their blessed Master, Jesus Christ.

Our part is to assist each husband and wife wherever we can to know that they will grow spiritually very much faster when striving to serve unitedly than each could alone. For alone they are incomplete—that is, the one complements and supplies certain soul qualities and powers that the other lacks, else they would never have come together—being so different.

You may not realize this now—some of you who do not yet know the soul of your husband or wife. We have seen numerous instances where a wife deemed her husband far beneath her spiritually, and when the quickening came to the husband, he

proved to be much more advanced than the wife—
especially in living and practicing what he knew.
Similarly, where the husband thought the wife
knew nothing about Truth, when the time of her
quickening came she showed herself to be much beyond him in true spiritual understanding.

After coming together in the Work, however,
these inequalities begin to disappear, as each learns
to know and supply spiritually to the other what
each lacks and needs. Thus they complement and
round out—as two-in-one—their united channel for
service under our Blessed Master, and are in a position to accomplish what He intended from the
beginning.

Practical Work

The time has come to give definite exercises that
will help to lift the consciousness to that of the
Master within.

Those of you who have earnestly sought to gain
a realization of the meaning of the words "Be Still
and Know—I Am—God," as suggested in the earlier
articles and in *"The Impersonal Life,"* may already
have caught a glimpse of this consciousness, for
these magical words have helped many to enter it.

In order to prepare your mind for as clear an understanding as possible of what follows, reread
chapters II and XVII of *"The Impersonal Life."*
This will also help you more easily to get into the
attitude of mind necessary to comply with the suggestions to be given. Then read carefully all that

is stated, seeking to grasp its inner meaning, before attempting to obey any of the instructions.

Stand or sit at ease in front of a mirror and look at your reflection therein. Look particularly into the eyes and try to see and note the intelligence shining out of them.

Try to realize that that intelligence is your mind or soul, but that *You* who are Spirit are much more than that intelligence or soul, whose mind is now thoroughly alert wondering what is coming.

Also realize that in very truth what you see in the mirror is but a reflection—an appearance—of what your mind thinks is You. But the Real You, being Spirit, cannot be seen, and instead is *that which sees and knows all things.*

Now slowly and very positively—trying as you voice each word to realize fully the deep meaning and significance of the *command* in them—speak to that intelligence which you see looking out of the eyes in the mirror as follows (you can say it aloud or silently to yourself—whichever is the most effective to you):

"Be *still* and *know*,—I Am—*God*. Know that *I* am, and that *you* are not at all—as a separate being. *I* am not your body, mind or soul,—*I* am Spirit. I am that which animates you, which lives you, which is your intelligence, which is your power to be and to do all that you are and do.

"*I* am your Real self—your Only self—I, the God of you. *You* are only a portion of *My* Consciousness, dwelling within a focalized center of My Mind, which you call your self. The proof is, you are nothing, know nothing, can do nothing, only as *I* inspire and empower you to know and do it."

Continue thus to talk to that intelligence—saying whatever you feel led to say, letting the words speak themselves—with no thought or effort on your part. Keep on talking to it until you find that you have the full attention *of your mind,* that it is actually listening to you,—when you need look in the mirror no longer, but may close your eyes, for your mind is listening and you can now talk direct to it.

As you continue you will suddenly realize, as your mind follows all that is said, that it is hearing some deep truths which *you* of yourself never knew before; and with a flash of illumination you will become mystically aware that That which is speaking is from a Consciousness that seems to *know all things,* that that Consciousness is I Am, God within you, the Real You, and that what is listening and hearing is what you formerly thought was you, but which is only your brain mind which believed itself separate from God's Consciousness—That which is All in all.

Thus has your consciousness for the time being been lifted from the lower brain mind to your higher divine mind—its true home, where it "sees" as You, the Master, wish it to see, and it knows as You know.

Try to grasp the deep significance of every word of the above, and until you do, read it over again—and still again, before proceeding to do what is required. Then practice it faithfully until you get the realization. If you are determined to get it, it will come.

Practice will eventually make it easy to enter the higher consciousness *at will*—by simply commanding:

"Be *still* and *know*,—I Am—God."

CHAPTER 8

"I, If I Be Lifted Up,
Will Draw All Men unto Me."

THERE are many earnest students who, while believing God to be all in all and the life and intelligence in all living things, yet also believe in the power of evil and even fear its power. Such do not want to accept or believe God as in any way responsible for man's actions, especially if they deem such actions to be evil.

We know that we are venturing upon dangerous ground in making that last statement, from the viewpoint of many who still adhere to old orthodox beliefs on the subject; but you will soon perceive our purpose in making it.

Of course it is only the limitations of the human mind that prevent most people from really *knowing* that God or Good is *all there is*—that God is *One*, not two (good and evil), and hence such think themselves separate from Him, thereby unwittingly classing themselves with what is not God and therefore not good.

It is because of such faulty reasoning that it becomes necessary to make clear a great truth—make it so clear that all who read will never again fail to know that their God is One and is All, and that

115

all that Is, is good—to those who see with a single eye.

First it must be understood that all that follows is directed to and is intended only for the followers of Christ and for those who seek to know and follow Him. All others cannot possibly understand or apply what is given herewith.

We now recall to you what our great Master and Teacher taught us regarding Himself:

"I can of myself do nothing."—John 5:30.

"Believest thou not that I am in the Father, and the Father in me? The words that I speak unto you, I speak not of myself, but the Father that dwelleth in me he doeth the work."—John 14:10.

If these statements be true of Jesus, they must be true of all men; for He is the Exemplar and the Wayshower sent to humanity by our Father to teach us the truth of being.

While it is true that the I Am or God's Spirit in man spoke the above words to Jesus' disciples and speaks them likewise to every awakened soul, it is also true that the Christ Spirit is not "born" or awakened in all men. Yet that Spirit is God's Life or the Light that lighteth and dwelleth in every man, even though the darkened mind of man as yet comprehendeth it not.

Therefore God's Life and Spirit is *All in all,* for there is no other life or spirit but His. Hence if He *is* all in all, He must *do* all that man does, or

cause him to do and say all that he does or says—
but for His own wise and loving purpose, and which
purpose man with his "separate" mind is wholly unable to comprehend.

*"When ye have lifted up the son of man, then ye
shall know that I am he, that I do nothing of myself,
but as my Father hath taught me."*—John 8:28.

Truly when we have lifted up our human mind
so that it knows the I Am or Christ within, then it
knows that it is nothing and can do nothing that
the Father, through His Spirit in us—the I Am,
does not lead or cause us to do. It is when lifted
to that consciousness that Paul refers to in the 10th
to 12th verse of the 13th chapter of 1st Corinthians:

"But when that which is perfect is come (the perfect
understanding as quickened and taught by God's Spirit
—the I Am, in awakened man) *then that which is in
part shall be done away with.*

*"When I was a child, I spake as a child, I understood
as a child, I thought as a child; but when I became a
man I put away childish things.*

*"For now we see through a glass darkly; but then face
to face: now I know in part; but then I shall know even
as I also am known."*

Man in his limited understanding calls everything
more or less evil that does not measure up to his
standard of good. forgetting that in reality "there
is none good but God," and not realizing that unless
we see God in everything we cannot see good in
anything.

He also forgets that it is only ignorance of the
truth or of the great Law of Being that causes any-

one to condemn a thing or condition as evil, for we have only to recall much that was called evil in our childhood days by our parents and grandparents which greater understanding and common usage now accepts without thought of condemnation, and which therefore must have been "lifted up" to the present standard of "good."

To the thinker it can be seen that God, being all *in* all, is gradually from *within* man (or infant humanity) teaching him that *all that is,* is good—because *He* is all that is; teaching him just as fast as man is able to bear it and accept it as good, and then to use such knowledge only as He directs—thus lifting up man's understanding and drawing him close to Him.

Man thereby in time grows in wisdom and understanding and learns that there are not two powers in the world antagonistic to each other—God and Devil, or Good and Evil. But that there is only one—a very wise and mighty Power, from Whom all other powers spring and derive their existence or reason for being.

Think this over and you will see that it must be so, for no two equally active and antagonistic powers could long exist, for either they would soon destroy each other, or the more powerful one would master the other and compel it to be its servant.

Therefore evil, when once understood as an actual force in the world, must be permitted—aye, must have been created and is being utilized by the One

Who Is Power, and Who created all and is over all—
for a very wise and benevolent purpose, and which
it behooves everyone of us to study in order to get
a glimpse of that purpose.

A thing or a force is evil only so long as we do not
understand the law of its being and therefore cannot
control it. Such was lightning, electricity, steam,
fire, the winds and the waves, before man learned
to control them and afterwards to make them serve
him. See what good and useful servants they are
now, as a result of being studied, understood and
wisely controlled.

For the same reason a wise man, instead of fighting, rebelling against, or running away from what
appears to be evil, will seek to know it for what it
really is—a force permitted by God to try, test and
develop man's strength of character and to teach
him wisdom; and never to tempt him—as is at-
tributed to God's "adversary."

But do not forget that evil, like any other uncontrolled force, is destructive, and therefore its nature must be fully understood, and whenever possible it must be prevented from doing any active
harm. Evil is a negative force, and according to
the law of its being is attracted only by forces of
a negative nature. It is well known that fear,
worry, anxiety, anger, envy, jealousy, greed, etc., all
of which are negative, attract forces that are inherently evil. But know this—evil cannot hurt or
touch one of positive mind who knows his part in
God and Good—who knows that God is All, and

that not only is there nothing therefore to fear, but that God is *always* a loving and protective power that will take care of all whose minds are stayed on Him.

One who knows this ordinarily needs do nothing but stand aside and watch the law work, realizing that in time evil will destroy itself.

It is our hope eventually to have all who are journeying with us to know evil for just what it is— that it exists everywhere outside the Kingdom of God's Consciousness, which is all Love, and that by entering that Consciousness—the consciousness of the I Am within us, we can look right through the seeming evil and see the good that it hides.

This particularly applies to the seeming evil in the personalities around us. Until one is poised in the I Am Consciousness so that one always sees through the eyes of Love, the imperfections of another stand forth more or less glaringly, thus distracting the attention and preventing one from seeing the good in the other. But when we have given ourselves and all of our personal ideas wholly over to the Loving One within, He gradually frees us from such separative forces and permits us a glimpse of Himself in the souls of others. Those favored ones who are vouchsafed such glimpse ever afterward cannot help but keep their hearts wide open, letting His love pour out when contacting others, ever seeking and longing to see Him again in all the souls they meet.

Of course the knowledge of God being all there

is must become a fixed part of our consciousness, in order to cause us thus always to seek to see and know the Christ-self of our brother. It is magical in effect when one really looks for good in another—one can always find it; when one really seeks to know God, in one way or another He will surely reveal Himself.

GOD, CHRIST, AND THE HIGHER SELF

Some have written us about not differentiating in *"The Impersonal Life"* between God, the Father, Christ, and the Higher Self, the I AM throughout its message apparently speaking for each and representing all, so we propose herein to give the reason for such non-differentiation.

It has also been remarked that in accepting the Impersonal message one is expected to jump from mortality to the God-head, in fact to the Absolute, without recognition of any of the intervening stages.

While this in a way is true, for we accept—nay, know—God as *within* us, as our very Self, we do not deny that there are many stages for humanity as a whole to pass through before even mastery of the mortal nature is attained, not to speak of Godhood.

But the Impersonal Life message is not for all humanity, any more than is the message in this book. For comparatively few individuals of the hundreds of millions of humanity are as yet able to receive and understand the truths they contain. These truths are given out to awaken and call forth

the chosen of the Lord—the teachers and servers
of humanity, preparatory to the ushering in of
the New Day or Eon.

Make no mistake, you who hear and feel within
the leap of your soul at these words, you need
not go through these many stages, taking eons of
time; but you can know and be your God-self now,
here, in this life—if you will follow Christ Jesus,
the One sent of the Father to lead and show the way
to all who have the courage to follow Him.

In order to help explain the identity of God,
Christ and the Higher Self, we quote part of a letter received from one of our earnest ones that is
quite remarkable and very illuminating, and clearly
brings out the most important phases of the subject—so conclusively that we find it unnecessary to
add anything to it. The first part of what follows,
while not definitely relating to the subject, is so
good and helpful, we are including it:

"Sometimes I have felt that I have made little
progress, and from the positive side this is probably
so. It has been a process of 'killing out,' a getting
rid of self. Years ago I used to say that I would
rather be myself than anyone else; I envied none,
no matter how miserable I might be I would not
change with any other soul. Then I passed through
a period when I felt I would gladly change with
many souls; and now I am at the point where I do
not prize individuality at all in the ordinary sense.
To be an onlooker, yet a worker too, beholding the

splendour and reflecting it, shedding it forth, yet utterly invisible and unconscious of self,—that would be my choice.   It would not trouble me to know that when I pass from this life I shall cease to be, except for my ability to know and feel, and to accomplish.   I could even be content never to meet my dear ones in person; if I could be assured that they too had entered the consciousness of God.

"But I have a feeling that we lose our individuality only to find it again, since each of us is an attribute of God, hence distinctly individual.   But until one develops the true Being, it must be wonderful to rest in non-being; it would be like a night's sleep replete with dreams.

"I understand now what you mean when you say that we should make no distinguishment—that God, Christ and the Higher Self are all one.   They do not differ in themselves but only in us, according to each·one's ability to understand.   They are different ASPECTS, that is, they are different only as they vary with the position of the beholder.   Which is really no difference, but only an appearance of difference.

"Boundless Being, The Supreme, the Seven Creative Logoi, the Solar Gods, The Logos, these are different states of consciousness, ONE CONSCIOUSNESS being in them all, but perceived in varying degree, according to the plane of manifestation. The consciousness is the string upon which all the beads of being are strung,—it is a rosary of realization.

"Intellectually I have been in great confusion trying to differentiate, but the true mystic does not bother about the different planes and manifestations, because he goes back of manifestation and above planes to the INMOST. If we learn by study, by experience, we must contact all planes; but if we learn by faith and intuition we are unaware of the rungs of the ladder by which we climb. The true mystic does not think of the ladder at all, only of the goal. AFTERWARD, when we KNOW, it will be interesting to examine all this learning, for the pattern is wonderful; but we see clearer after we have reached the top.

"Ever you must return to the clear, open vision; ever you must renew the eyes in love, vast, undying, limitless love, sensing it as the one power moving in and through and BEYOND the Universe, pervading your life."

WOULD YOU HEAL YOURSELF?

My child, dost thou believe that I am—I, and I alone?

Then thou must believe that all that thou art, I am—that thy body, thy mind, thy life, thy will, thy self,—all are Mine.

Then thou must be I, My Self. Which means that thou canst not be separate or different in any particular from Me. Only as thou thinkest thyself different canst thou be other than I am in any phase of thy nature.

Then naturally, if thou thinkest thyself as *not*

different but *one with Me,* so shalt thou *be,* and thou shalt express My nature.

Be still, until thou gleanest the full import of these words.

If I am thy self, then if thou wilt but thus *know* it and let Me think My thoughts, speak My words, and do My will in thee—which I will aways do if thou keepest thy thoughts of a separate self and will from thy mind—then thou wilt soon learn to be thy *true* self and wilt consciously join thy mind and will with Mine, and I will work through thee and My mind and will shall become thine, and thou wilt know thyself as I Am, even as My beloved Son, Christ Jesus, showed My Self to thee.

But before thou canst be and do this, thou must accustom thy mind to the knowledge of thy true nature as very Christ living in thy body and ruling thy consciousness and the consciousness of thy body. Thou must strive unceasingly to permit no thoughts to enter thy mind and no feelings to influence thy heart that thou knowest are not Mine.

Yea, thou must speak to thy mind as I am now speaking to thee, and must convince it by words of truth whom thou art—must lift it up into the consciousness that thou knowest to be Mine and thine.

Thou must even persuade the consciousness of the organs and parts of thy body that thou art now allied with God, the All-Good, thereby wiping out of their consciousness all the old separative thoughts of imperfection and not-good, and promising that henceforth only the good and perfect thoughts of the God thou art will be sent them, in order that the All-Good of the One Life may manifest in and through them in perfect harmony.

Then thou must practice daily, hourly, seeing thyself, feeling thyself, and being outwardly the all-good God that thou, thyself, art in reality.

Yes, thou canst do this, by saying and *meaning* it as thou sayest:

"Be still, and know—I AM,—God."

Saying it again and again—and realizing truly thyself as God—to the consciousness of the organ or part of the body that still yields to the claim of separation. Say it until it is freed from such false claim, and *know* that it must obey and let go; for error cannot stand before truth spoken by one who *knows*—any more than darkness can remain where there is light.

Then in order that I may use thee as a channel for the freeing and healing of others, thou must practice keeping thy heart open and letting My love pour out and radiate from thee, as light radiates from a powerful arc lamp.

Thou wilt thus become a moving center of influence for good that will affect all who meet thee, for My love-life in the midst of thee will touch and quicken the love-life in the midst of them, and they will be lifted up and made to long for and to come close to Me in consciousness, even though at the time they know it not.

Ah, do I hear some ask, How canst thou open thy heart and let out My love?

Dost thou not love someone or something—thy mother, thy sweetheart, a dear friend, a babe, a kitten? If thou knowest not as yet that thou hast a heart, study carefully thy feelings when thou seest such a cherished one,—note the warmth and welling up in thy heart of something precious and wonderful there.

Dost thou ever feel kind, or long to help some suffering or needy one? When such feelings compel thy attention, know that it is My love in thy heart opening it and asking to be let out. And if thou yieldest, thy soul will rejoice, for just that much more is it freed from self.

From much yielding to such feelings I shall in time teach thee to keep thy heart always open for My use; for in such a heart I come and make my abode and there live My life, do My will, and manifest My Self, unhindered and unlimited by the separate mind—love having long since dissolved all sense of difference and separation, and lifted it up into oneness with My mind.

Thus as My mind in thee is lifted up do I draw all men unto Me.

Harmony

In the preceding chapter we told in the article "Husband and Wife" about married couples coming more closely together in this Work through the truths taught and the Spirit of Service engendered, thus rounding out and complementing each others' characters.

The following, written by such a complemented couple, tells how to bring about the union of consciousness between husband and wife that must be in disciples of Christ:

"If there is any situation in your immediate circle in which there is a decided lack of harmony, you must work that out into Harmony, or you cannot truly teach anyone the precepts of the Higher Law. For Harmony is the first Law, the *supreme* Law, and it eventually must be lived to the Nth degree.

"Without harmonizing the position in which you stand here and now, how can you expect to touch other souls into Love and Harmony who come to you for help? To teach a law you must first learn it and then live it.

"First Law: Cleanse thyself first of all inharmony. Bring thy body into subjection to thy mind, thy mind into subjection to thy Spirit, and thy Spirit into subjection to thy God. Let the Harmony of God flow down through thy point of contact—thy Spirit, through thy mind into thy body, and out to all those with whom you come into contact through the spoken word or the creative word. The word must be spoken.

"*In the beginning was the Word, and the Word was with God, and the Word was God. The same*

*was in the beginning with God. All things were
made by Him (the Word) and without Him was
not anything made that was made.'*

"God created all things by the spoken Word. He
said, *'Let there be light, etc.'* and there was light,
etc. We in contact with God can create Perfect
Harmony, if we *speak* the positive word of Perfect
Harmony. Say to thyself:

*" 'I am a child of my loving Father-God, a
brother of the Lord Jesus Christ. I as my True
Self walk and talk in Perfect Harmony with Them.
Let the words of my mouth, the thoughts of my
mind, and the meditations of my heart be acceptable in Thy sight, O Lord, my Strength and my
Redeemer.'*

"SECOND LAW: Then when thou hast created
Harmony in thyself, begin to help the one nearest
and dearest to thee to harmonize himself (or herself) by holding him (or her) in your thought in
Perfect Harmony with the Father and the Son.
For a little while go apart and in the quiet away
from that person, preferably when he or she is
asleep, speak out loud these words:

*" 'My dear one, we are One with the Father and
the Son, and in the Oneness of the High Consciousness of the Holy Spirit we walk and talk with Them.
Let there be perfect Peace and Understanding and
purest Love between us, that we may clearly manifest that which the Father wills.'*

"Slowly that inharmonious mind, soul and body
will become more and more harmonious, and one

day your dearest one will say something that will permit you to speak these words to that one face to face. But be careful, go slowly. Wait! Wait! Wait, I say, on the Lord in perfect trust until that one speaks to you the key-word that will open the door so that you may enter in. Do not force that door. If you do you will be 'thrown out' as-it-were. Jesus Christ said, *'Behold, I stand at the door and knock. If any man hear my voice let him open and I will come in and sup with him.'*

"Knock gently. Wait. Knock again, and wait. Wait until your dearest one hears and answers your knock, saying, *'Come in.'* Knocking means knocking at the door of the heart or subconscious mind until it hears, and to do that we must wait until the subconscious mind is free from that tyrant, the conscious mind—when it is asleep. And then some glorious day thy dearest one's subconscious mind will be wise and strong enough to explain to its conscious mind about the Christ standing and knocking at the door of the heart, and cause it to open the door and tell Him to *'Come in.'*

"And then, and only then, will the Christ in thee and the Christ in thy dearest one enter in and sit down and sup together in Perfect Harmony.

"And thus your trying situation will vanish like mist before the sun. For just as the rays of the sun directed on the mist dispel it and we see clearly, so the Rays of God's Love directed through us will destroy that mist of inharmony in another, and suddenly we will see clearly face to face."

On reflection you will see from the above that this method can be applied not only to husband and wife, but to child or parent, brother or sister, friend or enemy, business associate or customer, whom you would help to come under the Law of Harmony. All that it needs is to use words suitable to the conditions needing adjustment. You will find that you need change none of the words, and need add only what the Loving One within inspires.

Remember that in Spirit you are *One*, not only with the Father and the Son, but with the Higher Self of the one whom you would quicken and help; and following the words, "Let there be perfect Peace and Understanding and purest Love between us, that we may clearly manifest that which the Father wills," you can add:

"You are not bound by any claims of the flesh, or of the world, or of the separate mind, for these have no existence in Spirit. Let the perfection that you are in Spirit and your own good that awaits expression now come forth, that the Father may be glorified in the Son."

The oneness of consciousness in Spirit of you and your brother is *actual*, as has so often been shown. Therefore by simply KNOWING this, and talking as above to the *soul* of another, the soul *will* hear and when the brain mind is quiet will convey to it what was received from you—even as when in the quiet of meditation you find thoughts flowing into your mind reminding you of things forgotten and what you need to know.

But you must let your Higher Self do the talking through you; your personal desires and human love and anxiety must be wholly replaced by a yearning to help and serve the highest in the other. Only through such an impersonal love can your Real Self reach and impress the soul consciousness of the other with the truth of what you will say, so that it will push forth to the outer mind.

While speaking to the other at night when the brain mind is asleep makes it easier for the soul to accept, yet at other times whenever spoken with positive power and confident knowing, it will also accept, especially when you continue speaking until the conviction comes that it has heard. Then cease and rest in peace, thanking and praising God for His many mercies.

A persistent practice and proving of this method will bring remarkable results, and we urge every reader to begin at once to put it to the test. This is a wonderful work you can do. We pray that our loving Father will guide you and make you into an efficient laborer in His vineyard, so that you may become capable and ready when needed for larger and more universal service.

CHAPTER 9

"Where Two or Three are Gathered Together"

THOSE who have traveled with us this far and have faithfully studied the various articles and followed the suggestions given are beginning to perceive that there is a plan and purpose back of everything stated, and that all is tending toward and preparing the earnest and persevering ones for a definite work.

They see that this must be a Spiritual work—from all that has come to them, and that it of necessity must be performed by and in the mind, under the direction of the will of one who has taught the mind to be a perfect and obedient servant.

If we have been persistent in urging aspirants to practice regularly the mental exercises and to observe faithfully the meditation hours, it has been only to help them speedily attain that end. And if those who have been mentally lazy or who have discontinued the practice before gaining complete obedience, yielding to the mind's claim that it is too strenuous or that it cannot see any need of such regularity, they will learn, when asked in the near future to do what will be required of them, why they are unable to help and to accomplish what those who have been faithful are doing easily and with such manifest results.

For in this Work only trained minds and wills
will be able to accomplish anything, either for the
Master's Cause, to which you have dedicated your
hearts and lives, or for yourselves, when the need
is upon you. And the practical work we have been
giving you has been to enable you to experiment
first on and with yourselves and then in helping
those nearest you, in order to prepare you for wider
and sterner service, when the time arrives that we
will be called upon to assist the Master and our
Great Brothers in Spirit in Their Work for humanity.

Before you can do that you must learn to work
first under the Master's direction in an intimate
personal way in your own life. Remember you
have not chosen to do this, but *He has chosen you,*
because He needs you to accomplish what He has
been especially preparing you for; and if you faithfully listen to and obey Him, you will become more
than a servant to Him. He will then call you
"Friend," and will endow you with powers that will
enable you consciously to *co-operate* with our
Brothers in Spirit in the definite Work for which
ALL are now making ready.

After you have truly learned to obey and to wait
upon and serve Him, and have given all your
own affairs over into His keeping, so that now you
always know His voice when He speaks, then you
will be ready and able to work with others, and
will sooner or later draw to you those who belong

with you and who will meet with you for group study and practice of the teachings.

Only a deep yearning to serve will bring this about—a putting of self aside in a desire to be used by the Master in every way possible. This yearning of course is inspired by Him and is your feeling of His desire to use you; and if you yield up self and obey all leadings He gives you, you will soon find He will bring you in touch with one or more earnest students who have the same yearning in their hearts.

This must be,

"For where two or three are gathered together in My Name, there am I in the midst of them."—Matt. 18:20.

It is *He* that brings such together for *His* purpose, which gradually He will unfold to you, as you learn to know His will in group study and service. How to work in a group by losing all consciousness of self and personality, and thereby attaining unto *group consciousness,* is the next higher stage for those who seek to be brothers in Christ.

From this you will see that groups will form themselves naturally—that is, under the Master's guidance. But all must first learn to know and obey His leading.

A glimpse of the purpose and possibilities of group work is given us in the two verses preceding the above words of the Master, in Matt. 18:18–19.

"Again I say unto you, That if two of you shall agree on earth as touching any thing that they shall ask, it shall be done for them of my Father which is in heaven.

"Verily I say unto you, Whatsoever ye shall bind on earth shall be bound in heaven; and whatsoever ye shall loose on earth shall be loosed in heaven."

Can you conceive of the vast power at the command of a group of consecrated souls who have learned to know "who they are and of what they are a part;" have learned how to "speak the word" in the service of their Father in Heaven and to *loose* for Him those who are bound and held in darkness?

It is true that each individual can work alone and can accomplish great things; but think of the far greater power for good where five or ten, or a hundred, or a thousand, or ten or a hundred thousand, are combined in a definite act of mind and will, with their Brothers in Spirit back of, directing and pouring through them the power of Their Divine Wills!

And that is what this Work of the Brotherhood, through us and through other similarly consecrated groups, is preparing its members for—those earnest ones who feel the strong urge from within to do everything possible to make themselves fit and worthy to be used.

This does not mean the formation of any outer organization—far from it; for remember, we said that even when small groups are formed it will be "under the Master's guidance," and that "all must first learn to know and obey His leading."

All that we are doing is to help you to find and to know Him, and then to learn to know His voice and to obey His leading. After that gradually *He* will bring you into the consciousness of "who you are and of what you are a part."

If this recalls to you some dim memories of a home far beyond mortal ken, and arouses an eager longing to make yourself worthy and fit, we are glad; and we trust that you will let nothing hereafter interfere with the training that the Master is waiting to give you, so that you will be truly ready when the call to action comes.

All possible help will be furnished those who feel the yearning and urge to work with others and who wish to draw to them or find those who belong with them. But first study and meditate earnestly upon the above, and ask the Loving Master within to bring to you or lead you to your own, and it may not be necessary to call upon outside help.

Suggestions for group study and work will be found in the appendix.

The Soul

Because of the necessity of students understanding clearly the terms commonly used by metaphysical and esoteric teachers and writers, and especially by ourselves, we will explain the meaning of such terms as we use them from time to time.

The soul, probably more than any other aspect of Divinity in what we know as man, is the least understood. Most students as well as teachers have only a hazy idea of what they consider is the soul, and if required to give an exact definition or explanation of it would be wholly at a loss—at least to make themselves clear.

In order for us to explain and for students to come into a definite understanding, so that hereafter they will always have a clear-cut idea of just what is meant by the soul, it is essential to know something of its birth and development. Try to realize, however, that it will be necessary for us to treat of the soul in terms of consciousness and not of form, for the soul can only be fully understood by considering it as a phase or expression of the One Consciousness.

We have a real starting point and a record of its birth in the second chapter of Genesis, where it is written that Jehovah God formed man out of the dust of the ground and breathed into his nostrils and man became a "living soul."

If you will remember, in the first chapter is given a symbolic story of how consciousness evolved up through the mineral, vegetable, animal, and finally into the human kingdom, when man made his first appearance in the world, formed in the image and likeness of God—or of the Elohim, the Gods who were the actual creators of man's form (*"Let us make man in our image after our likeness"*)—as the next stage for the use and expression of the fruits of this higher degree of consciousness.

Man's body, although thus humanly formed, was still of etheric substance and possessed all the characteristics of its former animal nature. But God blessed these newly formed beings called man. and said unto them, "Be fruitful, and multiply, and replenish the earth, and subdue it, and have dominion over the fish of the sea, over the birds of the heavens, and over the cattle and every living thing that moveth upon the earth." That is, they were to learn to have dominion over every feeling and impulse in the sea of their emotional nature, over every thought of their minds (birds of the heavens), over their animal appetites (cattle), and over every earthly condition surrounding them (things moving upon the earth).

Then God—the Elohim—rested, and during many long eons of time man continued to develop and unfold, to fit and accustom his animal consciousness into these new human forms, multiplying in vast numbers and gradually over-spreading the face of the earth. As time passed these forms began to grow more and more concrete and thereby to show forth outwardly on the plane of matter as they actually were on the etheric plane—this etheric state being the final stage of Spirit *involving* in matter before unfolding into visible, material expression— thus preparing them as the physical habitat of man.

In other words, the first chapter of Genesis gives a symbolic outpicturing of the *involution* of Spirit into matter, while the second chapter begins the history of the *evolution* of Spirit, now expressing itself as the consciousness of matter, back again into the pure consciousness of Spirit.

It was at this stage—commencing in the fifth
verse of the second chapter—that Jehovah God,
Himself, took charge, and calling upon His Sons of
Mind (the Sons of God) to assist Him, He sent
Them to earth to superintend under His guidance
the spiritual development of these human beings
made in the *form* of His image and likeness (the
Elohim were of course also in His likeness) but not
yet endowed with those Divine attributes of consciousness—Reason and Choice—which would enable man to *evolve* into the *spiritual* likeness of his
Father in Heaven.

Expressing this in another way, in the first chapter of Genesis we have the portrayal of the creation
of *mortals,* or the generation of the sons of man;
and in the second chapter the creation of the first
immortals, or the beginning of the *re*-generation of
the Sons of God. In the pre-Adamic race—the race
of mortals—consciousness had by this time unfolded
sufficiently in enough individuals to warrant Jehovah God creating the beginning of a new and
higher race—that of Adam and Eve; and by sending His Sons of God down into the bodies of such
individuals and giving them these bodies to live in
and to possess for the purpose of evolving them into
His likeness spiritually, They thus endowed these
mortals with "living souls," changing them thereby
from mortals to immortals.

From this you will gather that all of those having
human forms were not then (and are not now) endowed with fully conscious or awakened souls, for

a soul is only fully developed when self-consciousness has unfolded in the mind to the point where it
can be quickened by the Holy Spirit, or where it is
ready to be taught from *within*. Then only can a
Son of God, or the Higher Self, enter the soul and
live in it, thereby making it into a "living" or
awakened soul—the Son of God thus being "re-
born" and taking upon Himself the regeneration or
rather the redemption of the soul consciousness in
which He has involved Himself.

THE "FALL" INTO GENERATION

From this you will also be able to see that the
so-called "fall" of Adam and Eve was really the
conscious descent of the Sons of God into these
human souls, thereby into generation, in order to
evolve the consciousness expressing through them
into *re*-generation, or into Their consciousness, and
then later into Their Father's consciousness. The
consequences of this "fall" into generation, which
need not enter into this article, are what the soul is
now working up through, and whereby, under the
direction and instruction of the Higher Self, a Son
of God, it is gradually gaining the understanding of
the true meaning of both generation and regeneration which this experience is intended to
teach.

Our previous explanations have made you aware
that there is an intimate relation between the soul
and the love-nature; and you can now comprehend
that not until the love-nature is quickened and unfolded, and man is "re-born" by the Christ Spirit

entering into the soul, does the soul awaken and
man become a "living" soul, and thus begin his return journey to his Father's home, its Higher Self's
—a Son of God's—consciousness.

If you will read this and ponder over it carefully,
you will be startled, perhaps, by the thought that
many are living today who, while they are mortal
men, are not "living" or "awakened" souls and consequently have not attained immortality; they are
not yet "re-born," their Higher Selves not living in
their souls, but only overshadowing them, much as
some of the domestic animals are overshadowed.

Yes, this is only too true, as you must admit when
you try to talk of spiritual things to many of those
around you.   They not only can not understand,
but seemingly do not want to understand or listen
and think for themselves, and perhaps consider you
a "little cracked on religion," when you talk of such
things to them.   But this does not mean that in the
course of the ages they will not evolve along with
the race into immortality, their final destiny, or that
certain ones among them will not "ripen" and come
into soul fruitage before their fellows; for as is
manifest throughout all nature certain members of
a species mature and ripen faster than others.

Returning to our subject, and to the fifth verse of
the second chapter of Genesis, we have seen how
man's etheric body was growing concrete and sub-
stantial, and his consciousness had developed an intelligence that could be directed and used for his
further advancement; but if you will note "no plant

of the field was yet on the earth, and no herb of
the field had yet sprung up, and there was no man
to till the ground." Which means that the planet
earth had grown dense and material enough so that
it was now ready for the habitation of physical man;
but nothing as yet grew upon its surface, and there
was no man to till the ground and cultivate the
plants and herbs, even if there were any growing
upon the earth.

Therefore everything being ripe and ready, Jehovah God, exercising the power of His Creative
Will, breathed forth into the earth a new cyclic Life
Wave, and "there went up a mist from the earth,
and watered the whole face of the ground" (watered
the etheric substance with a new energizing Spiritual Force), causing the vegetation of all kinds that
had been created in etheric form (as recorded in the
first chapter of Genesis) to come forth into manifestation and to grow *out* of the ground. Likewise
as a sufficient number of human beings had now
evolved from their animal consciousness to self-
consciousness, He caused man's etheric body to slow
down in vibration, and thus to become dense; and
out of this same etheric, spiritual substance (dust),
the basic substance or *ground* from which all matter
springs and out of which was now growing the vegetation of the earth, man's physical body was
formed.

It was when man—the pioneers of the race who
had evolved into self-consciousness—thus became
fully manifest on earth and had grown accustomed
to his new habitation and environment, that Je-

hovah God breathed into his nostrils the breath of
life and man became a living soul.

This means that it was then that the Sons of
Mind first gave to man his mind, which made him
conscious of his identity as a "self," and also They
assumed jurisdiction over man's consciousness and
became responsible for his further evolution; but
that it was only in the case of the few highly evolved
souls—there being comparatively few Adamic men
at that time—that They entered into and possessed
them, thus making of them *living* souls and consequently changing them into immortal beings.

If you will remember, however, it was right after
man became a living soul that Jehovah God placed
this new man in the Garden of Eden and called him
Adam, which means he entered a new spiritual consciousness, higher than that of earth, where every
good thing grew and provided him with all that he
needed for his physical, mental and spiritual sustenance.   In other words, these Adamic men were the
pioneers or the first appearance of a new and higher
evolved race of *living* souls, *immortal* men, all
others being ordinary human beings or *mortal* souls,
still sleeping and bound up in the sensations of the
flesh.

The vast masses of these other human beings,
the Sons of God *overshadowed*, directing and guiding them much as the other and lower grades of
Divine Beings did the animal and vegetable kingdoms.   But while the latter served as Group Souls
to all of the individuals forming a certain species of

animal or vegetable, and thus guided their evolution, a Son of God became individually responsible for but one human being, acting as its overshadowing Spirit.

THE REASON FOR REDEMPTION

Now there was a very significant reason for Jehovah God calling upon these particular Sons of God to perform this great task of redeeming and uplifting the consciousness of these human souls. For way back many world periods before the earth was They were part of the humanity of another planet, the same as we are part of the humanity of earth. And They in the ignorance of Their then human nature, in Their countless lives on that planet, committed many sins and crimes against God and Their fellow men, for everyone of which They were held responsible by Their Father God, and everyone of which some day They would be required to redeem—even as we are responsible for and must redeem all that we have committed in this and our many past lives.

In the course of innumerable eons the souls of the humanity of this ancient planet evolved in consciousness into oneness with Their Higher Selves, then into oneness with the Ruler of Their planet, and finally into oneness with the Ruler of the Solar Universe, Their Father God. In the meantime They were gaining vast experience in the building of forms for the use of the consciousness and in the directing of its unfoldment while expressing in the multiplicity of mediums in the various realms under Their charge, and in all their different stages of development, from the elemental and etheric up through the mineral, vegetable and animal kingdoms.

During such experience They earned and attained many high degrees in the spiritual and celestial Hierarchies, including that of the Elohim, eventually reaching the exalted state of "Sons of God." Finally through the knowledge, power and understanding gained, the time came when They were prepared and ready to take full charge of Their own former miscreations of that long ago world period, which in mercy had been lifted away and deposited in the outermost reaches of consciousness in a realm known as the "eighth sphere," confined there in densest darkness where they would do as little harm as possible, and where they formed the nucleus of what some day would be a new planet.

Imagine a great compost heap of vegetable and animal refuse lying decaying and putrid under the sun, rain and snow, season after season—what a vast amount of energy is being generated, which, when this refuse matter is deposited in a barren field and plowed into the soil, will sweeten, enrich and renew it, giving it new life and enabling it to bring forth rich and bounteous harvests.

In much the same way was this great compost heap of the foul sins and crimes of that ancient humanity lying rotting and offensive, generating new life forces in the darkest realm of consciousness, awaiting the time when they could be used in building a new field of evolution and in providing the energy and substance for the new humanity that later would be grown by and harvested from it.

In fact this cosmic compost heap you can now gather was what originally constituted our planet earth, and those Great Beings Who were responsible for it and all that compose it are the Sons of God Who are actually the Higher Selves of every soul on earth. They naturally are responsible not only for our consciousness but for that of every living thing on the planet, as well as for the earth itself. For is not all of such consciousness what was originally that of Their miscreations of the dim past, which They are redeeming out of the darkness of ignorance in which they were given birth and are lifting back up into the light of the Father's Consciousness?

Read the last six paragraphs again carefully, so that you get their full meaning, and then go back and study what precedes them. You will find it will help to make many things clear that were not grasped in the first reading. It will also enable you to understand why a Son of God necessarily assumed the direction of the vast aggregation of the centers of intelligence grouped together and comprising the consciousness of the trillions of cells of the human body, every one of which was a sin or crime, His own miscreations of that former world period, and all of which had evolved up through the three lower kingdoms of earth life to the human stage of development. These kingdoms, however, were still closely related to these cells because of this body that they formed still containing their actual elements—as the mineral in the bones and teeth; the vegetable in the hair and nails; and the animal in the flesh, muscle and ligaments.

But try to realize that up to the stage when the animal body changed and became formed and shaped into the image and likeness of the Elohim, there was no actual mind inhabiting these bodies, that the directing of their lives and activities was done by the Minds of the Elohim Who individually had charge of certain whole species of animals, even as before other and lower grades of the Elohim overshadowed and directed different species of the vegetable kingdom, and similarly species of the mineral kingdom.   There was no actual directing mind *in* any animal, but there was an elemental soul animating each.   However, many animals of a species were under the direction and control of an overshadowing Group Soul, which means of a conscious intelligent *outer* Mind capable of directing and controlling the elemental forces of nature,—a Mind which could be no other than that of one of the Elohim—the Great Beings above mentioned.

This is explained so that you can understand that, even though man's body was formed in human shape, man was still only a super-animal, and that it was only when man was overshadowed and guided exclusively by a Son of God that he became endowed with a mind and thereupon was given the power of becoming a "living" soul; which means that his soul was then given the charge and direction of his own mind and body, and was made responsible for them by His Higher Self and for the life forces animating them. In other words it was not until the Sons of God took charge and gave man his mind that man became a self-conscious entity, with the possibility of attaining immortality.

We have led you through this long roundabout journey in order to show you the many elements and factors that enter into the constitution of the soul; for the above-mentioned aggregation of centers of intelligence, comprising the grouped consciousness of every cell of the body but dwelling in the body now as a composite and at the same time an individual self-consciousness, is—when guided and directed by the Higher Self—what constitutes the soul of man. In other words the soul is the "intelligence" evolved out of the experience of consciousness working up through the mineral, vegetable and animal kingdoms and combining all into human or self-consciousness, with this intelligence now capable of working with and being used by the Sons of God, Who as his Higher Selves are directing man's spiritual evolution.

By this time you will perhaps have perceived that the consciousness of man is evolving in and through him along three distinct lines at one and the same time. First there is the consciousness of the cells of his animal body; secondly the consciousness of the human mind or intellect, and last the consciousness that is responsible for and is causing and directing all—the overshadowing Holy Spirit, through the Sons of God.

We might say that the soul is now functioning

through the self-consciousness of the human mind
and using it as a medium for its outer expression,
having evolved up through the various kingdoms of
consciousness comprising that of the different cells
of the human body, and having built into its consciousness all the intelligence acquired from such
kingdoms of consciousness; and that it will continue
to evolve and unfold through and from its earth
experiences until it is lifted up into the consciousness of the Sons of God Who are serving the Holy
Spirit as the soul's Higher Self and Teacher.

Expressing this another way we might add that
the consciousness of the soul has evolved up through
the density of the material or outermost realms,
through the etheric and emotional realms, into the
mental realms, and is now supposed to be about
midway between the lower and higher realms of
mind; which explains why the soul is constantly
swayed and torn between its lower and higher
natures.

Remember that we are speaking now only of living or awakened souls, for the unawakened and un-
regenerate souls are only existing or, we might say,
sleeping in their mortal consciousness, the consciousness of the vast majority of the race today being
down on the lower emotional levels.

From the beginning there have been the few who
are far in advance of the masses of humanity. The
race unfoldment ranges from the Immortals or
Super-men, down through geniuses, or high intellec-
tuals; through the average intelligent mortals in our

highly civilized nations; then through the backward nations with their large masses of the uneducated and ignorant to the few barbaric peoples still upon the earth, the latter not far above the domestic animals in intelligence.

You must also realize that even among the most highly educated or cultured and supposedly most intelligent are very many who have not yet fully mastered all of the qualities of their animal nature, —for instance, their appetites for food and drink; witness the gourmands and drunkards even in our "best society." So that it is a case of the soul, once awakened, having to unfold and lift up—as it progresses—the consciousness of the cell centers of all of the lower kingdoms that still comprise its being, and that it cannot itself grow without turning back, as it were, and helping along the laggard qualities of its own nature and thereby of the lower kingdoms to which it is related.

From the foregoing you can gather much that will explain and clarify the meaning and exact status of the human brain mind or personality— the mind that is "overshadowed" and reflected in man by a Son of God—the mind's Higher Self, an actual Son of Mind; also called the Holy Spirit— the Christ, the directing Mind of Jehovah God, Himself.

In other words it is God's Mind or Consciousness reflected down through a Son of God, through the soul, into a physical brain; the human mind being but the soul in expression on the physical plane,

and through the soul a Son of God and very God
Himself also expressing.

This means that the soul is *you*, is *your* consciousness, as you are when quiet and uninfluenced by any
outer thoughts; a consciousness that is therefore independent of your human brain, which it uses only
to express itself in the world of matter. You are
ever trying to bring the consciousness of your human
mind into oneness with your consciousness, which
if you are a disciple is one with the consciousness
of your Higher Self, a Son of God, who is one with
His Father God's Consciousness.

The human soul in each succeeding manifestation
on earth of necessity builds for itself, under the direction of its Higher Self, a new body with a new
brain mind, appearing in each earth life as a new
and different personality. In each personality the
soul seeks and gains new experiences, from which
through its brain mind it is taught by its Higher
Self many lessons whose spiritual essence is built
into soul consciousness. Thus gradually the soul or
ego is taught all that the Higher Self can teach it
on earth, and it knows all that its Teacher knows,
when evolution on earth is finished and the soul of
man has become *more than man*.

This pertains only to individual man, for when he
reaches this, his divine estate, he turns back and,
along with all of his Brothers who have reached that
same estate, he helps the souls of his younger
brothers also to reach it. After long eons of time
evolution accomplishes the awakening and unfold-

ment of all on earth—Jehovah God's original plan and purpose, and all mortals have become living souls, and all souls have grown to be super-men; and earth no longer contains for them any consciousness which could hold them in the human estate or which needs lifting up into Oneness with their Divine Consciousness.

There is so much of vital and far-reaching truth in the foregoing, that we earnestly urge every student who seeks a clear, reasonable and satisfying explanation of the soul to read it repeatedly, slowly and carefully, until the exact meaning is perceived.

We know that it is all very abstract and requires deep concentration to penetrate to the meaning behind the words, and that it is different from anything elsewhere taught; therefore it is necessary to bring to its study an open mind cleansed of all formed ideas and beliefs, in order that its truths may be fully grasped.

But persistent study will bring results that will happily repay you for the time and effort expended, for you will gain an understanding of a subject that savants and philosophers back through the ages have spent their lives seeking without finding, but which is clearly shown in this and the succeeding articles.

Desire

"What things soever ye desire, when ye pray, believe that ye receive them, and ye shall have them."
—Mark 11:24.

Whence come the desires of the heart?

Ask yourself that question and try to answer.

From where else could they come but from Me, the I AM, God within you, Who abides deep within your heart?

For the heart is the entrance to the Kingdom of My Consciousness, and from it come all the issues of life—those that matter and affect your on-going and aid Me in the accomplishing of My purpose for you.

Could any desire, then, coming from the heart, be other than good?

Nay, for *all* such desires are inspired by Me, and are for your good—or they would not be given you.

Must this not be true of Me, God, your all-wise, all-loving, all-powerful and ONLY Self? For am I not ever seeking to manifest My Self in all fullness in man, whom I made in My image and likeness for the sole purpose of such manifestation?

Ask yourself, if you will, what *is* a desire and *why* do I give it to you?

Can you not see? It is My sign to you that I purpose giving you or outmanifesting for you *that which already exists* within you in Spirit, or in My Mind, and of which the desire is but the reflection. Aye, it is My *promise* of so doing.

Think, could it be otherwise? Could a desire *be*, if its fulfillment were not already accomplished in My Mind? What possible other purpose could I have in permitting your mind to see it, if not to *bring it forth?* And if I thus make you aware of

My purpose, it is but to prepare your mind so that it will co-operate with Me in the bringing of it forth.

For desire and its accomplishment are one and the same. Every desire, once born in the heart, is already fulfilled in actuality—that is, in My Mind, and but awaits *your acceptance of it* to come forth into manifestation.

One who *knows* this, instead of longing for and seeking and straining by mental and material means to bring it about for personal use, merely *calls it to him, accepts it, and possesses it,* and in loving appreciation thanks God for being permitted to use it and to assist Him in His Purpose.

All he needs to do, after visioning clearly that for which his heart yearns, is to *speak aloud* the words:

"Let this desire of my heart, that—(naming it definitely), and which is already fulfilled in my Father's sight, *come forth* Now in all its fullness and perfection, that the Father may be glorified in me His son."

Know, My child, that this is a simple law, but how hard and difficult you have made it for it to work for you and for your good! By your anxious fears and seeking to obtain and use for your own selfish ends, you have but covered the fulfillment with a cloud of darkness, hiding it from the outer light, and thus preventing your seeing that which only awaits your recognition of the truth of its being to come forth and bless you.

By possessing it is meant *feeling* and *acting* as if
it is already yours, *as it really* Is, letting no thought
or feeling contrary to such consciousness of possession for one slightest moment be entertained by
your mind.

By thus going about in that consciousness, you
become a powerful attracting magnet—aye, a cosmic vortex—toward which all the powers of mind
and all the forces of nature speedily rush at your
voiced command to fill full and complete that which
temporarily seems a lack or need.

Know likewise this truth,—All that I have is
yours *now,* and always was yours. Therefore great
riches of the Spirit are yours, and when I reflect in
your mind from a desire felt in your heart an image
of that which will fulfill (fill full) a need in your
life, know now that as I thus promise so shall it Be
speedily—according to the degree of your co-
peration with the law.

But before you seek to prove this law, be sure
that your desires spring *from your heart,* and are
not from the selfish and separate mind. For a use
of the law for selfish ends will surely bring its own
retribution. Learn prayerfully to distinguish your
personal desires from *My* desires for you.

That is not hard to learn, for My desires are always for your soul's good—and for the soul good of
others, and never to benefit the selfish personality.
To realize this, however, self must step aside, and
you must learn to view your desires as if they were
the desires of another. Nothing is ever good that

will take from or deprive another to benefit self. It is much better that you yield to what seems a selfish desire on the part of another, than to deprive that other of it—if such would benefit self.

On the other hand it is wisdom to withhold from a selfish personality that which would only feed its selfishness, if such withholding in no way benefits self. This last, however, requires great strength of mind and an understanding heart, which has learned to turn to Me for guidance at all times.

CHAPTER 10

"Except a Man Be Born Again"

IN THE preceding Chapter we tried to point out the place the soul occupies in the unfoldment or evolution of consciousness, and incidentally to explain the meaning of the soul.

We now wish to treat of the soul in relation to the following statements of our Master and Teacher, and which will help make clear the true meaning of the soul, as also will the understanding of that meaning help to explain the Master's words:

"Verily, verily, I say unto thee, Except a man be born again, he cannot see the Kingdom of God."

"Nicodemus said unto Him, How can a man be born when he is old? Can he enter the second time into his mother's womb, and be born?

"Jesus answered, Verily, verily, I say unto thee, Except a man be born of water and of the spirit, he cannot enter into the Kingdom of God.

"That which is born of the flesh is flesh; and that which is born of the spirit is spirit."—John 3:3-6.

Try to realize that a soul is not a "living" soul until it has been born spiritually. Man is a soul, but not until he is born again, or as it is in the exact translation, born "from above," he is not truly alive spiritually. And as in reality all is Spirit, then man, or the soul, until he is "born of water (the symbol of baptism or the descent of the Holy Spirit) and of Spirit," is unborn, or is still in the "flesh."

"That which is born of the flesh is flesh; and that which is born of spirit is spirit."

All of which proves that there are two types of souls or of men on earth at the present time—*un*-born men, or men of flesh—mortals; and *re*-born men, or men of spirit—immortals.

Think this over carefully in connection with what was stated in the preceding chapter, where it speaks about the descent of the Sons of God and Their entering into and possessing the souls of men, thereby bringing about a re-birth of the soul; and then compare and relate it all with the birth of the Christ in the heart, as pictured in the first two chapters.

We are endeavoring to show clearly what constitutes a "living" soul, that man is not alive until the Holy Spirit descends "from above" into the womb of the soul—still largely animal in nature —and impregnates it, when soon a new being comes to birth—the Christ child, which grows, thrives, and reaches maturity, and finally takes full possession of the soul with its mind and body, all then forming a perfect instrument for Its use.

Remember, the Christ, or the Holy Spirit, is your *Real Self,* Who is a Son of God, a Ray or Reflection of the Father, sent down into the soul to redeem it and lift it back into the Father's Home—into His Consciousness.

You may ask, what determines the readiness of
the human soul for re-birth, or when does the Holy
Spirit descend into it, and why are so many as yet
apparently unborn or unaware of the true spiritual
life?

In answer, we ask you, why do some roses bloom
earlier than others; why do some branches on the
same stock put out buds before others?

You reply, because some roses and branches develop before others.

Yes, it is all a question of growth and development, and that is under the care of different grades
of great Spiritual Hierarchies, Who are given charge
by our Father-God of all cell life and its growth
and manifestations, including its growth and development in preparation for the use of the human
soul.

We pointed out in the earlier chapters that all
life in its highest aspect is an expression of the
Father's Love, and that not until consciousness had
unfolded to the human stage in a fully developed
soul, was His Love able to make Itself felt and
understood in anything like Its true nature.

And then only when the soul through the mind
could be taught the nature and purpose of life as
Love, was it possible for a Son of God to quicken
and teach it, and later to enter it and to be born
in the consciousness as its True Self, and thereby
become an *expresser* of Divine Love,—which means

that the Christ-Self could enter in and possess Its own.

You may wonder at living or immortal souls having been created at the very beginning of the human race, when seemingly so few of such are manifesting now after all these many ages. But you must realize that the book of Genesis is an allegory, a symbolic out-picturing of stages of growth where each "day" of creation in reality took milleniums to complete. Hence man, though created in the sixth day, undoubtedly was hundreds of thousands of years developing self or soul consciousness. Also you must remember that as our Father can work and teach on earth only through His human instruments, He had first to quicken some souls into efficient instruments, so that they could be used by Him to teach their younger and lesser developed brothers, and thus could assist Him in the evolution of this new humanity.

In the beginning of the race very few were thus quickened or ensouled by the Sons of God, but through the long ages that have elapsed since, perhaps one-third of the human race have unfolded into immortal souls. During the many ages to follow, however, all will evolve into that state.

REINCARNATION

Many find the study of the soul to be one of fascinating interest, and there is a reason for this interest. For the soul is the ego, the self, the seat of consciousness in man, and when the soul becomes aware of itself, it can never rest until it knows all about its nature, its source and destiny.

Because of this restless desire to know—this urge to unfold its consciousness into the fullness of realization, it ever seeks opportunity and means to grow and unfold in wisdom, which is the true word for soul knowledge. This urge is the urge of all life— the cause of all growth, for it is the Idea ensouled in the heart of each living thing which must grow and unfold Itself until It attains and expresses the fullness and perfection of Its nature. That is the law of life. None can escape its operation.

Also because all living things on earth can grow to their fullness of life only on earth, then only by repeated lives on earth can this fullness and perfection be attained. Witness this demonstrated in all nature in the seeming death and rebirth of the trees, grass and vegetation, season after season. Remember it is the souls of the trees, the grass and the vegetation that put on new bodies each year, in order to express the nature of the Idea hidden within their hearts and which outpictures Itself in their "fruit."

This applies as well in animals as in man. In animals it is the soul of the species that reincarnates in the different generations of animals, until the fruitage stage or perfection of the animal Idea of that particular species is attained. Think of the evolution of the animal Idea of the cat species from the ferocious jungle tiger to the household pussy-cat.

In man the soul has become individualized in the human mind, and its consciousness has unfolded to the stage where it can be taught to co-operate with the Intelligence that is directing and assisting it to its fruitage stage.

It can be seen, from the many eons of time that have elapsed since the birth of the human soul, that in one short lifetime on earth it would be impossible to gain more than a rudimentary knowledge of the soul's purpose while in that particular body, time and place of incarnation, even by an average intelligent soul, not to speak of early representatives of the race when there were no books and but few teachers who knew.

Therefore, it stands to reason, the only way a soul can come into the fullness of wisdom is by repeated lives on earth in many different types of bodies, in many different ages and conditions, giving opportunity for a great variety of experiences, from all of which can be garnered the lessons that would bring wisdom—when the essence of such lessons had been fully digested and assimilated and thus built into soul consciousness.

In order that this great truth can be fully impressed upon those who read, it will be necessary to recapitulate what has been previously stated and thereby point out the essence of the article on the soul in the preceding chapter.

From what was shown, the soul is the sum-total of consciousness that has evolved up through the mineral, vegetable, animal and human kingdoms of consciousness to the point where He who originally gave birth to this consciousness could take full charge of its final evolution on earth. Those who were responsible for such soul creations are the Sons of God, Who when They were the humanity on a planet similar to the earth in a previous world period, long before the earth was, committed in Their ignorance many sins and crimes against the law of God, even as man is committing them today.

These sins and crimes, all centers of consciousness—and all consciousness is God's Consciousness, remember—naturally had to be redeemed by those who gave them birth in the realm of mind, and had to be lifted back once more into their true consciousness. These evolved sins and crimes of consciousness have now been gathered together, under the direction of the Sons of God, by the lesser Creative Hierarchies, the Elohim, as described in the first chapter of Genesis, into the trillions of cells of the human body, physical, astral and mental, each, as it were, an entitized center of consciousness of such past mis-creations, into and now comprising one composite center of consciousness—the Soul.

This conglomerate consciousness—the human soul—now capable of being consciously and intelligently ruled, a Son of God then personally took charge of, and when fully developed into love consciousness, actually entered and possessed as its Higher Self, for the express purpose of leading its consciousness back into its true state—into the Father's Home—into His Consciousness.

This They are accomplishing by having the soul, under Their direction, build and incarnate in successive human bodies in different ages and conditions, so that from the experience gained on earth, They can teach and explain to the soul through the brain-mind, the medium expressly developed for that purpose, the meaning of it all,—that all life, all minds, all centers of consciousness, which means all manifest things, are parts of and one with God's Mind, in which all live, move and have their being; and that only by so living that Love is allowed to rule, motivate and direct all activities of the human consciousness can it come into conscious oneness with His Mind.

Eventually thus They—the Sons of God—lift up the soul consciousness first into oneness with Their (the souls' Fathers in Heaven) consciousness, and then finally into oneness with God's (Their Father in Heaven) Consciousness; thus bringing *all on earth* back into Their Father's Home.

And now for the real purpose of this long dissertation on the soul and this explanation about its incarnation in matter.

You have seen that it is the soul only that incarnates—not the Higher Self; That, a Son of God, stays in the higher realms of consciousness where, through the brain-mind, It directs the life and teaches the soul the lessons garnered from the experiences of the personality while living in the human body.

Of course the personality knows nothing of past

incarnations, only as the soul, while dwelling in it and using it, has developed its brain-mind so that the soul can bring through to its brain consciousness the memory of former lives as other personalities. But this is only possible with very old and advanced souls—Initiate disciples.

How many who read realize—actually know—the truth of what has just been stated? Are you but an "awakened" soul, in your understanding, or are you conscious of being the Self—the *Higher* Self of the soul, aye, a Son of God?

Think! And if you do not know, go back to *"The Impersonal Life"* and read, study and meditate until you KNOW.

It is true that all souls must be born again— *from above,* yet permit us to tell you that no more "living" or immortal souls need be *re*-born in other physical bodies *from this time on*—except in the families of the "Elect," and then only for a particular purpose and to do a special work. But all re-born or immortal souls must soon come into the full consciousness of their Real Selves—that they may know "who they are and of what they are a part."

This means that all such souls are here to do a work, and that work is now soon to begin. This also means that having come here to do a work, they need necessarily "go no more out," or in other words "die"; and when they do come into the full consciousness of their *Real* Selves they will realize all this, and will compel their brain-minds and personalities to "get busy" and will make them into perfect instruments for the work that lies ahead.

This is the reason and purpose of teaching you the real meaning of the soul, so that now you may in "dead" earnestness seek to know "who you are and of what you are a part."

Therefore study these articles on the soul until you get their actual meaning. If you are fully determined to know it, you will be shown from *within*. Then you will be ready for additional and higher truths that will be made known to you in succeeding articles.

The Personality

In the silence of my room, one day, some years ago, while meditating upon the mystery of the One Life, and trying to realize that my personality with its human mind and body is but the instrument I, an Immortal Soul, have built and am using while expressing through my present state of consciousness, I, or rather this mortal, personal phase of me, that part which concerns itself with outer, separate things, seemed to be led into a vast, wonderful room, my conscious self now having become, curiously, an onlooker, a seeker of knowledge.

This room seemed to be semi-circular in form, with high walls, forming a series of panels, oval-shaped at the top, each exquisitely beautiful in the sheen of marvelous colors that radiated from it; in each a dominant shade or tone so merging into

those adjacent that all produced an impression so
wholly indescribable, because so unlike anything of
earthly experience, that my mind was enthralled
and dazed by the brilliancy and beauty of it all.

As I gazed I became dimly conscious that in each
panel were pictured wondrous scenes, all seemingly
alive in their strange, intense vibration of colors, in
one fiery pink predominating, in another deep, azure
blue, another emerald green, another solar orange,
others brilliant indigo, or richest purple, or pure
blood red, or blinding yellow; but each interspersed
continually with scintillating flashes of every other
color, so that a startling impression of unreality
crept into my mind; while at the same time the
alluringly attractive interplay of thoughts and emotions, sensed as being outpictured in the colors rather
than actually seen, of loves and hates, of aspirations and disappointments, of hot passions, unful-
filled desires, crazed fears and the whole gamut of
suffering, held me spellbound and wholly unable
to gather all together into an intelligent conception
of what it was about.

I seemed to be led into the center of what now
appeared to be a great rotunda, the other half of
the circle seemingly having closed in behind me—
this also being sensed rather than seen. I found myself standing there in the center and gradually became conscious that before each panel and merging
into it as if a part of it was a figure.

While wondering at it all, lost in the beauty of
the strange, unearthly coloring, there slowly shaped

in my mind the query, "Why am I here, and what have I to do with all this?"

A figure seemed to detach itself from the panel at the extreme right. It approached and spoke. There was something vaguely familiar about both the figure and the background or scenes in the panel, which sense deepened as I listened.

"So you have come also? He must be finished with you and needs you no longer—else why should you be here?"

"What do you mean?"

"The Lord must have completed another phase of the Father's Work and I see that you have furnished Him opportunity to do much that He was not able to do before."

"I do not understand."

"You have a more refined body, a cleaner brain, and a better trained intellect. He was enabled to express His nature more easily, without so much hindrance as we were to Him. But that is natural, for you are the soul of that which we earned and provided for you. In you is gathered together all that He had accomplished in and garnered from each of us, from the simple animal soul-body of the first, long since disintegrated, down to me, who was the last before you."

"Please explain who you are, who these others are? There is something familiar about you. I should know you, but I do not seem to recall your name."

"No, you do not know my name, but I can tell you of many things that you would recall as in a dream. For I, before the Lord called you into expression, was the cumulation of all that He had evolved through the others; I am but the personality or the soul's body that the Lord, your Real Self, used last. Before me came the others, including all those who have become as shadows," pointing to the dim figures in the mists of the panels at the back of me to the extreme left.

"You are now standing in the Hall of Memory in the Temple of Life, as your mortal mind would conceive it, wherein is gathered all of the knowledge of the past, and where it can be fully digested and assimilated by the soul during its sojourn here between incarnations of earth life.

"On these panels are pictured the experiences of each previous incarnation and of the personality which was used in the unfolding of the soul's consciousness while it was enmeshed in a human brain. Each new brain and body enabled the Lord to teach the soul more of His Divine Idea, and in each new personality He manifested more of His Spiritual Nature."

"But who then *are you* and the others, and *who am I?*" I asked in a panic.

"I see you have not yet learned the Truth, even though I have heard the Lord many times teach it through you. You as you now deem yourself are but mortal mind's creation. You are what that mind, separate in consciousness from the Lord, has conceived your human self to be, the thought-built son of man that was born only to die as a separate self, after the soul has lived and learned enough with us in this world of memory to assimilate *all* the Truth taught in yon pictures, which are the true records of its past lives for its and our teaching."

"But I thought I was destined for union with God; I understood He was All in All, that He was my Real Self? But He has gone and left me! After all His teaching and all my understanding, am I now no more than you and the rest?" I cried in an agony of desolation.

"Yes, as you are now, involved in the fear thoughts of your mortal mind, you are no more than we. For you and we are the thought creations of our mortal, separate minds, given life and being by our ignorant misuse of the life breathed into us by the Lord. But remember, *all* life is His Life, *all* mind is His Mind, and *all* substance is His Substance; and when we *really* know this and *abide* in this knowledge, then it is that we cease as separate personalities and become one in consciousness with Him, our beloved Lord and Master, Who all the time is and has been our Real Self.

"That knowledge is almost a reality to me and to you—when you are in your normal consciousness, my more than brother; but when it *is* a reality, can *we* go on and leave our other selves here behind—for you know that they also are His disciples? *Can* we?"

"But you say when we really know our true identity we cease as separate personalities. How then can we stay behind to help our brothers?"

"How did Jesus return to His disciples after giving up His mortal personality? Even as did He, so can we, for those personalities are all phases of the soul—our soul, which the Lord is lifting up and making one with His Consciousness. Even as He made the union with His Father-God, and now lives and works in humanity, so can we work with Him —a Son of God, our True Self. For do we not by union enter into His Consciousness and therefore into His Being, and is not His Mind then our Mind, His Life our Life, His Will our Will, His Personality our Personality?

"Then let us, beloved, let go of our sense of mortality and really know our Divinity. Let us give up utterly to Him, and enter into the joy of our Lord, so that He can live His Life in us, do His Will in us, and be His Self in us on all planes of consciousness."

The scene faded from my mind and I slowly returned in consciousness to my self and to the room where I sat. But for a long time afterward I felt the uplift and thrill of this strange experience in which I was thus taught the meaning and purpose of the personality and of the long, long journey of the soul back to its Father's Home.

The above experience is of great value to those who can grasp its real meaning. Read again and again until you get its inner significance.

The Light

Looking up into the heavens on a dark night we see millions of points of light, which science claims are suns and stars, or planets, each supposedly the dwelling-place of some kind of intelligences similar to the humanity of earth.

We assume that there must be life and intelligences on these planets, else they would not shine or give out light. In reality, however, we know nothing about them, only that they shine and emit a radiant, scintillating light, some of them a much more brilliant light than others.

We like, on such a night, to imagine that the canopy of heaven is actually that—a vast black curtain spread over the earth, and that the points of light that we see are little holes in the curtain through which streams the Great Light of Heaven.

Some of the holes are larger than others, permitting more light to shine through; and we like to think that during the course of ages by such powerful and continual shining the Great Light will not only wear the holes gradually larger and larger, thus permitting more and more light to penetrate, but that it will wear the curtain very thin, so that the earth eventually will be blessed by always being in the light.

Let us all ponder over the thought of this wonderful Light back of the curtain, where it is always gloriously, radiantly shining, and where no darkness or even the faintest shadow could possibly be. Such must it be in the Kingdom of Heaven, where dwell the Angels of Light, those who know not darkness or the troubles, inharmonies, sorrows, sufferings, sins, crimes and unhappiness born of and bred in the darkness of earth where we dwell. Surely this light must be striving ever so hard to penetrate through the curtain in order to give us children of darkness all the light possible.

Now let us consider men's minds, how they are in truth holes or openings into the great Universal Mind, through which the Light of God's Perfect Love is ever trying to pour in order to illumine man's consciousness. Many millions of men's minds we know are only tiny pin holes, others are fair sized apertures, while a few, comparatively, are large and wide open channels through which the light of Divine Mind pours freely, and from the light that they radiate we feel and know that they are Illumined Souls.

Now let us carry you a little farther, and say that all of these lights that we see in the heavens are in reality only reflections in the outer world of mind of the lights of our centers of Mind shining in the heavens of Consciousness *within;* that in very truth the dark curtain that separates us from the great Light is the curtain of our mortal minds which in their ignorance think themselves separate from the One Mind. But this curtain is only a self-created curtain and in reality exists solely because men way back in the beginning turned their backs to the Light and consequently now see in memory only the darkened reflections of the radiant bodies of their fellows that were in the beginning— before they turned to this world of shadows. They do not know that these shadows are caused by their belief in separation which keeps their faces ever turned away from the light so that they see only with the darkened sense of self and know no more the light that shines within.

Back through the eons a few in each age awakened to the truth that they had been walking in their own shadow, and they then faced about and were flooded by the light of the sun of their own being. They learned in very truth that they were of the Light—a part of the Sun of God, could walk in Its Light, could live in that Light and could partake of all of Its blessings. Aye, they knew that they were Sons of Light, Sons of Mind, Sons of the God Who is The Light which lighteth every man in the world.

Through the glory of the illumination that followed they learned that their minds were truly one with the One Mind, that there never was and never could be any separation—only as they turned again away from the Light.

CHAPTER 11

"Now Are We Sons of God"

IN THE last two chapters we tried to tell you all about the birth, source, constitution and nature of the soul, and if you truly studied all that was given and noted carefully what was shown you *from within* as you read, you will have arrived at a more or less clear understanding of your own soul, its relation to your Higher Self and to your human mind and body.

You were shown that the soul dwells in the human body, and that the Higher Self dwells in the soul—that is, in an awakened, or re-born soul.

Naturally, however, the soul cannot live in a body, for the body is mere flesh; so that it must mean it dwells somewhere deep within the consciousness of the human mind, which does have its abode in the physical brain. And when we tell you that what is commonly known as the sub-conscious mind is really the consciousness of the soul, or is all that the ordinary student and most psychologists know of the soul or its consciousness, it will help you to place the soul definitely—by relating what you know of the sub-conscious mind with what herein has been shown you about the soul.

Now as Mind includes within itself all realms of consciousness, it does not take much of an effort of thought to realize that you, a soul—the thinker, *must* dwell *within* Mind, and that you are a center of consciousness of Mind. Which means that you *are* consciousness; and that in order to express your self or your soul on the earth plane, you had first to create a "separate" mind or mental body in which to dwell; and then that your mind had to create for itself a physical body with a human brain in which *it* could dwell, in order that you as a soul could function as a self-conscious separate unit of Mind. For try to realize that the human mind in the sum total of its consciousness—sub-consciousness, ordinary consciousness, and super-consciousness—is really the outer reflection of the soul, through which or by means of which the soul expresses itself.

We are trying to have you grasp the fact that the soul dwells deep within the mind, or deep beneath the surface of the conscious mind, and rules and operates from there. Psychologists and metaphysicians glimpsing this truth created the term "sub-conscious mind," in their efforts to give a name to what is actually the soul.

All this implies that deep within the consciousness of mind there must be realms where the soul actually "dwells" and which must be its real home. And it must be a *real* home, for we have seen how many times in physical incarnations it has built bodies to house its "separate" mind, in which it involved itself while seeking the knowledge which would finally free it from its earth attachments, and which knowledge could be gained only through ex-

perience in earth lives. And that after each earth
life it would return to its home in the inner realm
of consciousness, there to digest and assimilate the
essence of the lessons gained from such earth experiences.

Gradually through many such experiences it
learned that it could partially free itself and return temporarily to its home in Mind or Spirit—
for Mind (with a capital M) is really Spirit. Such
freedom occurred first at night when the brain
mind slept, and then later it was found that in true
meditation, when the brain mind was stilled, the
soul was able to escape for a brief period to its soul
home in consciousness.

Now if there are realms in consciousness where
the soul dwells, naturally all souls must dwell there
and they must live, think, speak and act there; even
as we would think, speak and act—all men being
souls—if we were wholly freed from our body consciousness and from the influence of our brain
minds, which still think in terms of personality and
of separateness and thereby ever tend to keep us in
such separate consciousness.

We will consider at this time only the souls of
disciples or re-born men, and the realm or home of
such—the soul-plane of purified or immortal souls
—where we would have you realize that such souls
actually live, even as their human personalities live
here on the earth plane; but that there they appear
to each other as young, beautiful and perfect—as
their ideal selves, all living the purest life of loving

service, having only one thought and purpose—how they can help their younger brothers and how to grow wiser and stronger in order the better to serve their beloved Master, Christ Jesus.

There the souls of disciples, according to their stage of unfoldment—for they always keep on unfolding—are taught by their Elder Brothers, or by their own Higher Selves, the essence of the experiences passed through each day in their body consciousness, or the higher truths that they are to bring down into application on the earth plane. These Elder Brothers may be either more advanced disciples, or Masters of Wisdom. Often the Lord Jesus will be in their midst personally instructing them, or blessing them with His Presence.

Stop here and meditate awhile on what you have just read, and see if you can get any inner confirmation of it.

From this you are beginning to perceive that this soul plane must be a realm very much like your concept of the Kingdom of Heaven. Therefore you will be glad to know that it is indeed the first realm in the Kingdom, and that all purified souls are actual members of the "Community of Saints," the "Great Congregation," the "Holy Ones," spoken of in the Bible; also known as the Great White Brotherhood of the Spirit, and the Great White Lodge. This will be evidenced to all disciples who have unfolded their soul faculties, by seeing all there gowned in robes of purest white, and by the predominance of white everywhere.

In the December, 1928, Paper, which inaugurated this Work, and which forms the first chapter of this book, the Master sent forth a call to all those who were earnestly seeking the Kingdom and who were ready to make this seeking the first and supreme thing in their lives.

Many disciples heard His call in their hearts and began their journey with us to the Kingdom. Some have traveled with us all the way up to this point, and nothing could now induce them to turn back, or halt.

Many aspirants, however, perhaps a greater number, were not equal to the requirements of the journey. They started unprepared in mental equipment. The traveling into the far country of Mind was too hard going, necessitating too much concentrated effort to which they were unaccustomed. And Meditation was a strange and uninviting land for them, because of the many wild and uncontrolled thoughts there encountered. Besides, regular and systematic traveling was more than they had counted upon; they much preferred to take long and enjoyable side trips into the interesting realms of thoughts of other minds, or to stop at some former traveler's home that had been built by the wayside. They forgot that call they had heard in their hearts —that Loving Voice that had so thrilled and inspired them and had given them the wondrous vision of the Kingdom—their Father's Home, where they knew He was waiting with welcoming arms and loving heart for their return.

But all those who have been truly with us—all aspirants and disciples who, when they heard the Master's call, were not only ready and eager, but who were never happy unless they heard that Voice again speaking in their hearts,—they have earnestly sought by faithful study and application of all the suggestions given to find and know the Beloved One abiding in their hearts, so that they might wait upon and have His guidance every step of the way. And many of such dear ones have been given unmistakable evidence of His influence and His abiding presence in their lives.

It is for these faithful ones that the above information about the soul and their soul home has been given. Such have not been left without encouragement at any stage of their journey; but now that we are nearing the goal they are told these glad tidings in order that they may press on unhesitatingly until the full consciousness of the Kingdom is reached.

How may those who read know that they have reached this stage with us? Surely those who have evidence of the Loving Presence within their hearts know! Have they not been hearing His Voice, and have they not been lovingly following Him and seeking to obey His every suggestion?

Then know that while doing this He has been leading you straight to the Kingdom—the Kingdom of His and your Father's Consciousness.

Many have written us of visions and dreams— soul experiences that tell plainly of His guidance

and of His love. Some have even been vouchsafed
visions of our Blessed Lord, Christ Jesus, others
have felt His Presence, while others have clearly
heard His actual words of blessing. A few have
already been privileged during meditation in their
Group meetings to rise directly in consciousness to
the soul realm and there to be with their Brothers
in Spirit in full awareness of Them.

We have had word from several Groups of two
or more members in their Group being so privileged
and actually seeing the same things; and in one particular group, starting with two members being able
to do this, gradually additional ones opened to this
consciousness until six were able to see and to report to the group while seeing, and thus to compare
notes of their experiences in the soul realm.

We tell you of this for the reason that from what
we have been shown we feel, owing to the powerful
force now being poured down upon Earth, which is
affecting every human soul, stimulating and quickening into undue activity both the highest and the
lowest in them, that before very long it is going to
be the common experience of every true disciple.
We mean, that *every such disciple* will be open to
the soul realm and will come into conscious contact
with their Brothers in the Great White Brotherhood
of the Spirit, of which our Beloved Master Jesus, is
the Supreme Head and Life.

This because the time is rapidly nearing when all
such disciples must come into the knowledge of
"who they are and of what they are a part," in order

that they may become fully prepared for the work that lies ahead, which in their soul consciousness they pledged the Master they would do.

We know that many who read may feel discouraged and fearful that none of this applies to them, thinking because so far they have felt no tangible evidence of such quickening, that such opening of the soul consciousness is unattainable for them.

To all such we say, that if they desire with all their hearts and souls to enter such consciousness, solely in order that they can the better be prepared for service, and if they have set aside regular hours for meditation and faithfully at that time try to enter and abide in the I AM or Christ Consciousness, it will not be long before they will attract to them or be led to one or more whose souls harmonize with their souls and who will form with them the nucleus of a Group, which then may meet for a mutual study and practice of the teachings.

For the next stage of unfoldment of the worthy and prepared members of the human race is that of Soul or Group Consciousness, which must be attained, or at least comprehended, before the consciousness of the Brotherhood of the Spirit can be given.

This means that while in time, by intensive meditation, one can unfold alone and contact the consciousness of his or her own Group on the soul plane, without meeting with other personalities on the outer plane, yet it can be seen how much easier it will be accomplished when a group of earnest students—if only two or three—can meet and work together on the physical plane.

Some again may feel discouraged when reading this, because of not being acquainted with any who are interested in this Work. But let them not be disheartened, for remember this is not our Work but the Master's, and He is not only directing and preparing you for your part in It, but is guiding and caring for all who belong in the Work. When you are ready, have mastered personality and have so submerged self that you can work in true harmony with your *soul* companions, then He will bring them to you or you to them so that you will *know* each other, and all will be arranged so that you can meet and study together. All you have to do is to pray daily that you may become wholly worthy and prepared, and then to obey all that He from within tells you to do in every detail of your life. As Group Consciousness is the enlargement of the Christ Consciousness and is your next step, you can see that He within you will do all possible to help you to attain it—if you do your part.

Those Groups that do not feel any inner quickening or have had no evidence of the Master's Presence in their meetings may know that it is because of the presence there of personality, of gossip, or of personal feeling of some kind or other toward one or more of their fellows, which prevent the perfect harmony and peace that must prevail before the Master can make His Presence known.

One further word—let none think that we are giving any suggestions that will open the consciousness to the astral, the planes contacted usually by those dabbling in spiritualism; for as we are now speaking to *disciples* who have found and are waiting upon and serving only the Christ within, through His Power and Presence you will be carried far above the astral, through the mental planes, to the causal plane, which is your soul's and therefore *your* true home.

In our next Chapter we will tell more about the soul planes, more about the Kingdom, and more also about the lower planes—which will help you to know their difference and enable you always to avoid the lower ones and to discriminate between them, when that comes which would entice you down into such planes. Not that the lower planes have not their part and place in the unfolding of consciousness, but that purified souls will rise naturally above them—unless still held by their attractions.

As a help, in the light of the above, read over and study *"As a Flower Grows,"* by Mabel Collins, keeping in mind that the ethereal plane, as she terms it, is the causal plane, the plane or home of purified souls—of disciples (see page 14), and many new truths will unfold to you.

That home is yours, if you are a true disciple of Christ, and it is ever open waiting for you. When you want it more than anything the world has to offer, then will you be permitted to enter it consciously and to go in and out at will—not before.

Let no one be discouraged. Every soul, who longs
to find the Kingdom and who is earnestly striving
as much as circumstances permit to win his or her
way there, is known, is lovingly watched and helped
whenever possible. None is ever left without guidance, as you may learn from what follows.

Teachers

You have asked, My son, why the necessity of
teachers, when I am always within and ready to
make known to you all that you need to know.

Think, have I not always provided teachers for
you? Have there ever been any periods in your life
when you have not had teachers? If not recognized
as such, has there not always been someone close
who required of you the performance of certain
duties, who was ever a monitor of some kind pointing you to that which you needs must do, if you
would accomplish that which is before you to do,
and who thus taught you and saw to it that you
learned your lessons?

Do you doubt this? Then think of your parents,
and teachers in school, college, university; of your
superiors in factory or office; of partners or associ-
ates in business; of wife or husband or children in
the home; of friends in society, or of the Pastor of
your church; or of others whose opinion you respect
and value. Have they not all had a part in mould-
ing your character—in teaching you tongue-control,
gentleness, poise, patience, self-restraint, uselessness

of worrying, faith in self, and the hundreds of other qualities that I could build into your soul only through such teachers?

Yes, I use every possible medium to teach you the laws of being, which must be learned if you would make yourself measure up to that ideal I am ever holding before your soul's eye, and ever urging —compelling you from within to be.

For, is it not always *I within* you Who assent to or confirm the judgment or instructions of these outer teachers, permitting you to accept only that which *I* wish you to accept and believe at the time; *I* thus being to you the real teacher and the final authority to which you always turn, consciously or unconsciously, for such assent or confirmation?

You may sometimes rebel and run away from the condition in which I have placed you, and where best you can learn the needed lessons; but even then it is I who cause you to choose unwittingly a much harder condition in which to involve yourself, so that you may have opportunity to think and perhaps repent and maybe later to turn to Me for guidance and release.

But you say, what of those who have turned to Me and have found and are waiting upon Me, and who seek only to learn of Me and to serve Me? Need they other teachers, either on the outer or the inner planes? Need they Divine Teachers— Masters of Wisdom?

Listen, My son. There never will be a time when I shall not teach you through others; for so long as you work with and for others there will always be some above you to help you in such work and to prepare you for the next grade ahead. Through them *I* shall ever teach and help you, for remember *I* am the Real and *only* Self of all men; for *I am All in all.*

Being the Self in you I use all men to accomplish my purpose for you; even as I use you to help all others.

Never forget that I am *that* Self, that I AM THAT I AM, that *I* that is in every man—in every disciple, in every Teacher on earth or in Heaven,—in every Master, every Angel, every Son of God.

And when you realize that through each and all of such you can reach *Me* and be one with Me, even as you can reach and be one with Me in your own soul, then you will know that I am the ONE and ONLY Teacher for you and for all men—I, the Christ of God in Man.

A PERSONAL LETTER

Here is another letter from one whom we have quoted before. It is remarkably clear in its understanding of what has been stated regarding the "Sons of God," and is most helpful because of the writer's loyalty to our dear Lord and Master, Christ Jesus, and her knowing and unequivocably declaring His true part and place in the cosmic life of the earth and of all humanity upon it.

In parenthesis we have added our comments upon

her thought, in order to amplify and emphasize the high truths expressed.

Dear Friends:

Your letter and the remarkable Lesson just came. The vision under the head of "Personality" is the strongest meat you have given us, and will require study and careful thought in order to be fully understood.

I've felt for years that the true soul does not reincarnate until the last. I am reminded of some words by A. K. Mozumdar in his book, *"The Life and the Way,"*—"Behold the permanent form through which *thou* art now passing."

Ordinarily we would think of the "I" or the soul as permanent and motionless, while the forms would appear transitory and fleeting. But the truth may be that the forms or personalities are preserved— not the physical of course (*until the Soul learns all its lessons from these personalities and their experiences—see the article on the Personality*), while it is the soul which passes on, passes through or transmigrates. Yet even *this* is not the Higher Self. Then there would be three,—the manifestor, the manifesting, and the manifest.

It came to me once that in the individual life there must be that which corresponds to the Cosmic Christ. *It does not incarnate until its final manifestation (or rather manifestations—for after the soul has earned union with its Father-in-Heaven, a Son of God, then it or they may manifest for a spe-*

cial purpose having to do with the race) but remains
above or outside its successive bodies until the end
of its evolution.   When it does incarnate (*in a
physical body; before it was incarnate only in the
soul*) we have the manifestation of one of the Sons
of God.   I never read this, it is just my very own
idea.   And Christ Jesus is the culminating incarnation of the *Cosmic*, not the individual, Christ; hence
so much greater than the rest of us.   Which explains
why He said, "I am the Vine, ye are the branches."

Just as you say, "They, the Sons of God, lift up
the soul consciousness, etc."   You might have said
the soul *consciousnesses*—plural.   For it is evident
that when a Son of God is lifted up he draws with
him all his previous or lesser selves.   But Christ
Jesus did—or does—even more; He draws His disciples, *the Sons of God*, who in turn draw their disciples,—the   Infinite   drawing   the   infinitesimal.
"And I, if I be lifted up, will draw *all men unto me*."
The greater includes the lesser.   *He* includes and
draws us all.

Jesus was the culminating manifestation of the
Universal, or shall we say the planetary, Son of God.
Whether He is Cosmic in the sense of universes, I
would not say; but He is the "beginning of emana-
tion and the end of immination," the Alpha and
Omega for this earth, if not for the whole Solar
System.   So each of us is simply a pocket edition,
a miniature copy of the Great One, and except for
His Spirit—the string upon which the beads are
strung—we would not be what we shall be,—we
would not "awake in His likeness."

This idea is apparently a little different from yours, but I think there is a point where they could be made to harmonize. It may be the same thing seen from a different angle—a different aspect. (*Yes, there is no difference—it is only differently expressed.*)

One thing I know, we must always admit the supremacy of Christ Jesus. You know what Paul said of those who erred, "Not holding the *Head*." It is not enough to see Christ as supreme, we must see Christ Jesus! Jesus as the epitome, the last Son of Man and the first "Son of God," must be understood. I say the last Son of Man—not that there will be no more, but that Jesus was the last of His line, the *Cosmic line*. The rest of us are the Body. He was, and is, *the Head!* You know what the angels said to the disciples when Jesus ascended; they spoke of His return and said it would be "this same Jesus."

That means a great deal. It means that as Jesus, Christ finished the sacrificial work; as Jesus He will come to rule as before He came to serve.

It cannot be that it will be by natural birth—by reincarnation—that Jesus will return, for in that event it would not be "this same Jesus." I will not undertake to say how it will be, but it will not be a re-embodiment, since His incarnations were complete at His last appearance. (*She clearly perceives here a great truth.*)

Now all who are to be "His at His coming" will either be here still in their last manifestation or *they will come with Him.* Those here will be changed, will assume their glorified or soul body, while those who come with Him will already possess it. They will not be reincarnated. They will have finished their work before passing on.

I look for Jesus to become the Ruler, King or Governor of this planet, in the outer sense. The Jews and the world will be unable to see anything at first of an outward manifestation; "the Christ in you" is only for the Church, the true Christians (or disciples of Christ) in or outside of all Churches—the Members of the True or Invisible Church.

He, Christ Jesus, will be a Spiritual Being, such as He was when He appeared to His disciples after the resurrection. Not a Spirit, as He said, having flesh and bones, but it will be the immortal, incorruptible body, having life in itself.

There is a natural Israel and a Spiritual Israel. The natural Israel must pass through a natural—a national tribulation. I think the tribulation of spiritual Israel is Spiritual.

You know, according to the New Testament, the "elect" are to "escape the tribulation," and to "stand before the Son of Man."

Because I did not escape but had to be tried (*She says she passed through 15 years of tribulation. What disciples have not been through much tribulation?*) I doubt if I belong to the Sons of God class. That is, I mean I'm not of those who may be said to "sit upon the Throne." I'll have to be content to "stand before it." See Revelations 3:10 and 7:14–15. These, who have come out of great tribulation and *washed their robes*, are *before the Throne*. The overcomers sit upon it, they reign with Christ, while the others *serve before Him*.

G. P. B.

CHAPTER 12

WE ARE COME UNTO MOUNT ZION

"Ye are come unto Mount Zion, and unto the city of the living God, the heavenly Jerusalem, and to innumerable hosts of angels, to the general assembly and church of the first born, who are enrolled in heaven, and to God the Judge of all, and to the spirits of just men made perfect, and to Jesus the Mediator of the new covenant.
—Hebrew 12:22-24.

WE PROMISED in the preceding chapter to tell you more about the soul plane, more about the Kingdom, and more about the lower planes of consciousness.

We will consider first the Kingdom, and refer you to the opening paragraph of the first chapter where was said, "These words are addressed to all those who are seeking the way into the Kingdom of God —the Kingdom where a Great Love and Wisdom, the serving and inspiring of others, and the utter forgetfulness of self is the natural life of everyone who dwells therein."

Think on these words that you may grasp their deep import, for in them lies the whole essence of the Kingdom consciousness. And the Kingdom of God, you now know, is a state or realm of consciousness.

You have learned that the way into that con-

sciousness is the way of Love, or by following the
Christ within the heart Who will lead us into the
Kingdom there. You have found that by following
and obeying Him, Love gradually expands and pre-
pares the consciousness of the human mind so that
the Light of Divine Mind penetrates through and
illumines it, thus enabling it to see with His eyes
and to know with His understanding.

Likewise you have been taught the true meaning
of Service, and many of you have been led its way
and have been used to inspire and heal and bless
others, thereby learning to forget self and the real
soul joy of selfless service.

All such consequently are experiencing in their
outer consciousness what their souls actually are
living in their soul consciousness—that is, their
souls are now living in the Kingdom and working
from Its consciousness, else they would not be so
serving in the outer.

But you must remember that there are many
grades of Servers in the Kingdom. Note what is
stated in the verse at the head of this article. All
in the Kingdom are disciples as was shown in the
article on "Teachers" in the last chapter. Always
there are those above to teach and help their
younger brothers on all planes up to the highest,
our Lord and Master, Jesus Christ, being the Supreme Teacher of all Teachers and Masters, of all
Angels and Archangels, of Cherubim and Seraphim;
for *"He sitteth on the Throne with the Father and
from thence He discovers himself in his state and*

glory, as the great Ruler of the world, the King of kings, and Lord of lords, our Saviour."

We have shown that the highest soul or causal plane, the plane of purified or re-born souls—of disciples of Christ—is the first realm in the Kingdom. This implies that there are many realms beyond—realms or states of consciousness higher than that of disciples. This of course is so, as a higher state of consciousness is always enterable when the soul can comprehend in and be taught from it. You need only to look back a year or five years to the state of consciousness you were in then, and compare yourself then with where you are now, to see that then you were not ready to comprehend what you are being taught now, even as a year hence you may be in a much higher state of consciousness.

We have stated that disciples are purified *souls*. Try to realize that we mean souls, and not *personalities*. For such souls may have much in their personalities still to overcome and bring into harmony with their soul natures.

In fact, the Higher Self—a Son of God—now living in and actually being the soul of a disciple, having purified the soul consciousness and united it with the Higher Self's Christ consciousness, the soul's next immediate task is to bring the brain mind's consciousness—the actual disciple—into oneness with its soul consciousness, which is now one with its Father's—the Higher Self's—consciousness.

This accomplished—and we know it is accomplished only by purging the personality of all phases of selfishness, feeding it the "bread of adversity and the water of affliction" until nothing of self is left that can suffer—then the Great Consummation of the Three-in-One, the Divine Trinity, is effected,— the Higher Self, soul and human mind, or the Father, Son, and Holy Spirit, are now all one in consciousness, and hence are a perfect channel and instrument for the Father's use on the earth plane— the sole object of the present physical embodiment of a disciple.

A disciple, therefore, is always taught and directed in all his activities from the soul realm in the Kingdom. From there either his own Higher Self or other Teachers and Masters of Wisdom teach and guide him in the work of the Brotherhood to which he has dedicated himself, or help him to overcome and perfect in himself the qualities still needing to be brought into harmony for the Father's use. The Higher Self calls upon others to aid in the technical details that require supervision on the lower planes—even as a workman in a factory is taught or directed by a foreman, rather than by the Factory Manager, although when something of special importance is required of the workman the Manager will give him personal instruction and advice.

To all faithful ones who persistently strive to overcome self and who endure to the end are given this promise:

"And therefore will Jehovah wait that he may be gracious unto you; and therefore will He be exalted,

*that He may have mercy upon you; for Jehovah is a
God of Justice: blessed are they that wait for Him.*

*"For the people shall dwell in Zion at Jerusalem; thou
shalt weep no more; He will surely be gracious unto thee.
At the voice of thy cry, when He shall hear, He will
answer thee.*

*"And though the Lord give you the bread of adversity
and the water of affliction, yet shall not thy teachers be
hidden any more, but thine eyes shall see thy teachers:
and thy ears shall hear a voice behind thee saying, This
is the way, walk in it."*—Isaiah, 30:18–21.

All experience of whatsoever kind brings steady
growth or unfoldment and expansion of consciousness for the disciple, whether he is aware of it or
not. For when he thinks he is growing the least and
has no opportunity to meditate, yet is faithfully
striving to put the teachings into practice, apparently with many failures, his growth would be very
apparent on the soul plane to those who can see the
light that he radiates. An intense desire to become
worthy and an earnestness of purpose manifesting
in a continual striving to overcome faults and weaknesses, count for such much more than is generally
realized.

This applies equally to aspirants in their search
for Truth. It is the motive and the faithfulness
with which the seeker *persists* despite failure that
attracts the attention of Teachers on the inner
planes, and which brings the help needed, when
facing the problems of the daily life. While aspirants have not won to the plane of purified souls,
yet being souls they live and are active in the inner

planes of being exactly as their human personalities live and mingle with those interested in the same lines of thought on the physical plane.

Try always to realize that the soul must be in the inner realms just what its reflection—the personality—is in the outer, for it creates its home and environment first in the soul realm of consciousness, manifesting or outpicturing them within, on the mental or one of the astral planes, according to its spiritual growth, and then without on the physical plane; the inner and the outer being really one —the same consciousness manifesting on different planes of being. The only difference is, on the inner planes that which manifests is divested of all pretence, the soul stands forth naked and has no personality or mask to cover and hide its real nature, and similarly all else there are seen in their native purity.

From this it will be seen that the soul automatically finds its own level or plane of consciousness, be it one of the abstract or concrete planes of the mental realms, or in the higher astral realms, assuming that the aspirant has evolved beyond the lower astral, where self and the darkness of ignorance rule.

It is now time to dissolve some of the mystery and by the same token some of the condemnation and stigma that attaches to the astral plane. For the astral is merely the plane of consciousness from which come all desires, feelings, emotions and passions, including love.

Ponder on this statement. Can you not see that this being so, then every human soul is involved in the astral plane every time he lets any desire, feeling or emotion of whatsoever kind rule him and influence his thoughts, words and actions? The same way exactly as he is involved in the mental plane when some thought or idea claims his attention and rules his mind.

It is only when the psychic centers are prematurely opened—where spiritual growth has not opened them naturally—that there is trouble and the conscious soul is not always able to control the functioning of these centers, and it "sees" and "hears" or "feels" things that are not natural. But that is no harder than it is for one who is not "psychic" but is *mental,* and who has not learned fully to control his mind, and thoughts unbidden and unwanted come in and have their way with such. The only difference between the two is that the first named "sees," "hears" or "feels" psychically, while the other "sees," "hears" or "feels" *mentally,* but to each they seem as real as if in the physical.

The answer to this in both cases is mind-control, which must be gained before one can make any headway on the path to the Kingdom. In other words, the disciple sooner or later realizes that he must be able actually to stand guard at the door of his mind and admit only the thoughts and feelings he desires to entertain, and then must learn so to rule and train his mind that it thinks and holds only the perfect thoughts he wishes to outmanifest in his body and affairs.

We hope by this time that every student of these articles has realized the vital importance of mind-control, and has faithfully practiced the exercises given in the large meditation sheet, until he has proved to himself that he is master of his own mind. All students might as well know now that without such control *conscious* functioning on the soul and higher planes is impossible.

FEAR

This brings us to the consideration of the greatest obstacle that stands in the way of progression on the inner planes—which means to the Kingdom of God; for the Kingdom, remember, is within the mind or within its consciousness.   That obstacle is Fear.

The moment you let fear enter the mind, you are sucked into the emotional or astral plane, and unless you are able calmly to face it there and see it for just what it is—a craven creature of your own imagining, which has come to you to be fed, for it has no life but what you give it by recognition and tremblingly entertaining it—you had better cease meditation and go about active work of some kind that will require your mind's full attention.

Every disciple must learn, the moment *any* fear of whatsoever nature appears, to detect it immediately and to call it forth into the open, compel it to stand in front of him as it were, so that he can look

it squarely in the face and see it for the cowardly
thing it is—usually some form of *selfish* quality that
is being disturbed in its mental dominion and thus
seeks to maintain its hold over the soul.

From all this it should be seen that the way pictured is the road of mastery, is the conscious tread-
ing the Path inward to the Kingdom as *ruler of
your own mind*. Have you ever noticed how a positive personality not only attracts people, opportunities and all good things to him, while weaker
and negative persons unconsciously always step
aside and give him the right of way?

It is always so with the one who is master of his
own mind, for he has compelled and taught it to
serve him, and other minds instinctively recognize
such and render obeisance. Weaker souls are the
slaves of their minds—of their thoughts and emotions.

In true meditation one has such control of the
mind that he can focus its attention on whatever
he wishes to study and know. All the forces of
mind fly to aid such a positive soul. Therefore such
meditating can be done anywhere, at any time, and
in the daylight, and needs not darkness or some
quiet place. Such a soul can free itself from all
consciousness of the outer at will, and is able to
enter such realms as it chooses.

When thus freeing itself, the soul automatically
rises to the realm which is its soul home, and where
it always goes and works at night when the brain

mind is at rest in sleep.   There it sees and knows its soul companions and does whatever is required of it at the time by the Higher Self, even as when in the outer consciousness, although all activities in the inner will be of a soul nature necessarily, and are not concerned with personal interests; the brain mind of course, being unaware of such activities, except of what may come through in dreams, or if psychically unfolded of what may be seen in visions.

A disciple or awakened soul along with its brain mind will learn eventually to enter the inner planes consciously with definite purpose either for study or service, and will always have not only the conscious co-operation of the Higher Self, but of Great Souls and Helpers, and often of the Master Jesus, Himself.

As before shown, where two or more are gathered together in the Master's Name, He is actually in their midst, as are other Great Souls and many Brothers on the inner planes.

This will point you to the necessity of regular hours and places for both meditation and group meetings, for when it is known that such meetings are faithfully held they are always attended on the inner planes by those who seek to provide the necessary Light and Inspiration that the disciple wishes to bring through to his brain consciousness.

Think on these things, and then compare with the negative sitting in the dark of the ordinary seance room of spiritualistic circles, where members

seek messages from deceased relatives or others
through a Medium usually unconscious in a trance
state, his or her organism wholly controlled and
utilized by disembodied entities on the astral plane.

Not that the phenomena of such seances have not
given to the student much necessary information of
scientific value, and that all souls influenced that
way do not gain significant and needed lessons from
such experiences. But it is not the method of
learning of the disciple of Christ; for he seeks to
master self and all his mental and psychic forces,
in order to use them solely in the Master's Service
in uplifting and enlightening his fellow men.

THE LAW OF PROSPERITY

Many doubtless would like an explanation of the
principle or law back of tithing, and we believe that
all will be interested in knowing this law, for it
applies to all phases of human endeavor.

This law reduced to simple words is, *"As you
freely give, so will you freely receive."*

In other words, like so many laws difficult to
understand and obey, it is a matter of right *thinking* and *trusting*.

We all of us believe in God as the Source of all
things. But some of us cannot quite see Him as
*"our Supply, our Support, our Sufficiency in all
things,"* as so wonderfully taught by H.. Emilie
Cady.

Why—if we accept Him as the Source of all?

Is it not because we do not try to prove Him as such—truly and definitely try to prove Him?

Jesus, our Master and Teacher, has told us many times and in many ways of actual promises of the Father to those that love and trust Him. But we do *not* believe Him or we would prove it by *acting* as if we believed.

This is peculiarly true in the matter of material supply. How many really—unquestionably—trust Him? How many take no thought—are not anxious —at some time or other about what they shall eat or drink, or wherewithal they shall be clothed, realizing that their heavenly Father knows their need of these things; and as commanded are seeking first the kingdom of God and His righteousness, fully expecting all things to be added unto them?

Is it not so that instead of such expecting most earnest students go about *trying* to trust Him, but with so many sub-conscious doubts and fears that they actually drive the Good waiting to manifest far from them.

It resolves itself to this—and think these words over carefully: Until we learn that *all that we have* comes from the Father *within* and is for *His use,* and not ours, except for our immediate needs, and we then *act in that consciousness,* KNOWING that as we *use all* in His Service more and plenty will be given us for further use, we may find our present supply cut off or grow less, and we will be allowed to feel the stress of lack for awhile. It is as if we must keep the stream ever flowing, and as we give out, more and more will be poured in.

This has been proved by so many, especially by tithers, that it is known to them as an actual and workable law. We all of us have to learn that just as we pinch and hold on to money we automatically stop its inflow to us.

By learning thus to give or use money freely and fearlessly from a consciousness that *knows* that by every act of our giving we open the gate, as it were, for more to flow in and in even greater measure— for such is the actual way it does flow—naturally we not only never hesitate when our heart urges us to give, but we learn to love to give.

From a study of the above you will plainly see that it is purely a matter of attaining the right consciousness—that of absolutely trusting in God as our supply, or in the Law, if you prefer. For many have discovered that there is a law of loving giving which automatically brings its sure returns.

And you might as well know now that our Loving Father, being always our Highest Self, is putting us through all of these experiences that seem so hard solely in order to bring us to such trust in Him. For He longs with a great longing to have us give up self utterly, so that He can *be all* things to us and can *do all* things that He wishes to do through us and for us.

A tither is one who gives a tenth of his income back to God, seeking to support such phases of His

Work as enlist his heart interest. There are many notable instances of those who have attained to such faith and trust in Him that they have prospered to an almost incredible extent.

The law of giving, however, does not pertain to money only, but is a phase of the greater law of Love, whose outer manifestation is Service. And Service naturally is pure giving—not only of money, which is the least that we can give in actual value, as it deals only with *effects*, but of spiritual help, which reaches into and removes the *cause*.

We cannot impress too strongly upon students the vital importance of learning to live and work with this great Law of Loving Service, letting it rule in every thought, word and act. It is the basic element of discipleship and leads directly to the Kingdom.

In the next chapter we will make clear the practical use of this law, showing how in it is hidden the Magic Secret of attaining success, prosperity, health, happiness, peace and oneness with the Father.

To fortify and strengthen you, read the Master's own words regarding it all in the 6th chapter of Matthew, especially beginning with the 19th verse. *Study* it carefully, chiefly in order that you may see that our Father requires of us an absolute trust in Him, even exhorting us not to lay up for ourselves treasures upon earth, where moth and rust corrupt and where thieves break through and steal;

but to lay up for ourselves treasures in Heaven. For where our treasure is, there will our heart be also.

RECEIVED IN A GROUP MEETING

"My children. I am come that you may have life and that you may have it more abundantly. Open now your hearts and receive Me, for I am waiting to come forth in each of you consciously, so that you may not only know Me, but that you may know I am your Self, your one and only Self.

"The time is come that all may know Me, if they will. Receive Me, oh My children. Look for Me not in some far off time or place, but realize that I am here *now*—here in your hearts; I am that Love that is pushing forth to enrich and bless you, to supply you with all good and useful things needed for My harmonious and perfect expression through you.

"Open wide your hearts and acknowledge Me there—look to Me there constantly. Ever keep your ears turned to Me there, listening for My voice, waiting thus upon Me and Me only, as you go about your tasks, or when quiet comes and you would know My will.

"For I promise I will not let any go unfed, unhelped, unsatisfied, whose hearts are fixed on Me; for even as you receive all of your life, health and strength from My life in you, so can you receive the fullness of My life, not only as perfect health and strength, but as perfect care, perfect supply, perfect expression of My perfect nature—when you yield your mind and self over wholly to Me.

"I bless you, My dear ones. My love ever surrounds you and will always go before you, lighting your way and making easy your tasks—if you will but trust Me and let Me lead and guide you in all your ways."

CHAPTER 13

"As a Man Thinketh in His Heart"

IN THE last three chapters we devoted much space to making plain the meaning of and the part that the soul plays in the unfolding of consciousness; and we hope that all have studied and meditated upon what was stated until it is perfectly clear.

Until you know yourself as a soul, and can distinguish yourself from your mind and its personality and know your identity with your Higher Self, you will not be able to grasp intelligently all that follows.

We will assume however that all can do this, and also that all have an intimate acquaintance with the teachings of *"The Impersonal Life,"* so that if you are not yet conscious on the soul plane you will be more at home when we speak of and show you how to apply some of the Impersonal truths to what has been taught about the soul and about the Kingdom.

We have led all aspirants to the entrance to the Kingdom—at least we have told what is to be met along the way that leads to the entrance, and those who accompanied us should have gotten a clear glimpse of its reality. We do know that some have truly found the Kingdom and have entered it and are able to go in and out at will. Consequently we are very happy, and great joy reigns in the hearts of all Brothers within the realms of Spirit. For They have been watching and helping all steadfast travelers every step of the way with Their love and spiritual guidance.

In order that you may better understand the realms through which we have passed, we will recapitulate a little; for it is necessary that all know just what is required before they can go further.

We started from the physical, or outer rim of consciousness, and began our journey *inward* toward the center of being, where lies the Kingdom.

Unconsciously we passed through the six inner planes of the physical world—the two planes of the chemical region and the four planes of the etheric region, which supply vitality to the physical organism.

Then all aspirants passed easily through the three lower planes of the Astral World or Emotional Realm, commonly known as Purgatory; for it is supposed that all have won past the enticements of their lower or animal natures, which express on these planes of consciousness.

The next plane is the Borderland, that between the three lower and the three higher planes of the Desire, Emotional or Astral World, as they are variously called.

If any are still of a highly emotional type, it has been and will be most difficult to get beyond this

realm, for their feelings and their reactions thereto
will hold them so that they cannot free their soul
consciousness to permit them to concentrate and
thereby to penetrate the Mental World with its
first four concrete planes constituting the first, second, third and fourth heavens. These planes comprise the realm of mental forms, as distinguished
from the three higher planes—the fifth, sixth and
seventh heavens, which comprise the realm of abstract thought, also called the Causal Realm.

Similarly until one has been able to free the consciousness from its interest in the form side of
things, and can concentrate and meditate easily
upon abstract ideas and gain light and understanding therefrom, one is held in the concrete realms;
while those who become engrossed in the beauty of
tones and ideas—as is the case with many musi-
cians, artists, poets and other writers—and who
cannot penetrate through to their spiritual realities, are held here, although they have reached the
entrance to the Kingdom.

We merely mention these different heavens or
realms of consciousness, not giving any detailed description of them here, referring you to Theosophical
or Rosicrucian teachings—whose terms we have purposely used because they are definite and explana-
tive—for the relation each bears to the various
stages of soul unfoldment.

On our journey inward we have now reached the
Causal Realm, consisting of the three planes of
the abstract Mental World. Beyond the Causal

Realm is the first Spiritual Realm; but the last of the three Causal planes, the one next to the Spiritual, is the virtual entrance to the Kingdom. It is the plane of purified souls, the natural soul home of all disciples and of members of the Great White Brotherhood—of Just Men Made Perfect.

Here dwell the purified and perfected souls of all things, the ideal state, all Spiritual realities made manifest in their purest soul forms. Which means that here everyone is perfect in his or her soul nature—young, beautiful, wise, powerful and all-loving, all manifesting that phase of soul their Higher Selves intend to express.

From this you are recalled to the fact that even in this high and pure state you may or may not be fully conscious of your oneness with your Higher Self, your Father-in-Heaven. For remember, as a disciple you are no more nor less there than you are in the physical, for what your soul is *you* are, whether in the inner or the outer realm of consciousness.

In other words, if in your brain consciousness you are wholly in the consciousness of your Christ Self —can say with Jesus and *know it* as He knew it, "I and my Father are One" and "all that the Father hath is mine,"—then you are actually established in the Spiritual consciousness of the Kingdom, *beyond* the Causal realm. While if you are now looking to, waiting upon and serving faithfully the Christ within or any other Master or Teacher, then you are on the plane of consciousness of all disciples, the soul plane of the Kingdom.

We are trying to point out the fact that even if one as a disciple has awakened his soul faculties and is able to function consciously on the soul plane of the Kingdom and to see and commune with his Brothers there, he is still but a disciple and not a bit further advanced than his brother disciples who are not so psychically awakened, and he still has to turn to the Master for guidance and instruction when in need.

Indeed, one who cannot consciously see and hear on the soul plane may be farther advanced than one who sees and hears clearly; and to explain why this is we cannot do better than to quote from the Commentaries in the *Light of the Soul*, in the 3rd Part, on Patanjali's Sutras, No. 37, by Alice Bailey (see Appendix):

"These powers (the higher sight, hearing, touch, taste and smell) are obstacles to the highest spiritual realization, but serve as magical powers in the objective worlds. (Italics used as shown.)

"One fact continuously emerges in this textbook of spiritual development, and that is that the psychic powers, higher and lower, are hindrances to the highest spiritual state, and must be left behind by the man who can function freed from the three worlds altogether. This is a hard lesson for the aspirant to grasp.

He is apt to think that a tendency toward clairvoyance or clairaudience is indicative of progress and a sign that his practice of meditation is beginning to take effect. It might prove just the opposite and inevitably will, should the aspirant be attracted by, or attached to, any of these forms of psychic faculties."

Soul sight and hearing naturally means the ability to see and hear consciously with the *soul* faculties on the soul planes. There all the beautiful, pure and perfect things present everywhere would be seen and they would naturally greatly attract and even entrance anyone newly privileged with such soul sight.

But unless such realized that they were all expressions or outpicturings of spiritual realities, and then sought to learn and know what it all meant— what were the spiritual verities thus symbolized, such soul sight would indeed prove a hindrance.

On the other hand *spiritual* sight is the ability to see past and through all forms the ideas that they outpicture and embody, to see the spirit within the soul of things, that which is trying to express itself to the consciousness of every awakened soul. It is the highest seeing and that which awaits every disciple. It is the seeing of a Master—the power attained by every Christed man; and those who are beginning thus to see may know that they are far along the Path.

Now hear this great and most important truth,—

all true Masters and Teachers, whether on the inner or outer planes, even as Christ Jesus taught, ever seek to point their disciples to the Father within as the source of all life, all health, all supply, all wisdom, power and love, and that they should always look to Him only whatever their need.

"The Impersonal Life" plainly teaches this and impresses it very strongly upon the soul of all disciples that they should never allow themselves to be inveigled into looking elsewhere for what can only be found deep within their own souls.

You have been shown that in disciples, the Higher or Christ Self, a Son of God—actually a conscious center of God's Consciousness—resides in and rules the soul, and is the one Master for that soul. And while there may be many Teachers and other Masters higher than the soul in its present understanding, yet always within is *The* One, its Christ Self, its Father-in-Heaven, Who is its supreme Teacher and Master, and to whom it ever must turn for its final authority and guidance.

This will obtain not only on the soul planes but on all planes in the Spiritual realms until the final union of consciousness with God's Consciousness is gained.

Therefore all who now recognize and accept this great truth will never become enamoured with the wonders and beauties of the soul realm, when they awaken to its consciousness, where life is a pure joy and where the perfection of all things is perceived and fully appreciated by every soul there; but they will press on to the goal of the high calling of God in Christ Jesus, the heritage of every Son of God.

THE GREAT SECRET

In the preceding chapter we promised to make clear the practical use of the Law of Service, showing how in it is hidden the secret of attaining success, prosperity, health, happiness and oneness with the Father.

In it we indicated, but not in these actual words, that our present financial condition is the result of our thinking and *holding uppermost in our consciousness* the things we *believe* are so.

At this time we wish to state that *all things now manifesting* in our lives—in our bodies and our circumstances—are the result of our believing and thus holding in consciousness the ideas that gave them birth.

Meditate earnestly on these words and try to get their deep significance, for in them lies the secret of all success in any line of endeavor.

First we will state the Law:

"All manifest things are the result of thinking and holding in consciousness what we believe is so."

Then we wish that you were able to see in the inner realm of consciousness and could note how every thought is outpictured there, and that according to the clearness and vividness of its picturization in the mind of its creator and the life or feeling put into the thought, does it become concrete and maintain and attach itself to the one who gives it birth. If you could so see, you would be very, very careful what you think or say, and especially of what you *hold in mind* and feed with more life by your fears, worries, doubts or concerns about it, every time it claims your attention. However in lieu of such seeing, which may come later, we hope that what we have shown will make you just as careful, and will thus enable you to come more quickly into your heritage of true seeing and knowing.

There are many, even students of the higher life, who do not yet accept or admit this fully, because they are not willing to acknowledge that all of the present inharmonies in their lives are a direct result of their own beliefs—or of their past thinking crystallized into beliefs, these beliefs having thus become a part of their subconsciousness or of their *soul* consciousness.

Note the last,—if a part of their *soul* consciousness it means that on the soul planes they actually exist and manifest there. And everything *established there* in consciousness—for all planes are states of consciousness—tends sooner or later to outmanifest itself on the physical plane, in their creator's body and affairs. It must do that—for it is the Law of Creation.

Now we know that every aspirant is desirous of

eliminating from his subconsciousness or soul every belief or concept that is responsible for any inharmonious conditions now manifesting, and which, whether he knows it or not, is the direct cause of every fear, anxiety, or worry that steals into his consciousness to influence him.

And we know that his primary interest is how to do this; for he more or less clearly perceives that not until he has accomplished it can he bring his mind to that state where he can begin to build into his life the conditions he wants to manifest there.

We are now going to point out to you the one and only way this can be accomplished. And it is so simple that anyone can see how true it is. Then all that remains is for *you to do it*. Is it not so? And you *can* do it, *if you will*—if you want it badly enough.

Listen! We will repeat it again,—it is all contained in these few words:

"Whatever we think and hold in consciousness as being so will outmanifest itself."

Then is it not so that all that is needed is to stand guard at the door of our minds, and to *let in no thoughts or feelings that we do not want to manifest* in our bodies or circumstances?

This means that we must scrutinize carefully every thought or feeling that approaches, and if any are negative in any way—criticisive, condemnatory, doubting, worrying, hateful, jealous, angry, self-pitying, unhappy, sick, painful, or untrue in any sense to the ideal state we wish to manifest —refuse them admittance and shut the door in their faces.

And it should not be necessary to state that *voicing* such thoughts definitely and speedily outmanifests them; for the spoken word is far more potent than the thought and makes it *live* once sent forth on the breath. Then remember that by preventing such thoughts entering the mind there will be no impulse to voice them.

And here also it may be well to state that if any such thoughts come begging for admittance—the fearful, doubting, worrying, unhappy, self-pitying, hateful, jealous ones—it is only self crying out, thinking of itself first, not concerned about others. Think on this.

For remember *you* are a Son of God to whom none of these negative and imperfect things can. apply—and they are only creations of your human mind that thinks itself different from *you*—are but lies born of selfishness. Then turn your mind's attention to what you really are, and think of and picture in your mind your real qualities, knowing that *you* are a creation and image of God, your Father. This would be having in you "the same mind that was in Christ Jesus."

A good thing at such times is to sit back coolly, as it were, and study your mind, and watch all the thoughts that come claiming your attention, and learn to discriminate between them, to know their source, whether they are your own creations or some one's else; and particularly to note how many of the negative ones are your own, and how they keep coming back to you to be fed by more of the feelings which gave them birth and have kept them alive since. This will prove a very illuminating and helpful exercise.

Then when you have demonstrated to your satisfaction that you are learning to control your mind and can keep out not only your mental abortions but all tramp thoughts that used to come in at will, you can begin to build in the new conditions that you wish to have manifest permanently in your body and affairs.

This will entail calling to your assistance the Loving One within—if you have not called on Him before. For now you want to begin thinking only His thoughts, and to let His Love motivate and vitalize every one of them, so that they may be worthy and acceptable in the Father's sight.

Here the real joy of your efforts will begin to be felt, for the Master will give definite evidence of His co-operation by inspiring you with thoughts and ideas that you will *know* are from Him, and you will happily follow the suggestions they contain.

After considerable experience in such following, and perhaps with many failures, due to your unwittingly permitting other thoughts than His to get in—some doubts or fears or anxieties, the old bugaboos of former days, you will have trained your mind to trust Him, to make that trust the door-keeper, so that no other thoughts or feelings can get in, and you will gladly give your whole mind over to *Him* to use.

From then on it makes no difference what you do, so long as it is what *He* wills you to do, and you do that gladly; for *He* every day now proves that He knows best, that He can enable you to do all things, and can supply all things necessary.

Now let us get down to basic facts, and remind you again of what the human mind needs to be told without ceasing, until it finally accepts and *knows*.

Who are you? You are a soul, a center of the Father's Consciousness that now *knows* its oneness with His Consciousness. And you are now trying to teach your human mind that it is a center of your consciousness and one with you, who are one with the Father's Consciousness.

Being thus a center of His Consciousness, which always thinks and knows only beauty, goodness and perfection, the way to let His beauty, goodness and perfection outmanifest is to yield your conscious-ness over wholly to Him, so that *no thoughts ever enter your mind that are not all beautiful, all good and all perfect.* Then there will naturally be noth-ing to hinder your seeing with His eyes—being in His Consciousness—and knowing with His under-standing what He has had in store for you from the beginning. That is, there is nothing whatever then to prevent your own good from coming through speedily into manifestation.

Hence there can be no greater success in life than such letting go of all your own personal ideas and opinions and abiding in your Father's Consciousness, so that your highest good, which He has planned for all of His children who are able to give up self and the lie of separation, can come forth and be in the outer even as it already is in the Kingdom. And that good naturally includes real prosperity, the most perfect health, and the purest happiness.

Can you not see that this must be so—when your mind becomes a center in which nothing out of harmony with Divine Mind can enter? Then such a mind is a center into which must pour continuously the rich, healthy, loving consciousness of God Himself. Likewise you can then see how, when such consciousness enters, Love and its law of service automatically rule, and how success and happiness must naturally follow; for harmony then outmanifests, and that means harmony in every department of life. And then you will think no more about *getting,* but only how you may *give* to make someone happy. And you will be no longer concerned about prosperity, health, or happiness for self, for you *know* that as you give yourself —your mind and heart—fully to the Father for His use, He will provide everything necessary to enable you to do the Work He gives you to do.

Tithing it will be no more—for you gladly give *all* to Him, all that you have, all that you are, and all that you hope to be.

Think this all over carefully, a sentence at a time, until you get fixed in your consciousness the wonderful truths here shown.

It is all definitely confirmed in these words, *"As a man thinketh in his heart, so is he."* Also in these: *"If ye abide in Me* (in His Consciousness), *and let My Words abide in you* (think only His thoughts and hold them unwaveringly in consciousness—that is, *believe* them), *ye shall ask what ye will and it will be done unto you"* (you need not even ask—they will automatically outmanifest for you whenever there is a need).

Therefore, dear ones, watch carefully your thinking, especially the thoughts that you carry around in your heart about those closest to you, about your business, your job, your health, or any condition in which you find yourself.

These thoughts should be always and only *positive,* optimistic, self-confident, happy, kindly, fearless, seeing only the good in everything, and absolutely trusting in your Father to bring to you your highest good. For such are His thoughts for you and what He purposes for you, and anything *less* in quality or quantitiy you may know are of self, are separative, and have no part in His Consciousness.

CHAPTER 14

"Whom the Lord Loveth He Chasteneth"

WE HAVE been asked this question, "Why are all who long to serve the Great Cause of Humanity so oppressed by lack and limitation of one kind or another?"

The title to this paper will give a hint to our answer, and while it may be quite satisfying to some, yet until it is fully realized and its application to one's individual case is clearly understood it is but a sorry fact, if it can be proved to be a fact.

This we hope to prove to you, and we first would remind you that we have shown in previous articles how all earnest aspirants and especially all true disciples seek to be cleansed of all qualities of self and separateness that prevent the unhindered use of the personality by the Higher Self; and that they actually ask and invite such cleansing—at least in their hearts they do if not in definite prayers—so that they may become perfect instruments for His use.

Remember this must be so, with true disciples of Christ, for we must give up all of self if we would follow Him. And that means we must give up all of those things that hold us to the world, the flesh and the devil; for self is the only devil and self is wholly of the flesh and of the world.

Now try to realize that to have reached the stage of spiritual growth where we gladly do this, we must know that we have had little to do with such growth. It was something *within* us that was growing, and in order to grow some of the old confining and conflicting qualities of soul and the thoughts and ideas they engendered had to be loosened from our consciousness and be left behind—that such was part of the cleansing process. And if such loosing and freeing hurt, which is natural, we should be glad, and should at once seek to learn why it hurt —and the quality of self that was being hurt and was refusing to let go and was thus holding us back from the goal that awaits.

Keeping in mind the unconscious growth *within* taking place, we can then see if health departed, or financial reverses came, or some loved one was taken away, or one of the cherished desires of our hearts was suddenly removed, that it was necessary to bring such about first in order to awaken the soul, and then when that was accomplished the mind's attention could be turned to the Lord within, the Giver of all good things.

But, some may say, why should any of these things be taken away in order to turn us to God? We will let you yourself answer that question. Why did you not turn to Him before—really turn to Him? When you had health and money and loved ones and the desires of your heart, where and when did God come into your thoughts? Was He not then but a vague term, an abstract ideal, who intellectually stood as the fountain of all religious thought, but who actually had no *real* existence in your life? Yes, you accepted Him as the author of your being and that He was responsible for all things in your life. But did you really know Him?

Well, the time had come when He, *within* you, could prepare your human mind so that it could become conscious of Him, could learn to know Him as He *is*, and could eventually co-operate with Him; by first letting Him use you and all that you are and have, and then giving to you those qualities of mind and soul and later those things in the outer which He can use, not for your good alone, but for the purpose He intended from the beginning— for the good of all.

All must come to that consciousness, and if you have been brought to that place where He has accepted you at your word, has begun the cleansing process and has taken some things away that meant very much to you, it is a sure sign that *He* has called you, has chosen you, and is not only trying to gain your mind's and heart's attention, but is verily drawing you to Him.

"Whom the Lord loveth He chasteneth."

The Standard Dictionary defines chasten as "to discipline by pain or trial; to make chaste, to refine, purify."

Now none of the above means much unless you fully realize that the Lord is your Self—your Divine Self, that One *within* who has been growing you, who has been putting you through all the experiences of life, in order to teach, discipline, chasten, refine and purify your human and supposed separate mind, so that it knows its identity with You and Your Mind. It is no outside God doing this, no Great Being somewhere apart from you, but is the Real You abiding within the soul and from there directing all, inspiring every needed helpful thought, and permitting other kinds only for your mind's disciplining and its learning from the mistakes they cause it to make.

Until you have taught it thus to turn *within* to the Lord—the Self within, and to look to Him only there for everything, to wait upon His every will and word, God is not real to you and has no actual part in your conscious life.

"The Impersonal Life" has taught you all this, and if you have not already proved it, it is time that you begin to know that the I AM of you is your Lord, that He *is* your Self—your *only* Self. Many of you have earnestly studied the helps provided in the preceding articles and have faithfully striven to grasp the realization intended, but cannot quite close the gap between your human and divine centers of consciousness. Some, however, have been able to draw their minds back into conscious Oneness, where they recognize I AM as their Self, and their human minds as but instruments or channels formed for use in outer work on planes of consciousness outside the Kingdom.

We will try to give herewith a few additional

helps for those who feel they need only a little more light to enable them to close the gap.

Practical Work

First read again carefully the article, "Practical Work" in the seventh chapter. From it you will note the importance of learning *to talk to yourself*. For in such talking you soon find that something greater than your human self is talking, and that it is the mind that does the listening and thinking and understanding of what it hears. Practice will gradually bring the conviction that a higher or greater You is thus talking, for things will be said that your mind did not before know; and that will give you encouragement to continue until your mind recognizes that words of wisdom are being spoken— truths very much worth knowing and putting into practice in your life.

At such times it would be well to have a note-book handy to write in it such truths, so that they may not be forgotten, and can be available for study or giving out to help others.

Now when you thus talk to your human self and it learns that it is but the listener and the pupil, you can realize how You, as the Higher Self, are the real Teacher and Master, and that your human mind is the disciple. Also you can grasp, as you more and more prove it to your reasoning mind, that You are a Divine Being, are actually the Lord God, Who is the Chastener and the Discipliner.

For remember that it is God Who alone Is. The

human mind only thinks it is, that it is separate from You and from God; when how could that be when *He is all that* Is, and that in the consciousness of His Mind *all* live, move and have their being? Human minds are only centers of his Consciousness, are ideas in His Mind, just as your thoughts and ideas are centers of your consciousness.

Cease reading now and think on all of the above, until it becomes clear.

Then when you have grasped it, try definitely to realize your Self as That which is the innermost inner of your being, that *It* is your life, intelligence and will which is expressing your Self outwardly in and through your human consciousness as a personality, an instrument created solely to enable You to accomplish that which You came into human manifestation to do.

When you clearly realize this, then say to your human mind, and try to mean it and *know* it as you speak, what follows:

"Be still, my child, and come back in here where I am.

"Withdraw all attention from and interest in outer things and fix them upon Me, deep within the soul.

"Let go of your sense of self and separateness, think of yourself as a spiritual being and enter fully into My Consciousness, I Who am all Spirit.

"Know that you have no consciousness that is apart from My Consciousness; therefore you cannot be separate from Me—only as you mistakenly think so. For as you *think*, so does it seem to you to be—when you are *without* in the consciousness of such mistaken thoughts.

"Therefore, come back into your soul consciousness and abide here with Me. For your soul *body* is very beautiful, is perfect in every way—strong, healthy, harmonious, pure, radiant, glorious; for it is your *real* body, in which you really live and where you always are at night when sleep frees you from your physical body consciousness. It is so because I am there, because I created it as My habitation in the beginning, and because I dwell in it as your Self and therefore You when there are one with Me, and consequently are perfect *now*, even as I am perfect.

"And back in here in My consciousness you can see and know your Self in the perfection of My Image and Likeness, even as I see and know you; can see clearly that you are *not* separate—could not possibly be separate or different—from Me, your *Self*, your one and *only* Self.

"Think! I am trying to prove to you your actual and eternal nature, that your real body is perfect; that *You* can never really be sick because of its perfect purity; that in your soul home, which is your true home, all good things are yours; that there is no lack or limitation of any kind there, for in the Kingdom of My Consciousness, which contains only all good and perfect ideas, less than perfect ideas or conditions do not and could not exist.

"Can you not see that it is only because you *think* yourself different from your true Self, that you seem different?

"Remember what was stated in the last chapter, *'What you think and hold in consciousness as being so, outmanifests itself in your body and circumstances.'*

"Then your body and circumstances are now only the outmanifestation of your wrong and ignorant thoughts—and they have no *real* existence! Can you not see that, and that if you will but cleanse your mind of all those wrong and untrue thoughts and know yourself as you *are*—in your soul state, in your Kingdom Consciousness, you will actually be and see yourself as I have shown you are there.

"Ponder this for awhile until you get it. It will mean everything, if you persist and do get it.

"Now listen carefully. Having grasped the great but simple truth of what has been stated, then to You nothing without in the realm of manifestation is true or of any real importance; for the only reality is within in your soul state where I Am. Then you in your human self are nothing at all, for *I, your perfect Self, alone am!* You are only a human mind, an idea or center of My Consciousness that I created for My use in the realm of matter—which itself is but a composite idea in consciousness—in order that I myself might dwell and function in that outer realm, when I had prepared and fitted you as a perfect avenue for such functioning.

"You are nothing, can be nothing, and can do nothing only as *I* do it through you. Then why should anything really matter to you, you may well ask.

"Can you not see that it does not—cannot possibly matter, if you are nothing, and I alone AM?

"Then, beloved, why not let go and turn over *all* to Me? Let go of *everything,* and put all responsibility upon Me?

"You *can* do it, if you really try. Just think what it means not to care any longer; that you need not fear or worry or be concerned any more about anything, for I will take care of all.

"No matter what is the problem confronting you, just turn it over to Me. You do not know what a wonderful blessing awaits you, when you are able thus to let go and to trust everything to Me. For I *will* take care of *all,* even as I am doing anyway, and I will handle everything far better than you possibly could.

"Yes, when you have learned to trust all to Me —in a *positive,* living, powerful trust—I will arrange everything; for when you actually let go, and get out of the way, I can bring forth into manifestation the Good I intended from the beginning for you, in order to accomplish My Purpose with you.

"And when your mind thus becomes empty of self-will and of all self-ideas and purposes, I can then put into your mind My Ideas and My Will for you; then I can tell you what to do and your mind, no longer cluttered with fears, worries and concerns of self, can hear My Voice and can know it as Mine, and you will be glad to obey.

"Then I need chasten and discipline you no longer, for your mind has become cleansed and emptied of all ideas of self, and I can take possession and can use it for the purpose I had prepared and fitted it to be used.

"Yes, you then need do nothing but wait upon Me and need not be concerned about anything, for you will do perfectly what I tell you to do, because then I actually *will be You, and I will be doing it.* And I will take care of all and I will be wholly responsible for all; and you will know that you and I are One, and that I am God."

GROUPS

In the first chapter and also in later ones, we mentioned group work, and while then we did not definitely urge the formation of groups, we feel by this time that many are able to understand the significance of disciples of Christ meeting together in His Name and that they should be able to receive from Him definite guidance, or at least definite assurance of His Presence, should two or three earnest souls come together for the express purpose of fitting themselves for His Service.

As stated in the article in the 9th chapter, which we earnestly request all to reread and study, such groups will be brought together by the Master, when He finds those truly consecrated and desiring above all things to serve Him. Our part has been to help quicken and inspire in aspirants first the spirit and meaning of Service, and then the desire to do all possible to fit themselves as instruments for His use.

We have helped by providing exercises and instructions for training and disciplining the mind and emotions, and have stressed time and again the vital importance of faithfully mastering the exercises until the mind and all its faculties have become perfect servants of the will. We have also done all possible to make each aspirant acquainted with the Loving One within, Who is the inner assurance of Him Whom they look to outwardly, as it were, as their Divine Master and Leader.

Therefore, those who have failed to follow the suggestions given, because of its being too much trouble, of not wanting to take the time necessary, of having too many social or personal things that they let interfere, of being too mentally lazy to make the necessary effort, or of thinking such requirements unnecessary, will now have no one to blame but themselves when they find others have arrived at the entrance to the Kingdom, with their soul and mental faculties unfolded and well trained for service, proven by what such receive while meditating with other consecrated souls in group meetings.

An earnest study of the teachings and a faithful striving to follow and put into practice their truths, in every case has resulted in an expansion of consciousness and a consequent unfoldment of soul faculties. But not all souls unfold alike, which is natural and is better for the development of a strong and efficient group consciousness; for such a consciousness should be composed of different types of minds in order to be well rounded-out, just as a well rounded-out intelligence should have every faculty fully developed by studies and training along varied lines on many different subjects.

Group consciousness is the next step to be attained by disciples, and it can be attained only by actual experience in a group, where can best be learned, in association with other consecrated souls, how to master and deal with personality, and later how to utilize its forces in the Master's Cause. And all this under His direct guidance, remember; for where two or three are gathered together in His Name, He is actually in the midst of them—expressly to give such guidance and teaching.

Many in groups have had definite evidence of this, and happy are they to learn that others are meeting with experiences similar to their own. Many letters have been received, telling of their great joy at actually seeing and being blessed by the Master Jesus with a personal message for them, and which had a profound effect upon their lives. This and many other significant things have been told us, indicating that the Master is now calling out His chosen ones in ever-increasing numbers, and is getting them ready for what awaits.

Because of this, we shall continue to stress the great importance of all forming into groups wherever it can be arranged. And we know it can be arranged in most cases where the true spirit of Service is present in the heart; for when the heart wills, a way will be found, because the Master rules in and works from the heart, and His will is the only will of a sincere disciple.

In a later chapter we shall tell about the possibilities of group work, and will give definite suggestions for such work, including group healing, helping in personal financial and other problems, also in community, national and international affairs. We will give the law and how to apply it under the direction of the Master within.

CHAPTER 15

THE IMPERSONAL LIFE

THE first chapter of this book was originally issued as a Paper which was sent to a large list of metaphysical students, and which is still being sent to all new correspondents, as well as to all new students of the Impersonal Life message.

In that Paper we offered to send the succeeding numbers to all who were earnestly seeking the Kingdom and who were making that seeking *first* in their hearts and lives, and we invited all such to accompany us on our journey to the Kingdom, to which we promised to lead them.

Some of those who accepted our invitation and who have journeyed with us from the beginning know that we have reached the Kingdom and that the door is open wide to all who are able consciously to enter and to abide therein.

Again we wish to point out that it is the *earnest* ones, those to whom the finding of the Kingdom was really the *first* and *supreme* purpose of their lives, who are now conscious of the great blessings of the Kingdom, their Father's Home, that is theirs to possess and enjoy.

Those who made this seeking secondary to other interests and desires can now see why they are unable to grasp the full meaning of all that has been shown—why they cannot close the gap between their lower and higher consciousness and know the I Am or Christ as their Self.

In the last chapter we gave final instructions to enable all who were ready to accomplish this last step, and we expect others from time to time, as they digest and prove what the teachings contain, to find that they also have reached the goal; when we will be very happy with them, as will be all our Brothers of the Kingdom.

You who for any reason have not gained what your hearts seek, we urgently advise to go back and start over again, beginning with the first chapter, and not to leave it until you have made everything in it your own, fully digesting and proving each truth to your satisfaction, before passing on to the next. If you do this, we prophesy that you too will be enjoying the blessings of the Kingdom with your Brothers before many weeks.

Now we are going to ask you to consider with us some truths that may prove rather startling, at first thought, until you realize from what has been taught regarding the Soul that they cannot be other than as shown.

The first truth, assuming that you are a disciple of Christ Jesus and consequently are become an immortal soul, is that you are not at all what you think yourself to be. No, you are not the personality— not the John Smith or the Mary Doe—that the world knows; but you are using that personality, which your human mind created, and which now you are cleansing, developing and perfecting, as an instrument with which to accomplish that which you came into physical expression to do.

Try to realize that this must be so—if you are an immortal soul—that this present personality is but one of many you have similarly used back through the ages,—*but that these personalities were not you.* They were only characters you assumed for the purpose of accomplishing what you planned to do.

Well then who—what am *I?* You ask.

If you have not studied and meditated upon the several articles on the Soul until you have a fairly clear concept of yourself as a soul, we urge that you go back and study them until it becomes clear. In any event it were better to reread the articles in order to refresh your memory, so that you may grasp more easily what we are now going to say.

Remember, a disciple is a soul consciously being taught by his Higher Self, a Son of God. A *conscious* disciple is one who is in close communion with his Higher Self, the I Am, the Christ, and is often possessed by Him, and thereby is often in His consciousness. The more advanced the disciple the more he is used by this Master Self, and the more he learns to see with His eyes and to know with His understanding.

Such a disciple sooner or later is given to see and know "who he is and of what he is a part." This means that in time he will *know* himself as a soul having put on different bodies in different ages, creating personalities that played a part in the history of those days, probably most often an insignificant part, but perhaps one or more times of a prominent nature, according to the age and advancement of the soul. He will know this because it will all be unfolded to him as definite soul memories of those past lives.

Ordinarily a soul spends the few years of life in his mortal body and then retires and lives in his soul body for centuries before reincarnating again. But of course it depends on the soul—the number and frequency of its incarnations, for some souls because of their nature are given special work to do in connection with humanity, while others who ripen more slowly are not yet ready for the special training that can be gained only in strenuous earth experiences.

But this phase of the subject does not pertain to what we are seeking to explain. We want you to realize first that you are old souls—all of you who clearly heard the call of the Master when reading the first chapter, and who have been faithfully and earnestly following Him ever since.

Does this make you stop and think? Then hear this: Perhaps you were one of His followers when He was on earth in Palestine. Perhaps you have been His follower and even a martyr in His Cause in other lives down through the centuries since. Aye, perhaps you were among those who were taught, sung to, or who believed the prophesies about Him, voiced by Moses, or Abraham, or David, or the Prophets, and who long looked forward to His coming before He appeared. So that you love Him with a love that is not only of the soul, but of the Spirit, of which He is the very life essence; because He is the Holy Spirit, and your own Higher Selves are one with Him and one with the Father.

Remember now that we are not speaking of the John Smith or Mary Doe of your present life, but of the *real* you who are an old soul. If this has awakened a response deep within, you may find it not hard to accept that you were a living soul when He was on earth, maybe before He was on earth, and perhaps even in old Atlantis. Something may say to you, this may be possible. If something does not so say, then it may not be possible. But do not let yourself be fooled or get concerned about it, for it does not make any particular difference; it only gives you an idea of how old is your soul.

This will help you to know. Are you serving? How long have you been serving, and how many and whom are you serving? If you are an old soul you came here to serve, and love is the very essence of your life, so that you began serving in some form or other as soon as your instrument could be used. And the older the soul the more influence you radiate, the more souls you are awakening and helping into the Kingdom.

But do not let your age concern you, for the only thing that matters is—does your soul yearn to serve *now,* and is it straining to make your human self fit and worthy to serve?

Remember what the Master told us in the parable of the householder who, when paying the laborers in his vineyard, paid those hired the eleventh hour the same wage as those hired the first hour. Those who serve are all part of the Great Brotherhood of Servers; they are Brothers who think not of their wage or of their Brother's part, but are concerned only that they are pleasing the Master by perfectly performing their part.

That is the first truth we wanted to convey. The second is, if we are immortal souls, then we are also Sons of God; for remember that the Sons of God are our Higher and *Real* Selves, and it is They who are unfolding, developing and ripening our souls through the quickening of our minds and the purifying of our bodies, so that They can enter and possess us and live Their life in us, do Their Will in us, and *be the Self* of us.

And who are the Sons of God? They are reflections of God, His Holy Spirit, the Christ—God's Love poured forth into the souls of men, so that they may know Him, and may return to conscious Oneness with Him in His Consciousness.

Have you felt the Christ, the Loving One within you? Have you heard Him within your soul say:

"I am the way, the truth and the life. You cannot come unto the Father except by *Me.*

"For I am the love you feel in your heart urging for expression, and through this love is the only way.

"*I* am the truth of your being, and without Me—love—you are nothing, can know nothing and can do nothing.

"*I* am the life, and there is no other life but My life of love. All other ways, all other teaching, lead but to death—the sense of separation from the Father and Me."

Dear one, if you know Love, if you feel it as an actual presence within you, *you know your Higher Self,* a Son of God, Who is One with the Father, who is *You,* the only *Real* You.

Think! Who is John Smith anyway—he whom you call your self? Has he really ever done anything wholly of himself? Can he do anything? Who puts thoughts into his mind? Who causes him to listen to certain thoughts, to heed some and not others, to obey certain impulses and to let others pass? Who has been putting him through all these experiences of life, for certainly the John Smith part of you did not want to go through many of them?

Who has been doing all this, and what is His purpose; surely there must be one—a wise and loving purpose, or else why do it?

You say, God, or the Father, did it. But we say, *You* did it all. No, not the you that you know; but the REAL You—You who have lived in many bodies, have used many personalities like John Smith and Mary Doe; and when they were capable of being used, You accomplished with them the work You sought to do. This John Smith personality You are now finishing into shape so that You can soon take complete charge and possess him, can actually be the Self of him—*Your* Self, which You intended from the beginning.

But *You,* remember, are not John Smith, but are a Son of God, working and directing the John Smith part of you from within your soul, and *knowing the end before the beginning.* And that end surely is a wise and beneficent one, or why all the trouble?

Now listen, all you who are passing through trials and tribulations—no matter how desperate or severe or how pressing the need of help; for we are going to offer to you the surest and most effective help possible to give. For hear what the SELF of you has to say:

"My dear one, you have been clearly shown who *I* am, what I am doing and what I intend for you; and that you of yourself are nothing and can do nothing.

"Then, can you not now trust Me to do what is best for you, and realize that I intend only the best? For am I not preparing you so that I can enter in and be wholly *My Self* in you?

"Then think, would I permit any real harm or hardship to come to you? For remember, everything you do I cause or permit you to do, —I, abiding within your soul, which is within your mind, which is within your body—all belonging to and expressing *Me* only.

"That which is troubling you and seems so desperate, is only a final trial and cleansing necessary to rid you of all remaining qualities of self—of all its fears and doubts and personal concerns that are hindering My taking complete charge and possession of mind and heart for My perfect use. Can you not see that I cannot enable them—when they are so filled and stirred with such thoughts and feelings— to recognize and thus to help Me to outmanifest the Good for you and the Purpose I have intended from the beginning?

"Then let go, dear one, and turn *all* over to Me, your *Self*, your God *within* you—not to some God apart or away off from you. For I, your Self, am here directing all, caring for all and have been waiting so long for you to give Me full charge.

"Can you not realize that I will permit only that to manifest which is for your greatest good? For remember I see and know what is that good, and long with a great longing to have you to participate in it with Me."

"Simon, Simon, behold, Satan hath desired to have you, that he may sift you as wheat; but I have prayed for thee, that thy faith fail not."—Luke 22:31.

Stop! Read this all over again and try to get the great significance of it all before proceeding. For once the Realization comes it will change your whole life and bring a Peace and a Joy that is beyond telling.

BEING YOURSELF

We have been trying to prove to you first that you are not your personality, but that you are an immortal soul; and secondly that as a soul you are a Divine Being, a very Son of God, one with the Father and co-inheritor with Jesus Christ and with all other Sons of God of all that the Father has; that in you reside all the wisdom and love and power of the God-head. All these are yours to *use*, and but await your recognition and acceptance of this great truth, when you will begin *consciously* to use them.

And how am I going to recognize and how am I going to accept and thereby to use this truth? You ask. You intellectually see and know this truth more or less clearly now, but how are you going to know it so you *can* use it?

Think! How do you go about proving any rule or principle that you have accepted as being true? Let us see if we can show you by taking as an example how you learn to drive an automobile. Your instructor tells you the principle of the throttle, of the different speeds controlled by the gear lever, how to turn on the power and to start and stop the engine; the rules of the road and of starting on low gear first and changing to second and then to

high as you attain speed, and of turning and stop-
ping.

You hear all this and the first time it is all Greek
to you. But by his repeated telling and explaining
and your watching him do it, you get a more or
less clear *intellectual* concept of it all. Does that
enable you to drive the car? No, but it will help you
to make a *try* at it, for you will have grasped one
or two of the principles; and only after many trials
under the careful superintendence of the instructor,
and with many mistakes, you get a fairly good understanding of what is necessary to do.

But almost everyone has found that before he can
get up enough confidence to start out. alone, he has
to do a certain thing, and that is to sit down quietly
alone and "see" or visualize himself driving the car,
going through all the motions, meeting another car
in some unusual emergency and knowing instantly
just what to do to prevent an accident. After several times going through the experience of such
mental driving, you found actual driving would
come easy.

And in like manner, when, in the silence of true
meditation, *"seeing"* yourself an actual Son of God,
with all the consciousness and powers of a Christed
soul, acting, speaking and knowing as would Jesus
or as would your own Divine Self in your every
contact with others and in all conditions of life,—
when you had thus accustomed yourself to the *feeling* of *being* such a great soul, you would then find
it easy to gain control of and to drive, guide and use

your personality with its mind and emotions, its body and its sensations, which you are developing and preparing to be so used, and for that purpose only.

For try to realize that is all your human personality is for—the John Smith part of you; it is only to serve—when it is finally prepared and ready as you intend it—for the use of your Christ Self in the work which you came here to do as your part in the Divine Plan. Then You—the *Real* of You— will enter in and possess and *be* your personality, be John Smith or Mary Doe; aye, be another Christ Soul walking here among men in the flesh.

The Impersonal Life

We have shown you one way to be your Real Self by first mentally *seeing* yourself *acting* as a Divine Being would act, and in meditation so practicing such mental acting that it becomes natural and easy when you mix with others. Those who will prove this will be startled by the attitude of others, the respect and even awe they sometimes unconsciously manifest toward you.

Now we want to show you another way, or rather to give you other helps to aid you to arrive at the same place in consciousness. We want you to consider with us for awhile what is the Impersonal Life, and how to live it.

An article on "Impersonal Persons," in the March, 1929, Unity Daily Word is so excellent and fits in so well with our subject that we give it herewith in

full, interspersed with our comments, asking all to
read carefully and to try to see that everything
stated is as your Higher Self would have you be
and do.

*"How would you like to live in a world in which
there were no misunderstandings, no unpleasant
personal remarks, none of the thousand and one
situations which cause inharmony and personal dislikes? In other words, how would you like to live
in a world where people were impersonal, living
above personal consciousness? Would it not be a
heavenly world?"*

Yes, it would be an actual living in the Kingdom
Consciousness here on earth. Is that possible?
Read on and see.

*"In an impersonal world there could be no per-
sonal limitations. No one would look upon you and
see your personal shortcomings. You could not see
these in others.*

*"Is it not possible that this impersonal world ex-
ists right here and now? You do not believe it true?
Possibly you are in personal consciousness and, consequently, cannot sense its existence. Possibly
freedom from personal consciousness is the passport
that you need in order to enter this world."*

Stop here and think on this. Can you not see
plainly from this what may be holding you back
from your soul's goal—what is preventing your finding and entering the Kingdom? For the impersonal

world is really the Kingdom, as you will realize
later.

*"With such a goal in sight—the finding of an im-
personal world, a world of impersonal persons—is
it not worth an effort to become so impersonal that
you can find your place in this impersonal world?
Would it not be well to set out today to improve
your thought and your outlook upon life so that
you will merit a place in this realm of impersonality?*

*"How can you be impersonal? By seeing your-
self and others freed from personality. In personal
consciousness you have been bound to personal
shortcomings. You have seen your own shortcomings and those of others. In the great universal
consciousness you know yourself and others not according to your personal limitations but according
to Truth, according to the philosophy of perfection.*

*"Begin this very day to be impersonal. Do not
let your thought dwell upon personal limitations.
Do not think of personal failures of the past. Do
not think of any of the things that belong to the
personal man—failure, disease, age, time, blemish,
fault, the yesterday, or the tomorrow. Live a life
entirely separate from personal values.*

*"You will make a great discovery when you begin
to live the impersonal life. You will find that your
impersonal attitude toward yourself and others will
cause them to take a similar attitude toward you.
You will discover that your tendency to find fault*

*had served to attract faultfinding to you. Then you
will make another great find. There will be revealed
to you a mighty truth: that in reality there never
has been such a thing as personality and its limitations, that the eternal truth of man's perfection is
the only truth."*

That is, that the personality and its limitations
are but a personal concept and are ephemeral and
have no reality or permanence in consciousness, for
only the Soul Consciousness is real and eternal.

*"How can you make a practical application of
this doctrine of impersonality?*

*"If there is someone in your life with whom you
are always finding fault or someone who seems to
be finding fault with you, begin this impersonal
treatment at once:*

*"See the person concerned as loving and perfect.
See him as living with you in the impersonal world.
Possibly this personal situation will prove through
its transformation to be the key which will open the
impersonal world to you.*

*"The impersonal world is not a fictionary one.
In fact, the world of personality, with all its beliefs
in personal limitation, is the illusionary one. The
impersonal world is the world of Truth—the world
of reality, love, and perfection.*

*"The more you practice seeing perfection instead
of personal limitation the sooner will you enter the
impersonal world, the sooner will you be glorified*

through impersonal consciousness. You can see that the more persons you behold through impersonal vision, the more will your world be peopled with impersonal persons. Finally, the world of personal shortcomings, criticism, and personality will disappear and only the world of reality will appear."

It is then you will begin to realize "who you are and of what you are a part." For you will discover, through loving service that has now become your life, who your Brother Servers are, and you will be brought into contact not only with such Brothers who are serving outwardly among men, but with those who are directing and aiding from the Spiritual Realms. Can you not now glimpse the Great White Brotherhood of the Spirit of which you are a part?

"Truth teaches us to be impersonal. We learn how to rise above the world in which personal limitations are seen. We live in a world in which only the Son of God in man is seen and exalted. We live in a universe in which man does not think and act according to personal standards but according to the principle of Truth.

"How real this true world seems to us as we meditate upon it! We feel that after all there is an impersonal world peopled with impersonal persons, if we will but lift our vision and see this world through eyes of impersonal seeing."

Through much of such meditation and seeing— and only through such—when dealing with things in the outer world, you will find you need not be of it, but can live in the inner world and from there can direct all the activities of your instrument, the human mind and its body, in whatever is necessary in your outer life.

"You will find another thing. Once you have sensed the impersonal world, you cannot go back to living in the world of personality with all its limitations. You will not care to look at the seeming blemishes or faults of others, once you have seen them as they exist in Truth. You will have no desire to be critical, once you have been able to view your fellow beings through the eyes of God.

"In the impersonal world there is but one power and authority. Since it is the world of God, that power must be the power of God. His principle of Truth reigns supreme. All things must be observed through the eyes of God. We must see the people of this world as God sees them and know them as He knows them.

"Do you know any impersonal persons? That friend of yours who takes the impersonal attitude —does he not bring you just a little closer to heaven and to God? Does he not lift your thought just a little higher through your contacting him? You will find in this impersonal world that there is a strong influence always at work exalting your thought. You will find yourself being lifted up through this power—the power of Divine Mind."

For then you will verily be seeing through the eyes of a Son of God, of your own Higher Self, Who is truly God in You, through the medium of His Spirit, the Christ Love in your heart.

In the above, dear friends, has been shown you as nearly as can be put in words what is the Kingdom of Heaven. Wherever the words "the impersonal world" are used you could verily substitute "the Kingdom of Heaven," and it would apply perfectly.

This chapter serves in a way as a culmination of all that has been taught previously, for it gives you a true view of life in the Kingdom. Our great desire is that everyone study it, stay with it, and try with all your hearts, minds and souls to realize fully its deep meaning for you, and to BE and LIVE all that is herein shown. For you are now looking in through the door of the Kingdom—if you are not able to walk in and to be at home there, and you now know all that is necessary to gain admittance.

And LOVE is the Passport, and the only power that will enable you to enter.

CHAPTER 16

"There Am I in the Midst of Them"

SOME very momentous things were told you in the last chapter. So vital and far reaching were they that those souls to whom came the realization of their wondrous significance are changed beings. Never again will they think of themselves as John Smith or Mary Doe, for they now know that that personal part of them is but the instrument or vehicle that they have been preparing in order to do the work they came here to do.

They now see the purpose for which they have put their personalities through the strenuous training and discipline of their present life. They now realize the meaning of their having come into this Work—that it is the finishing process of preparation for the greater Work that is to follow.

Having given full instructions how to develop the mind so that it will be a good servant of a master will, those who have faithfully followed the suggestions and practiced the mental exercises indicated, have found themselves possessed of a power which, when put to use through the instrumentality of the mind, will accomplish for them anything they choose to do.

If you have not discovered your possession of such a power, it is only because you have not followed the suggestions, or practiced the exercises given, and therefore you alone are to blame for not owning the greatest thing you could possibly desire of a personal nature.

But of course such power is not given for purely personal purposes. If having it, you have assumed that *you* personally developed that power and have used it for personal and selfish ends, you probably by this time have learned your mistake, by having had taken from you all the things gained from the selfish misuse of that power.

But in Chapter 13 we showed you how to regain that power by the right use of your mind, and we call your especial attention now to the article, *"The Great Secret,"* in order that you may learn definitely how to apply what is taught therein and how to use it in group work.

If "all manifest things are the result of thinking and holding in consciousness what we believe is so," then all that is necessary to heal, to attain prosperity, success and happiness, is to think clearly about any or all these things and to hold them in your consciousness as being already in evidence in the Kingdom Consciousness, and they must outmanifest themselves.

Now we will try to show you how we may properly direct our prayers toward the healing and helping of others in group work.

First, remember, whatever we *think* and *hold in consciousness as being so* will outmanifest itself.

Then if we think *true* thoughts—the good and perfect things that God thinks of us—about any member of a group and hold these thoughts in our consciousness as actually being so *for one week*, they must outmanifest themselves. For hear what our Master promises:

"If two of you shall agree on earth as touching anything that they shall ask, it shall be done for them of my Father which is in Heaven. For when two or three are gathered together in My name, there am I in the midst of them."

It is assumed that all those who have accompanied us this far in our spiritual journey and who therefore are reading these words, are no longer desiring material things, but are seeking first the Kingdom of God and His righteousness, believing Jesus' promise that by finding the Kingdom and living the Christ life all things else will be added. They have sought to live and act according to this belief; but many perhaps have failed as yet to find the Kingdom or even to get a glimpse of some of the things they hoped would be added.

Can both of these statements of Jesus about asking of the Father, and seeking first the Kingdom, be consistently true? Let us see.

One of the most innate and natural urges of the human soul is to pray to or ask an invisible Father or Power—who, it *feels*, can do so—to supply a dire need. Jesus recognized this and on numerous occasions taught us how rightly to ask and to pray.

See Mat. 6:6–8, 9–15; 7:7–12; 21:22. John 14:13–14; 15:7; 16:23–24.

Yet He also says, *"Your Father knoweth what things ye have need of before ye ask."* Mat. 6:8. Why then should we ask?

Realize that Jesus sometimes was talking to the multitude, and sometimes to His disciples, and of course to the latter He would not talk as to children—as He usually did to the multitude, who really were children in Spiritual understanding. Study your bible and learn what He said to His *disciples,* for you too are His disciples; and then try to understand His meaning for you.

In the previous chapter we told you how He talks to His disciples today. If you have fully grasped the meaning of His words, then you know that you need not even ask or pray, but you give thanks daily to your loving Father for the blessings He is *now* pouring out upon you.

If you have not yet grasped His full meaning and cannot bring yourself wholly to trust Him as He asks of you, then we offer you the following prayer as one way that you may properly ask and pray to your loving Father to help anyone who has sought help from you and whom your heart strongly urges you out of a deep compassion to help.

"Dear Father-God, we know that .... is Thy beloved child, and that being Thy child Thou hast a rich abundance of all good things

waiting for him—every good thing that he (or she) needs.

"Dear Father, open his Spiritual eyes so that he may see and know and thereby may receive these blessings that await—that are all ready to outmanifest, when he thus becomes ready to accept them. Help him to know the truth, that he may be free forever from all lack and limitation of every kind.

"This we ask in Christ Jesus' name, for we know that as we have asked believing, our brother has received.

"We thank Thee, beloved Father, and we praise and glorify Thy Son in him, that He may now come forth and be His Self in our brother. Amen."

That which will help *you* more than anything else *to know the truth* about the one you would help, is to realize that he actually Is *a son or expression of God,* as we have proven to you in the preceding chapter; and so, when you pray to God for him, see and KNOW that the things you say of him *are* TRUE, for being true of God they must be true of His expression.

That is one way. You will note in the above that we ask for nothing material, but only for the Spiritual riches which *belong* to a child or expression of God. For you have learned from the previous articles that God is actually expressing His Self in every one of His children. And when a son of God once knows this, and lets go of all sense of separation and of all human beliefs in lack and limitation —none of which could be possible in an expression of God—he then connects his mind with God's Mind and thus permits the Good that is waiting to come forth into manifestation.

To those of you who have grasped the meaning of the Father's words, who know yourselves to be sons of God, who know that you are not John Smith or Mary Doe, and who therefore know the Divine power of mind and will that is yours, we now offer another way to help your brother—that of "Speaking the Word" for him. (See Appendix, "Speaking the Word.")

Read again carefully the two paragraphs preceding the last one above, about realizing that the one you would help is actually a son of God. Then know that he being a son of God, when you "Speak the Word" for him, motivated with deep compassion, HE WILL HEAR YOU *in his soul consciousness,* and will be reminded of the high truth you speak, and that the compassion pouring from your heart to him will impress the truth so strongly upon his soul consciousness that when the brain mind gets quiet it will push through from the soul to the brain consciousness, as an illumined thought from his Higher Self, and he will awaken from his dream of lack or limitation, and its cause and outer manifestations will disappear.

These words given you for such purpose when spoken with conviction and from a heart filled with love have helped many, sometimes with immediate and very startling results.

Please know that the words of the above Prayer and of the "Speaking the Word" Prayer, are but suggestions as to the true way of praying and speaking the word. Your own Higher Self may choose to change them to fit your particular need of expression. But they are wholly Impersonal and Universal, and the more their inner meaning unfolds to you the more conviction you will have, when praying and speaking them, that they will perfectly accomplish that whereunto they are sent.

The best way is to learn them by heart—whichever you choose to pray or speak. Then in your group meetings, preferably just before the closing part of the regular Prayer, let the leader of the meeting speak aloud the Prayer or the words of "Speaking the Word" for the brother or sister whom you wish to help, and each member in unison pray or speak them silently on the breath in whispers, thus uniting the vibrations sent forth in one powerful wave of loving and creative thought.

Then each noon for a week, if so decided, cease your work long enough to say *on the breath* the same prayer or words.

In very truth then, the Christ in the midst of you and of the brother you wish to help will be *One* in the Truth voiced, united by the compassion motivating it and whose creative power will outmanifest that Truth.

Try never to see or acknowledge the appearance of lack, limitation or inharmony in your brother or in yourself, but to see only the Divine perfection of the son of God which each soul truly is in its inherent nature.

We know the question that perhaps is back in the minds of some of those reading the above,— whether it will be right to pray or speak the word for each member of *your* group, *including yourself*.

Why not—if you truly need help and are earnestly seeking to make yourself perfect for the Master's use? Did not He teach us to ask our Heavenly Father to *"Give us this day our daily bread, and to forgive us our trespasses?"*

But always remember that a desire to serve must be first. If there is seeming lack, limitation, inharmony or dis-ease in body, mind or affairs, it is only because of that which you still think or believe and are carrying around with you in consciousness. Therefore your true prayer should be that your Spiritual eyes and understanding be opened so that you can see and know the Truth your Father wishes you to know, and thereby may become a capable, pure and selfless instrument for His use.

This first instruction in group work is of a simple kind, and is more to inspire the Group Spirit and to start you thinking in terms of group ideals. But as quickly as possible must the thoughts be lifted wholly away from self and its interests and needs, for no real group work can be done where the self is still in evidence.

Hence let the personal needs of group members be speedily placed in the Father's hands as shown, and then turn your whole attention to the real group ideals which will be elaborated in succeeding articles.

While all the above has been addressed to those who are meeting and studying in groups, yet it also is intended for everyone who reads these words. For we assume that all who have followed these articles thus far are deeply in earnest, have caught the vision, and are now letting nothing prevent their "whipping" their personalities into shape for the Father's use.

There are many who have not yet found their own group, who are studying and working alone, and who deem it impossible to find anyone who has the same interest in the Work as have they.

This is true only because of diffidence or backwardness, or perhaps of personal feeling against meeting and working with others. But are not such thinking of self first and of the Master's need of workers second?

Have they gotten any glimpse of the great Brotherhood of the Kingdom, silently working with all humanity, and have not wanted to be a part of Them, to work with and for Them, to know Them consciously—Those both in the flesh and in the Spirit? Think you, can you come into the true Christ consciousness without yearning to know and to work with Them?

As They form a great Inner Group, so do They seek to draw all Their disciples on earth into groups, under the Master's direction, and in such groups to develop Centers of Love and Light that will become powerful generators of force through which They can pour steadily upon the earth great cleansing streams of Spiritual fire that will eventually burn up all sin and selfishness now in mortal consciousness.

Those who earnestly seek to become an integral part of the Brotherhood of the Kingdom, will be aided from the Spirit by having their own soul comrades brought to them. But they must want it more than any other thing—want to be used and made fit and ready for the Master's Service.

Those who so want to serve and to find their soul comrades, need only to send out their call for them in the Silence, and as soon as they themselves are ready, their own will appear in some natural way, but so surely that they will *know* that they have been sent.

FROM "THE SPIRIT SPAKE"

Simplicity holdeth no temptation. Come nearer unto God! Trouble not! An infant counteth not the Nations of the earth.

Great joy cometh unto thee. Be patient! Await the Coming of the King. By joy shall the Kingdom of Heaven be justified.

Set thy love upon the Angels in High and Holy

Places; it shall find expression: the earth cannot hold Love; the sea cannot contain it.

Keep in the way of Angels. The Angel hath not any Will, neither of self nor any glory save in the expression of Divine Spirit.

God hath veiled Himself in thee as a human soul; let it be God. There is perfect peace in doing the Will of Him Who sent Me.

Dear Lord, make the place of thy dwelling holy!

Beloved! I would fain express Myself further unto thee. Wilt thou express Me? for thereby thou wilt free Me.

Trust in the guidance of the Angel. Why dost thou not more simply leave the direction of thy moments unto Him Who knoweth the Will of the Father.

I am a Father! Think not of Me only as God.

I await to shelter thine impotency. Trust in Me more simply. It is impossible for the Eternal Father to fail thee. Thy doubts, thy hesitancy are outside of thee and Me. Thou art in Me; while I am enfenced with everlasting strength.

Thou must learn to know thine own Spirit; it hath been as a stranger in a strange land; and all the way of thine ascent has been the retracing of thy wandering steps toward the place of Universal Spirit.

Those that perish are in multitude; but lo! the Saviours are few.

Redeem thine own soul, for God maketh a saviour of thee.

He calleth the saviours unto the desolate Mountain of Overcoming; but lo! how few there be.

Take up thine abode in the heart of another. Let thy gaze be toward the mountain-tops with the eyes which have seen sadness.

Be simple, be humble, be patient: the face of thy brother is toward thee; and the impress of the Divine Christ shall not be lost.

A Vision

Received by a Brother

This morning during my meditation I had this vision (everything seemed to take place within my body, nothing outside).

As I turned within and tried to recognize my Father's perfect image and likeness there—my Higher Self, my body seemed to become a temple, and I knew that within was an inner chamber, always shut to the outside world, in which dwelt the Image of my Father. The entrance to that chamber was a door which was very heavy. I then saw Christ going in and out of that door, but He seemed always to close it behind Him, so that I could not see within the inner chamber.

This inner chamber seemed to be in the very center of my body, yet at the same time deep within my mind and raised as on a high platform. This platform was surrounded by people on all sides, and I understood that these people were my thoughts, ideas and concepts about God, Christ, my self, my life and my fellow men. At times Christ would come out of the door and talk to the multitude, and at times He brought forth bread (Truth) sometimes small and sometimes large quantities. Then I saw different individuals in the audience come forward and accept from Him a portion of the bread, He would give some a small piece while to others He gave larger pieces, but no one received a full loaf. As these individuals carried those pieces of bread back to their seats they seemed to become illumined, according to how large was the piece accepted and carried away with them.

Some took pieces to those sitting in the audience who couldn't come forward themselves to get it. They too became illumined, but not to the same extent as those who carried to them the bread. As all the people passed out again into the world those who had received the larger portions stood in awe when they looked upon all nature, for they found they were one with all nature. While those who had gotten the smaller portions went forth more illumined than they before had been, and all nature seemed to respond to them—but they weren't conscious of it. While those to whom the bread had been carried by others received their first real appreciation of the light of truth; and even those who didn't receive any bread at all seemed to be more harmonious, but there was no more light of understanding than before.

Then these words came to me, as if Jesus were speaking them: "I am the Way, the Truth and the Life; no one cometh unto the Father but by Me. I am the keeper of the door of the Kingdom. I feed My own, and My own are they who recognize Me and give themselves into My keeping. I give forth the true Bread of Life as given to Me by my Father just as ye are able to receive it. I feed each with Light and Love and Understanding as they are given into my care, that My whole temple may become pure and holy and acceptable in the sight of My Father who is in Heaven, and that My temple may be ready so that ye may of yourself enter consciously by the door of the Kingdom and sit at My right side."

* * * * *

The above is an instance of how the Father within—the Higher Self—often teaches His son— the human mind, when the mind in true meditation turns within to Him for light and understanding.

The human mind, because of its sense of separateness, can receive Spiritual truths only in terms of form or pictures, so that such symbolical illustration is used that will best convey to the mind the truth sought.

The image or likeness of God—the Christ Self— of course is hidden from mortal consciousness deep within the mind, as in an inner chamber. Even when one is able to go in consciousness during meditation into the Silence, this inner chamber seems above our heads (or our understanding) as on a high platform. But in the Silence the Christ often comes forth and teaches or gives glimpses of the truths of the Spirit, symbolized by the portions of bread. These glimpses illumine all our other thoughts and ideas that we had before about the realities of God and life and nature, and every such contact in the Silence is a great inspiration and brings us closer to God and to the Kingdom and makes Christ more real and true to us.

Now read the vision again in the light of the above, and especially what the Christ spoke to our brother, and try to get the full meaning of His Words, remembering that the Christ is Love—God in man.

CHAPTER 17

JESUS, THE CHRIST

Another Easter Thought

WE HAVE fulfilled our promise and brought you to the door of the Kingdom. In the 13th, 14th and 15th chapters you were given the final instructions which, when earnestly studied until their great truths are fully *realized,* put you in possession of the "Great Secret," and enable you now to enter at will the Kingdom Consciousness.

This does not mean that you are able to *abide* there. To your great regret you have found this to be impossible as yet, but you know now that your supreme and constant effort will henceforth be to conquer every quality left of self that prevents your abiding there and letting the I AM—the Real You—abide and rule in your mind and heart.

Many of you understand clearly what we mean. Some of you may feel inclined to be discouraged, because you have noticed seemingly very little evidence of progress. But know that there is not one single soul who has earnestly followed with us and has tried to live up to the teachings given, who is not a changed being, and is so seen and known to be by those who are close and in a position to know.

Therefore, if you yearn to be of those who have

proven the power of the teachings, go back and beginning with the first chapter truly study each one,
determined to let nothing interfere or prevent your
getting all that each article contains for you. You
will be surprised at how much awaits the following
of such a determination.

Let us illustrate. One earnest soul, who had been
faithfully studying and trying to live the teachings,
had a great fear of dogs, for they always seemed
to choose to run out and bark at her. But one
day, when passing by the home of a particularly
vicious dog, and being in a high state of consciousness, her heart filled with love and not thinking
where her feet were taking her, she was startled to
have that same dog run up to her without barking
in an evidently playful mood as if he wanted to
be petted. And she also notices that babies and
children now confidently and happily come to her,
when formerly they would always turn from her
when she approached.

This is but one evidence of the change that
comes when one has learned to rule the mind and
emotions, and Love is permitted to enter and to
abide in the heart and to color thoughts, words and
acts. No one who *wants* to find the Kingdom and
who faithfully tries to follow what his soul tells
him are true directions can help but rise into a
high and blessed consciousness, where the illusions
of self and of separation from the Loving One
within will gradually disappear; and he will learn
finally to KNOW Him as the Love in his heart, and

will turn to and wait upon Him there, and will henceforth let *Him* lead him into the Kingdom.

*   *   *   *   *

This is the Springtime of the year when a new life impulse is pushing forth from within all nature. And all nature, including man, is being quickened so that it can respond to and can express that life in a higher form than that of yesteryear.

In man this is particularly so at this Springtime, and especially in all those who have felt the call of the Loving One within the heart. For great preparations are being made for the Resurrection Day this year, and for reasons that will later appear.

What we are now about to say may prove very startling to many who read, but all must accept it for just what it is worth to them. They either will or will not have an inner conviction of its truth, depending upon how far they accompanied us on our journey within to the Kingdom.

Sunday night after midnight, March 16th, (this was written in 1930), on the hills near Jerusalem, but on the inner planes of being, a great gathering of many thousands of souls who live in Spirit and those still having bodies of flesh was called together and addressed by the Master Jesus. The gathering consisted solely of the Workers—those who were being used to serve on the inner planes at night, and included every earnest soul who has consecrated him or herself to loving and selfless service and who is endeavoring to become fit and perfect for the Master's use.

The Master's talk was chiefly to impress upon each one present the vital necessity from this time on of each doing his or her utmost to awaken and quicken every soul that is seeking the Light, but whose human personality still wanders in darkness, where it is being misled by the enemies of Light.

The time of tribulation has begun and events will now follow one another with increasing severity, so that as many of the children of Light as possible must be drawn within to their true consciousness, where only they will be safe from the opposition and persecution that later will manifest.

He called upon all in the great multitude to stand together as one, to let Love alone rule and inspire every thought, word and act. The time is here when the thoughts of pure men will become as tangible things and we shall see their actual outward manifestations.

We have reached the apex of scientific unfoldment and we must stand ready, for great things are about to be given us. It will be as if our hands were guided, and we will be made to accomplish marvelous things. All who are pure and worthy channels freed from all clogging desires and beliefs of self will soon find themselves in the parts allotted us in the Plan for the saving and redeeming of humanity that we came here to fill, and for which all of our past lives have been a preparation.

We must above all be able to distinguish between good and evil. Those who purposely seek only the good will surely find and learn of wonders now inconceivable; for their eyes will be opened to the reality back of all outward seeming, and they will be enabled to work consciously with Those Who are directing humanity's emancipation.

After the Master's talk all were led to a great pool, which looked like heavenly blue water, but which on entering was of ether or a cloudy haze. It had a quickening and purifying power, for those submerging in it came forth with bodies almost transparent, and with one of the veils of matter still covering them dissolved.

Each week thereafter until Easter all were called to attend meetings where each was given another baptism in a pool of ether and another veil was dissolved.

All of the Brothers and Sisters attending these meetings and being addressed by our Beloved Master and by other Great Souls, have been formed into a great band of Soul Rescue Workers, for the special work given to us by the Master as above mentioned.

All of this you can now see is in a way a preparing of and helping to get worthy and ready those who are to participate in the great ceremonies of Easter Sunday morning, to begin according to our time on Saturday at eventide and to continue until after midnight; the ceremonies closing with prayers and chanting of hymns, and a full baptism of all the Brotherhood of the Rescue Workers of the Soul. The baptism will be in ether and soul perfume, which will cause the dissolving of one more veil covering the soul—and may it be the final one for many.

A great feast will be spread and all souls that are ready will be promoted into higher realms of consciousness. This means passing into a new Light and a further unfoldment of the Soul. It will be a soul initiation into the Higher Life—in which all will find peace, comfort, rest, happiness, contentment and plenty.

We mention all this now for a two-fold purpose, first that all may know that Easter and all it signifies is not merely man's effort worthily to celebrate the resurrection of our Lord Jesus Christ; but that it is a cosmic event, is an actual process of nature, and is all vitally connected with the unfoldment of consciousness, the consciousness of all nature—of the Christ life which is the force back of and which is unfolding all nature, including man as its culminating idea—toward a more perfect expression with each rebirth or re-embodiment after the sleep of Winter.

Secondly that you may know that each soul is an integral part of the consciousness of the Christ Life and that in the inner realms it undergoes an actual unfoldment of consciousness; and thereby each year *at Easter time* all souls who have earned it by loving and selfless service are promoted to higher realms of consciousness and to greater opportunities for service.

This and this alone constitutes growth, and all growth is Spiritual growth, or is an expansion of consciousness, which finally unfolds out of the consciousness of self and of material things into that of the Spiritual realities back of all physical manifestation.

From all of the above you get a glimpse of the real meaning of Group Work and of Brotherhood. For we have shown you a gathering of the great Brotherhoods of the Inner Realms and their many Groups that are working in the outer world.

When you can realize that in the Great Brotherhood of the Kingdom the life there is one solely of loving service—that service there is actually every soul's life, that there is no other thought or desire there that is not related to or does not revolve around service—you will understand what Impersonal Love is, and will surely feel that life begin to push forth in your hearts seeking to out-manifest itself here among men.

Those of you who feel that life now, that it is demanding expression and will not be denied, may know why there are brought to you, or you are led to them, those whom you can help and whom you are leading back into the Light. You are doing Soul Rescue Work here in the flesh as well as at night when your body sleeps. Some of you may be bringing back memories of such work.

And now do you see why you are called upon to
band together in Groups? It is that you may learn
to *work* in Groups, may learn to forget self and all
its petty personal feelings, likes, dislikes and concerns—even your desire for Spiritual growth, and
to lose yourself in a great longing to become fit,
body, mind and soul, for the Master's use.

Here is something for you to think over. Can
you imagine in the Kingdom any, even husband
and wife, trying to study and work alone by themselves, not associating with or working with others,
although wanting to serve the Master!

As it is there, so must it be here—if you would fit
into and work with the Divine Plan.

This however in no way is a reflection on those
who have not yet found in the outer their soul
group companions, but it is hoped it will prove an
inspiration to them to make greater spiritual efforts
to draw such to them.

CHRIST JESUS

In our different articles on the soul it was shown
that each "Living" or Immortal Soul is a Son of
God who as such had His real birth in another world
period eons before this earth was. We mean that
these Sons of God, our Real Selves, were originally
born then on some other planet, that our human
souls were born on this earth, as depicted in the
first chapter of Genesis; while in our articles on
the soul is shown how in the second chapter of

Genesis these Sons of God descended into our human souls and thereafter lived in them, thus making of them *"Living* Souls."

Consequently, all of us who are Immortal Souls, must be Sons of God *in our Higher Selves,* and as shown in the 15th chapter we have lived on earth in many bodies since that time, many, many ages ago, when we first descended from the celestial realms to dwell in our human souls.

Our Higher Selves then must be Divine Beings, and if Sons of God, they must be Beings very close if not like unto God.

Think! Must this not be so? And it is no sacrilege to state and believe it to be so, for remember we are speaking of our *Higher Selves,* whom we have heretofore considered as our *Christ Selves,* the Holy Spirit, or *God in us.*

Then if we have God in us, or if the Christ Spirit is the Light which lighteth every man that cometh into the world and is our Higher Self, what is our exact relation to Jesus, the Christ?

We will first picture Him as our Elder Brother, as the *"First born of many brethren,"* Rom. 8:29; as the *"First Fruit of them that slept,"* 1 Cor. 15:20; and then as the manifestation on earth of very God Himself. And we will show why these both are true and are not inconsistent one with the other.

Try to realize that your Higher Self, the I Am —the *Real* You, is a Son of God, or is the Spirit of God in you. Stop and think on this until a glimpse of its truth comes—if you do not yet feel it to be so.

In doing this, forget all about your personality. For in reality *there is no personality.* It is only a concept of your human mind which thinks itself separate from God.

Think of this Son or Representation of God in you, which is your life, your intelligence, your power, your ability to be and to do anything, as not only your Higher Self, but as your *only* Self, as God Himself, Who you know is *All in All.*

If you can realize this, then you will know, when you feel Love in your heart and let it abide and rule in your life, that you actually feel and in a way ARE *one with the God that you are.* For that Love which you feel is the Christ, God's Spirit or Reflection of Himself in you. And all Sons of God are such Reflections of God ever striving to reflect His nature in man.

When that Spirit, at what is called the Second Birth, descends and takes possession of your mind and body, and lives and rules in you, as it did in Jesus after his baptism by John in the River Jordan, then Love thinks, speaks and acts direct from the soul and definitely takes charge of the personality, and verily you become a Christed or an Anointed One.

So you see that seemingly Jesus was not more than what we all may be *in time.* Does not He himself tell us, *"He that believeth on Me, the works that I do shall he do also, and greater works than these shall he do, for I go unto My Father."* John 14:12.

And surely He is our loving Elder Brother, one whose soul is both older and farther advanced than those of other Sons of God, and He has attained a much higher degree of Spiritual understanding, power and ability to express His Father's Nature. Hence He was chosen to represent the Father and to give forth that new and higher phase of the Father's life which we now know as the Christ Life, and which was the life our Father intends and requires all humanity eventually to live.

But we must remember that Jesus' whole life and teaching was that *He only represented the Father,* and He gave *all* credit *to* the Father. This He stated in many ways similar to the following.

"I am in the Father, and the Father in Me; the words that I speak unto you I speak not of my self; but the Father that dwelleth in me, he doeth the works." John 14:10.

Therefore we can easily see that the Soul we know as Jesus of Nazareth was perhaps the greatest and oldest that has manifested on earth, because of His having been chosen as the vehicle for the Father's use in this latest and presumably farthest advanced stage of humanity's Spiritual unfoldment; and that He came to teach and show us the way and the Father's purpose for us in the present dis-

pensation, and over which He, Christ Jesus, therefore undoubtedly still presides.

Did He not say to His disciples after His crucifixion but before His ascension:

*"All authority hath been given unto me in heaven
and on earth. . . .*

*"And lo I am with you alway, even unto the
end of the world (to the consummation of the age,
in the Greek text)."*—Matt. 28: 18 and 20.

But we must also realize that at no time in the
unfoldment of consciousness of the human race has
the Father left His children without an Exemplar
and Teacher, one through whom He has shown to
the minds of men the highest expression of His
Life and taught them the highest ideals they then
were capable of receiving and manifesting. Such
were known in history as the Egyptian Osiris, the
Grecian Orpheus, the Persian Ormuzd and the Mexi-
can Quetzlcotl, and various others, each bringing
just the Light of Truth to the race and people of
his time that was to guide them until there was
need of higher truth.

There was a peculiarity in the lives of all these
Great Ones which is most significant. In the his-
tories of all are recorded two things, their Virgin
Birth and their Sacrificial Death.

Think of these great Sons of God, Beings of vast
experience in other worlds as well as on this planet,
who naturally when chosen to represent the Father

and to do His Work on earth among His children, were of such Wisdom and Power that each naturally would choose as a mother to give him a body one of high Spiritual development whose ovum he could stimulate, and which stimulation she could understand and respond to on the inner planes independent of physical contact with a husband; such Beings in fact thereby becoming literally their own fathers. Then they preside over the building of their bodies and the development of their personalities, and when both are matured, as recorded in the lives of some of them and shown in the baptism of Jesus, they enter and possess their bodies and then fully express their divine nature and begin their real work, that which they had been preparing their instruments to do—the work of teaching and showing by their lives the way the Father wills their people to live.

And then when their work is completed they give themselves as a sacrifice—become willing martyrs —for the Truth they came to establish, knowing that such sacrifice will serve not only to impress that Truth indelibly upon the consciousness of the race, but will inspire a devotion to Truth among Its followers which persecution and even death cannot destroy.

With all Saviours of humanity, we will note then three facts: There is the human personality, the vehicle in which they manifest themselves; there is the soul, long since possessed by their Higher Selves on the soul plane; and there is the Holy

Spirit or Power of the Logos, called by Jesus the Father, which fully descends upon the Higher Self and into the personality which It then uses to manifest the life and give forth the teachings intended for their people and race.

From this and from what you have learned from previous statements, all three of these facts can and must apply also to disciples of these Saviours. In fact in the Hebrew Bible and in the sacred writings of other peoples we have plenty of evidence of such descent of the Holy Spirit upon disciples, apostles, holy men—if some hesitate to admit that the Holy Spirit of the Christ is not present in the lives of many men on earth today.

If all of the above be true—and can anyone who has journeyed with us this far *feel* that it is not true—then if the Christ Spirit is manifesting in many today, it is more than possible that the souls of the Higher Selves of many disciples and apostles of these Saviours may be manifesting in human personalities among men today.

Why should this not be so?

You know that this is the end of one dispensation and the beginning of another. We are now entering the Aquarian Age, the sign of which is a man walking across the heavens pouring something from a pitcher down upon the earth. What is being poured is the new and higher life force which is being felt and is affecting everything upon earth, man especially, evidenced by the quickening taking

JESUS, THE CHRIST 285

place in everyone, compelling the spiritually minded to a more intense seeking for Light that they may understand what it is all about, and that they may learn to apply the laws they instinctively feel must now be put to use, if they are to make any spiritual advance in this lifetime.

On the other hand, those who are purely selfish-minded are likewise intensely seeking to gratify their selfish desires, whether it be for money, power, sensation, pleasure, sex-satisfaction, evil, crime; and none of such knowing where they are heading or what is impelling them to such seeking, for their selfishness has blinded their eyes and they have been foully deceived into believing that freedom and happiness lie that way.

It happens that we are not only at the end of a smaller cycle of about 2100 years, but of a large one of 25,000 years, thus bringing to a culmination mighty forces that have been in evidence for vast periods of time. But their day is done and they are now being superseded by higher forces, which is causing the breaking up of all conditions created by the old forces. You see evidence of this everywhere. Even the earth itself and all nature is re-acting to this conflict of forces, indicated by the earthquakes, volcanoes, floods, tornadoes and other seismic disturbances now manifesting almost daily in some part of the earth. Those who have eyes to see need only to look about and observe evidences of such changes taking place.

What we wish to indicate is that there are many

very old souls on earth today who are here at this time because of this most significant change; that they came here pledged to a definite work—that of preparing conditions for the New Age, or of being the leaders, teachers, and workers for the building up of the new order that will prevail in that Age. And all souls who have in them the Spirit of Service are those who will have a part in such preparing or building, and according to how much they are awakened to the vital importance of the work ahead are they now being "called out" and given the opportunity of fitting themselves for the part they are finally to play in the Great Cause. While others are becoming gradually aware that they are much more than they seem to be to themselves and to the world, and are reaching out for the knowledge that will make them understand the truth of their being. If many are receiving visions and prophetic dreams these days, it is only because of the Spiritual quickening that is being felt by every soul that is awakened and that is making them aware of their real natures and helping them to remember why they are here at this particular time.

Why then is it not possible that some of these older souls are the former disciples and apostles of Jesus when He was on earth; likewise some perhaps disciples of other Saviours? In fact it might even be possible that those of Jesus may have been disciples of the Saviours of earlier races. For if they are Sons of God, they came here to earth to redeem it and especially to redeem their own creations—

the humanity upon it. And naturally from the beginning since leaving their home in Eden they —the older souls—have ever been co-operating with these Chosen Ones of God to lift each race to a higher stage of consciousness.

All the great financial, industrial, political, educational, professional and other leaders who stand forth as characters of influence and force in the world today, are old souls, most of whom are not yet awakened spiritually, and many of whom are actually now unconsciously working on the side of the enemy. But soon the powerful spiritual forces operating within all humanity will either awaken them and remind them of their divine origin and cause them to join the Brotherhood of Light and Love, or will compel them to align themselves definitely on the side of the enemies of Light.

While in the great leaders consciously working for the spiritual upliftment of humanity may be found the workers, apostles and disciples of the ages, who are the earthly representatives of the Great White Brotherhood—although many of them may not know all this as yet, and through whom the Brotherhood is accomplishing that which is Their purpose in the coming world events incident to the changing from the Old into the New Age now taking place.

Is it then too much to think that at this time of special quickening all of these last mentioned souls are being called to meet and confer with their great Master and Leader, Christ Jesus? Do you see now why some are privileged in meditation to see and be blessed by Him and by other Great Ones in the Spirit, and some are granted the power of attending *consciously* such gatherings as described in the early part of this chapter?

Think and ponder over all of these things. If it is beyond the capacity of some of you to accept at this time, just lay it aside, and maybe later events or inner experiences of your own will cause a change or expansion of consciousness that will enable you to view it all from a different and higher understanding that will then be yours.

CHAPTER 18

CHRIST, THE LOGOS

WE WISH at this time to make it so clear that all may know, that Christ Jesus is an actual Presence, a definite Power in the consciousness of every human soul, whether they are aware of it or not.

To do this we must show that He is the Light which lighteth every man, and that He is the very Presence and Power of God—God Who is *All in All.*

In the previous article we pointed out much that should help you to arrive at that conclusion. We know that many already believe it, but we wish to make it more than a belief, we want it to be an actual part of your *knowing.*

There is plenty of evidence in the New Testament of all that we would say, and we will quote further from it only in order to make convincing what we shall prove, for more than anything else is it important that you know Christ Jesus as one with the innermost part of your own Self.

We will take the statement that God is All in All. We must either believe this or disbelieve it. We assume that all who have accompanied us this far believe it.

Then God must be both the unmanifest and the

289

manifest of all things.   He must be both the spiritual and the physical part of everything that is.

Think, must this not be so?

Then we must consider both of these two aspects
of God.   The unmanifest we will call the Absolute,
the Ineffable, Whom no man may know or even
comprehend.   But the Word—the Logos—is the
manifest God, or the God-Seed of all manifestation;
for all things as we know spring from a seed of some
kind.   And this God-Seed stands as an intermediary
between God and us.

Philo, the great Jewish philosopher who wrote at
Alexandria about 25 A.D., also speaks of the Logos
as having a two-fold aspect.   As representing the
Unmanifest God He is the Reflection of God, the
Creator of the Cosmos; but as mediating between
the Ineffable and us He represents humanity in the
eyes of God, and represents God in the eyes of humanity.

"He then is the Heavenly Man, the Door to direct
communication with God, the Prophet of the most
High, the Eternal Law, the Giver of Divine Light,
our Saviour.

"So long as the Logos exists, He is the way of At-
one-ment, the way of harmonizing humanity with
God."

St. John saw this clearly when he writes for us
these most significant words:

"In the beginning was the Logos and the Logos was with God, and the Logos was God.

"All things were made by him; and without him was not anything made that was made.

"In him was life; and the life was the light of men.

"And the light shineth in the darkness and the darkness comprehended it not."

In the remainder of the first chapter he shows clearly that he *knew* Christ Jesus to be the Logos, for he says in these unmistakable words:

"And the Logos was made flesh, and dwelt among· us, and we beheld his glory, the glory of the Only-Begotten of the Father, full of grace and truth."

St. Paul also saw deeply into these mysteries and gives many interesting details in his Epistle to the Hebrews. He says that God, *"Who at sundry times and in divers manners spake in times past by the Prophets, hath in these days spoken unto us by His Son, Whom He hath appointed heir of all things, by Whom also He made the worlds,"* and *"Let all the angels of God worship Him."*

When giving the genealogy of Jesus, St. Matthew in the first verse of the first chapter says, He is the *"Son of David, the Son of Abraham."* But our Lord Himself said, when discussing the matter with the Jews in the Temple, *"Before Abraham was, I am."* And in one of His prayers, *"O Father, glorify Thou me with Thine own Self, with the glory which I had with Thee before the world was."* —St. John 17:5. (Read all of this prayer.) And again, *"I came forth from the Father and am come into the world; again I leave the world and go unto the Father."*—St. John 16:28.

These statements are very significant of His exalted state in the heavenly realms and proves that He was fully conscious of His mission as the Representation of His Heavenly Father and that He was a Most High Son of God, which St. John explains as, *"God sent not His Son into the world to condemn the world, but that the world through Him might be saved."*—St. John 3:17.

Now we know that some would interpret this all to refer to the Christos, or the Holy Spirit in Jesus, and that it does not apply to Jesus the man. But we say that it is impossible to separate the title and the office of the Christ from the *man* Jesus, for what is the personality of flesh but the outmanifestation of the Soul? And what is the Soul in His case but the unfoldment and perfected consciousness of a very high Son of God—the highest that *ever before came into manifestation!* In fact so high that in Jesus the Father actually manifested more of Himself than was ever before manifested in the history of the world. Then would you say that Jesus was only a man? Rather can you not see that He was truly a perfect Representation of God in human form.

When Caiaphas, the High Priest, asked Jesus, *"I*

adjure thee by the living God, that thou tell us whether thou art the Christ, the Son of God," Jesus hesitated not at this great crisis in his life definitely to say in reply:

"Thou hast said: nevertheless I say unto you, Henceforth ye shall see the Son of Man sitting at the right hand of Power and coming on the clouds of Heaven."—Mat. 26:64.

Mark says that He replied, *"I am; and you shall see the Son of Man sitting at the right hand of the Mighty One."* While Luke has it, *"But from this time on the Son of Man will sit on the right hand of the Power of God."*

From this can anyone doubt Jesus' divinity, His being a very high Being descended into flesh to show us the way back unto the Father?

Listen to more of His own words: *"Neither came I of myself, but He that sent Me." "Whatsoever things the Father doeth, these also doth the Son likewise." "I am in the Father, and the Father is in Me. I am not alone, but I and the Father that sent me. He that sent me is with me."*

These words of Jesus are so highly significant, in the light of what has been said, that we hope everyone will get their real meaning.

In all of Jesus' teachings there is noticeable the insistence of that mystic unity of the Father and the Son: *"I am in the Father and the Father is in Me."* And that for which the Father sent Him was

solely to show all men the way back unto the
Father, and at the same time that He, Christ Jesus,
might be in each of us the way, the truth and the
life, preparing us for the day when He might lead
us into knowing the Father even as He knew Him.
*"At that day ye shall know that I am in the Father,
and ye in Me, and I in you."*

We have shown you in previous articles that only
through Love can you come to know Christ Jesus,
our Blessed Lord and Master; and we now say that
He is the actual expression, the perfect manifestation of the Father's Love in Man. He veritably is
the God-Seed planted by the Father in humanity,
and is the Light which dwelleth in the darkness.
But that Light—God's Love—must be lit in your
heart, before you can see and know Christ Jesus
there. With the lighting of that Light, then He
within you leads you unto the Father, and in time
you truly know that He is *in* the Father, and you
are *in* Him, and He is *in* you.

From this you must realize that there is a deep
mystical meaning of His being *in* the Father, of we
being *in* Him, and He *in* us, and we will try to help
you get a glimpse of that meaning. The fullness
of knowing can only be gained—note this carefully
—by *going within where He is,* where we may know
our oneness with Him, and with the Father. And
that each one must learn to do for himself.

How?

We have told you much about the Christ Consciousness, and how to find and know it. In that

Consciousness all who have entered it know that they not only *are Love*, but they are One with all that is.

It was in that Love Consciousness, and which was Jesus' natural consciousness, that He was truly one with the Father, for then He actually was the Father; for *God is Love*, and Jesus was God's way of showing humanity pure and perfect Love in expression.

Therefore when anyone is able to retire *within* into the Christ Consciousness—and many disciples are in the world today who can do this—they are truly *in* Jesus' consciousness, and He is *in* their consciousness, and both are *in* the Father's Consciousness; for then they are all *One in Consciousness*.

You have seen that Love is your Higher Self, that Love manifest is Christ Jesus, and that God is Love. They are the divine Three-in-One—the Father, Son and Holy Spirit. In Christ Jesus the Three-in-One were fully manifest, and because once manifest They are ever-present and available. That is, They are ever ready and able to manifest again as Christ Jesus to any who can receive Him.

Looking at it in another way, you know that your Higher or Real Self is always in that Love consciousness; for the Real You is a Son of God and is also a Representation of the Father, but is a younger to our Elder Brother, Christ Jesus.

Now think, the only difference between the Christ Self of Jesus and that of us is that *in Jesus that*

Self actually lived and *was* Jesus in the flesh, and the Logos or the Word had in Him become the flesh and dwelt among us—nay *now* dwells among us. While in us that Christ Self is not yet become but *is becoming* the flesh, and thus is making all flesh One; as in the Christ Consciousness, that of our True Selves, we are already One.

Therefore, in that deeper, inner sense, can you not see that Christ Jesus is an actual Presence always with us in our higher consciousness, *where Love rules,* and is there an intimate part of our consciousness, for it is likewise His consciousness, as it is the Father's consciousness.

Let us then know Jesus both as the Christ, the Holy Spirit of God, the Logos, within us; and as our Elder Brother, a Son of God of supremely high rank in the Heavenly Kingdom which was "before the world was;" and Who is ever with us in those high realms "even unto the end of the world." And that He came to earth as the Great Redeemer for the present phase of evolution, for the purpose of expressing the Spiritual Love aspect of God, and of developing that state of Christ Consciousness in the human mind which will bring it to know its own "Sonship."

"He called himself the 'Son of Man,' but we can regard Jesus as the Lord of Humanity, the Great Master of Masters, for He is the *'Word of Power'* for the present age," as has been proven by all of His disciples back through the centuries since the beginning of His earthly ministry.

We have in the above freely used some of the thoughts of A. V. O. in an article *"Jesus—who is He?"* from *"The Inner Light"* Magazine of January, 1929, and from a booklet *"Christ the Logos"* by C. Jinarajadasa. We are grateful for the clear light they have helped us to throw on this most vital subject.

The Easter Ceremonies

In the last chapter, written before Easter of 1930, you were told of some of the services held in the inner realms preceding Easter. But such would not be complete without a description of the Easter ceremonies themselves.

Please know that each Easter morning there are ceremonies performed also in the physical by many pilgrims from far and near who come to Jerusalem to participate in them, few of course—the psychic ones only—being aware of the great throngs who are present on the inner planes, even as most group members are unaware of the invisible audience always attending their weekly group meetings.

The pilgrims in the flesh as is their custom began to arrive shortly after midnight, and by one o'clock they were coming in crowds, all anxious to be there to watch for the first break of day.

As for the pilgrims who were to come by "air route" on the inner planes, about 11:30 Saturday night many hundreds of the White Brotherhood might have been seen coming to all parts of the earth, drifting earthward to the many good souls in the physical who were ready and willing to give of their soul power in spiritual aid to all whom they would be called upon to help.

Every dear one in a Study Group and all true seekers of the Inner Life were visited by some of the Holy Souls and in their soul consciousness were carefully instructed and then guided over the thousands of miles between their homes and the place of worship on the hills near Jerusalem to the actual spot of the Crucifixion. While the journey was by "air route," or in other words in consciousness, and took only a few minutes, yet naturally a guide was needed for each soul or group of souls traveling together to reach their destination.

On their arrival they were grouped together according to the order of their spiritual endeavor. Those still living in the physical (many hundreds being also present who had given up their physical bodies in so-called death) were given the Holy Sacrament and a drink from the crystal waters flowing from the Holy Rocks near the spot where the Sacred Cross stood.

The great Leader of the Mission Soul Rescue Workers delivered a lecture and directed all the ceremonies on the inner plane for all Group Workers seeking the Kingdom.

When the pilgrims in the outer world had all arrived they began their worship by performing a litany, many praying, others chanting a holy anthem and all entering into the spirit of the meeting as a sacred memory of the greatest event of history. It all became so awe-inspiring that the very atmosphere seemed to whisper, "THE CHRIST IS RISEN."

The White Brotherhood and all the dear Souls on the inner planes bowed their heads in silent prayer and drank in the heavenly vibrations which were exquisitely peaceful and harmonious, far beyond description.

This continued until a trumpeter sounded a blast from a silver trumpet announcing the first streak of day. Then the praises in singing and chanting became so thrilling it would have reached heaven, were heaven above the sky of blue; these services continuing until the sun had risen above the horizon, when the pilgrims in the flesh began to wend their way toward town, to church and to early service.

The White Brotherhood on the inner planes remained on the scene. There was a low square platform where the old cross at one time stood. All were bade to abide in silent readiness, and while their heads were bowed in prayer a stir was heard in the air as of a slight breeze and all the atmosphere became saturated with the perfume of many flowers. Then there was a sound heard like the rustling of silken robes, and looking up we saw our Beloved Master had come and was standing right in our midst upon the low platform where once the cross had been, His own beautiful white light surrounding and radiating from Him.

He opened the service by offering a short earnest prayer, speaking of the White Brotherhood as His Disciples. His original Disciples were also among our number.

Then He addressed the Brotherhood and spoke of the work which He had to leave unfinished, and which He asked all present to finish.

"All ye are Sons of God and Sons of Man. All followers that come to Me in truth and in full faith I will bless and enable to do their part in the Work of upliftment and enlightenment of the children of our Father.

"Ye are not here to be ministered unto, but to take up the work of ministering—that for which ye have been prepared."

He dwelt long on the subject of true greatness, emphasizing the great need of true, brotherly love; of reaching out a helping hand all along the way; of teaching every soul in need about the All-loving and Ever-merciful Father, Who cares for all his children and who yearns to open wide the gates of the Heavenly Kingdom to all sincere and true toilers in His vineyards.

After He had finished speaking all yet in the flesh were asked to pass in single file in front of the Master, when He placed His right hand on the forehead and the left hand on the shoulder of each in blessing, giving to each the power to heal and to do good unto his fellow beings.

The Ceremony was closed with music and singing which was heard all through the atmosphere as though the heavenly hosts were singing with us. We then floated home, reaching it to spend the remainder of the night in sleep.

It is probable that not very many brought back any memories of this wonderful meeting. In fact only a few wrote us of distinctly remembering all that took place, although a number told of things that indicated they were more or less conscious of what was being experienced.

The reason it was so hard to bring anything back was because there is about seven hours difference in time, American time being that much earlier than Jerusalem time, and most minds were too engrossed with outer things on Saturday evening to receive little if any impressions of such experiences.

But we would say this, if this Easter has been the most wonderful of your life, if you have been brought much closer to our Beloved Master Jesus than ever before, and if there is now present within you a powerful yearning to serve Him and all humanity and which yearning cannot be stilled, know that unquestionably your *soul* was in attendance at these gatherings and that you have been so quickened by the profound impression made upon your soul by His words and by the mingling with and feeling the Great Love of the Brotherhood, that it must outmanifest in your lives and make you one with Them in purpose and in deed. It could not be otherwise with such.

CHAPTER 19

"BELIEVE THAT YE HAVE RECEIVED, AND YE SHALL HAVE"

WE HAVE been receiving so many letters reciting conditions of real hardship, both of a financial and a mental nature, that we yearn to have everyone who needs find and use the always waiting help that is available to every soul willing to do his or her best to earn it.

In this article we intend to show clearly how all such may find that help and how they may apply it to their individual problems no matter what their nature.

In the article entitled "The Great Secret" in Chapter 13, we pointed the way to free yourself from all lack, limitation, inharmony, disease and trouble of every kind. Some have learned the Secret, have put it to practice, and consequently have found a peace and a happiness that is beyond human telling. For now they *know* with a sureness that nothing can alter that all that the Father hath is theirs.

Others, the great majority, and always those who need it the most, have never really tried to apply the Secret, chiefly because their minds are so filled with fears, anxieties and worries that hope or faith to back their efforts can not get in and stay long enough to inspire them seriously to try.

All such worriers, as well as the many others who are seeking the way out of their various troubles, we now with deepest earnestness entreat to read carefully what follows, and to strive with the utmost power of their souls to prove its truth.

Dear friends, if we should offer you wealth, health, happiness, and you knew you could have all of these for a stated price, would you not, if you had the price, give all that was asked and more to gain these priceless blessings? Can anyone doubt that you would?

Well we are doing that very thing,—we are offering you all three of these blessings, and you have the price asked, and can pay it—if you *will*. But you must pay it by doing something no one else can do but you—something requiring the intelligent and persistent use of your mind and your will. It simply means that you must begin to prove the truths of "The Great Secret," must henceforth let come into your minds no thoughts or feelings that you do not want to outmanifest in your body and affairs.

We recommend that you go back to "The Great Secret" and study it carefully until you get all of its intended meaning, or you will not be able to grasp the full import of what follows. All who persist in doing this, and who will not be satisfied until their Higher Self has shown them all of the marvelous truth that awaits them in what follows, will *know* that they have gained something that is worth more to them than anything else in the world.

Read again these words and try to realize that they are meant *for you,* that what they say *is exactly true,* and that *it is all possible for you;* and therefore that this we offer you is the biggest thing that could come into your life, and that it is yours for the *doing* of what is suggested. And there is not one who reads who cannot do it—*if he will,* and wants it badly enough.

We are trying to rouse you, dear friend, to make you see that you *can* have all of these things; we are trying to inspire in you the determination that you *will* have them, that you *will* do all that we suggest—if we convince you that *by doing it* you can have these blessings. If we have quickened in you such a determination then you are ready for what follows.

The first thing then must be for you from this time on carefully to watch and study your thinking and feelings and to let into your mind nothing whatsoever of a negative nature, and which you know has no part in your God-Self. All such thoughts and feelings come from *without* from other minds. Of course in your subconsciousness there are qualities that attract them, or they would not come. But you need not let them in to feed those negative and selfish qualities.

If such are not fed they soon will die of inanition, for they have life only as long as you give it to them by recognition; and when you no longer admit the thoughts and ideas they attract they will be supplanted by the opposite qualities that your new thinking will create.

When by persistent effort you have acquired the habit of shutting out all negative thoughts and feelings, you will more and more become conscious of inspiration from a high source making you aware of definite guidance and instruction. In other words, your mind now being cleansed of selfish and untrue thoughts which have no part in your real nature, your higher mind will begin to pour in the consciousness of your Divine Self.

Such watching and studying of your mind and its thought processes is one of the most important practices in which you can engage, for you soon will begin to realize your power to control and direct your thinking, and that thereby you are learning to be *master of your fate.* With this realization will come a new consciousness in which you will gradually be able to abide and from which you will more and more think, speak and work.

How will that consciousness begin to manifest itself? By what some call "hunches." You will have leadings, strong urges from within, that will claim your attention and which if heeded will always bring satisfying and happy results, but which if unheeded will end in sorry mistakes and often trouble.

Everyone receives such hunches. In other words everyone has guidance, but very few heed and profit

by it. There is not one who reads these words that
cannot recall many instances of definite leadings
which brought real inward satisfaction because of
obeying what he was impelled to do. And many
have noted that they receive guidance even in little
things, in matters seemingly unimportant at the
time but which nevertheless serve to impress the
mind with the fact that Something Within knows
what is best, aye, sees ahead and knows the good
which awaits and is eager to lead them to that good.

For instance, how many of you have been strongly
desirous of seeing a friend for some particular purpose, but at the time you were unable to go to him
or her or reach them by phone, when that friend
suddenly either called you by phone, or came to see
you; or something may have directed you to the
window and looking out you saw the friend coming
up the street or taking a car to his home; or in
other words some definite answer came to your
silent call which set your mind at rest?

Many are the instances of hunches obeyed which
have saved lives, prevented accidents, brought
friends together, won desired ends, proving that
some benevolent force was working to bring these
about.*

Now by such hunches or leadings we intend to
prove to you that every human soul always has
present *within itself* that which will unerringly

* There is an excellent booklet, *"Hunches, and How to Follow
Them,"* by the Eldredges, that will prove a great inspiration and
a real help in teaching how to watch for and know hunches when
they come. See Appendix.

guide it in every detail of its life towards its greatest good.

Let us reason together. You will remember in the 15th chapter how it was shown that your Higher Self is a Son of God who has brought your soul to its present state of unfoldment through many lives in many bodies, such as the one you now possess; but that the Higher Self, the Real You, chooses the time and the conditions into which again to incarnate to bring about a further development of the soul and to perfect an instrument in which You can do the work You planned to do of living Your Divine Life here on earth in a human personality the same as You are now living it in Heaven. (Read again carefully the first article in the 15th chapter.)

It was also shown how You in your Higher Self thus knew the end before the beginning, for all events in your life were planned and arranged by You toward that end. And we made it plain that the only wise thing for the human mind and personality to do is to accept this great truth and henceforth to seek to co-operate with You, to listen to and heed every leading which You give and which You are always giving it from within, as it has learned by the frequent hunches received when it learned to listen.

Then what is the answer?

First, to keep your mind clean of all untrue and negative thoughts. And secondly, to require it to listen to the Voice that comes from within. For just as surely as you prevent untrue and negative thoughts—those that the Real You does not want there—entering your mind, just as surely will your Higher Self put into your mind the true and positive thoughts that will attract to you the good which is waiting to deliver itself to you.

But this good cannot come to you until you want it more than anything else in life, which means when you are eager to do everything necessary to let it come—and will keep your mind clean and free of all thoughts that are not God's intended thoughts for you; for your Higher Self is God in you and He can work and express Himself only through a mind channel made clean and perfect for His use.

This of course means all thoughts of a negative nature about being poor, or sick, or weak, or discouraged, or lacking in anything; for such are untrue of God and likewise of a Son of God, who knows that all that the Father has is His.

We know how appearances hinder and flaunt themselves before you, making it so hard for you to believe or do what we have stated. But obstacles are given you to overcome, in order to enable you to develop and use your Spiritual power.

You must always remember that Spirit alone Is and that you and all things exist only in Spirit— that is, in the One Consciousness, nowhere else. Also that what you think and believe, and thus hold in consciousness, exists *to you,* and such always out-manifests in your life and affairs. Therefore you must see and believe only the true and eternal things—the things of the Kingdom, which your True Self is waiting to shower upon you, when you are ready to accept them.

By thus seeing and knowing, and *holding* only to the Truth, the Truth will surely make you free. Also by *abiding* in the consciousness of your Real Self—the God-You, and letting His Words only abide in and rule you, you need ask for nothing, for then all good things will pour in freely upon you.

A mind that refuses to be misled by appearances and persistently holds in consciousness only the good, the true, the beautiful and perfect things that exist in the Kingdom, will as surely as tomorrow comes see these things outmanifest in its owner's life.

Do you want them to manifest in your life? Of course you do.

Can you do the simple things required of you to attain them? Of course you can. For your Higher Self is a Son of God, has all power, and is yearning to help you to attain them. For then He will have in you a perfect instrument through which He can do that for which He has long been preparing you.

You can see how this applies definitely and perfectly to the financial problem. If as a Son of God all that the Father has is yours, then you must *abide* in that *knowing* and let no appearances of whatsoever kind affect that knowing. Conditions of lack are permitted principally to bring you to that knowing; for not until you learn to *know* and *to hold* to the truth of the rich abundance of all things that are yours as a Son of God, will you ever be free from the consciousness of lack.

Likewise is sickness permitted—in order to bring you to the knowing that a Son of God, an Immortal Soul, dweller in many bodies, is a Spiritual Being, whose life and intelligence rules the flesh and knows not inharmony and disease. When you truly realize that and think and hold in consciousness only the thoughts of eternal being, perfect health becomes your natural and permanent expression.

Likewise with such realization true happiness floods your consciousness, for then you will gladly let the life and intelligence of your Real Self rule, and will try no more to do or be anything yourself; for why try to do or be what a Son of God always will do perfectly and always *is* in all the glory of His Divine Perfection.

Can you not now see what this means *for you,* and that it only awaits your acceptance of this great truth—of your letting go, yielding yourself wholly to Him, keeping your mind and heart clean of all things unworthy of Him, so that He will have them always ready for His use?

Oh, dear friend, if we can only impress the great significance of all this upon you—so that you will

determine with all the might of your soul henceforth to permit no thought or feeling in your mind
that is not all good and which you do not want to
outmanifest,—then these words are not written in
vain.

If you would really do this, and it is the only way
to financial, physical and spiritual freedom, then
when any untrue or negative thought approaches,
say:

"Begone! You have no part in me. I am Spirit.
I harbor only the good and perfect thoughts of my
Father in Heaven."

And with a prayer to your loving Father that His
vision and strength aid you, begin this moment to
make your mind a pure and holy habitation for His
thoughts only, and your heart an abode which He
can fill with His love and through which love He
can inspire and direct every activity of your life.

JESUS EVER PRESENT

Every thinking mind must wonder how Jesus, our
dear Lord and Master, is always available and always ready and able to hear and to help every
earnest soul who calls to Him in sincere love and
trust.

Surely there must be many from all parts of the
world, and perhaps also in the inner planes, who
call to Him at the same time. So how can He hear
all and answer all?

First, we must try to realize that His Mind, because of his conscious Sonship, is omniscient; that

is, is all-seeing, and that to Him space and time do
not exist. We have some evidence of this in the
highest type of clairvoyance and in intuition. Of
the omniscient powers of intuition most of you have
had convincing proof. Surely then it is true that in
Him both of these faculties must be developed to
their ultimate degree—in the light of what is stated
in the preceding articles about Him.

Now recall that He is the manifested Love of
God, is the Representation of Love sent to human-
ity by the Father to serve as the Intermediary be-
tween humanity and the Father. In fact He, as
Love, is the *only* way unto the Father. We mean
this to imply that as Christ Jesus He is both the
Presence *within* us of that Love, and is the Way-
Shower and Teacher *without* Who is leading us unto
the Father. Therefore He is both the Way and the
Door through which we must pass to enter the
Father's Consciousness.

Think on this great truth until you glimpse at
least some of its deep meaning.

Now because of His being such an Intermediary
and the Way, He must be closely in touch with and
working in all the Inner Planes of Consciousness
between humanity's outermost and the Father's
own consciousness deep within. He has been seen
on the earth plane in the inner realms many times,
from the reports of those who saw Him on the battle fields in the recent War. And many others daily
report seeing Him in visions on various other planes
up to the highest that outpicture themselves to

human comprehension. And even in the highest plane He is seen *descending* through a brilliant sunburst of light surrounded by angels. But in all planes He comes to help, to heal, to instruct, to bless; wherever there are those who need or who are engaged in loving service, there does He appear and give definite proof of the Father's love for His children.

But how does He know when there is a need, you ask.

Do you know anything about vibration? Most of you do, those who understand about "tuning in" on a Radio to a certain wave-length to get what is "on the air" and is being broadcasted by a certain station.

Do you know that each human brain is a perfect receiving and a perfect sending station, and is exactly the same as a Radio built for both purposes? Only the human brain existed first, and there were certain human intelligences who studied the mechanism of the mind's working to such effect that they were able to produce mechanical instruments by which they could create vibrations that would go forth "on the air" both as sounds and pictures and would be received by reciprocal instruments built to record them, even as the human mind is constantly sending and receiving them.

You are continually sending forth from your mind station both thought and picture vibrations which are being received perhaps by many other mind stations attuned to receive them. And it is from other mind sending stations that you are continually getting the many thought pictures and suggestions which enter your mind station—if you do not have it shut off. The trouble is very few turn off their mental switches but let anything of whatever nature that happens to be "on the air" come in, and they may be hearing jazz music, jazz talks, and seeing jazz pictures all day long—just as some let their Radios run all day long, and most of the night also.

Now selfless love is the highest vibration known to man, and is the vibration above all vibrations to which Christ Jesus is attuned. Therefore when anyone in pure and selfless love directs their thoughts to Him, He receives them as your Radio receives what comes from the station to which it is tuned in. And to His Mind, being of the highest type, there comes also a vision of the sender accompanying his or her thought vibrations; even as television machines bring pictures of those speaking or singing amid the scenes that surround them.

You all know that this is done instantaneously. But Jesus' Mind, because of its being such a high type, is in no way limited, as are mechanical instruments, and He can receive and appreciate messages coming at the same time from many senders, and can answer them all by instantaneous loving thoughts and blessings sent in return.

And if you will think how television operates you can glimpse how in psychic visions the Master seems to appear before the various seers and to speak to or bless them, or whatever it is that He intends to convey. The fact in most cases probably is that He just sends His loving messages mentally and the human mind, being naturally far less perfect than His mind, receives and outpictures it according to the nature of its religious and mental training, believing Him to be personally present; even as some might believe a television picture was an actual experience enacted in their presence.

Those who have studied the processes of the human mind know that its nature is such as automatically to build mental pictures of every thought vibration that enters the consciousness. A thought thus becomes a picture, and on all the outer and inner planes of human consciousness what one really sees are the mind's picturized interpretations of thoughts or vibrations coming from the minds of others. These pictures or thought creations fill the astral and mental realms of mortal consciousness, and as they all have to be redeemed and lifted up into the Christ Consciousness, you can see what a work we have to do. But with the Master's help we who know are about our Father's business, which is carrying the Light of Love—of the Christ knowing—down into the darkness of men's minds, lighting them as fast and as much as is possible at the present time.

The above does not mean that Jesus does not actually visit and heal and bless by His personal Presence in the lower planes of the inner realms. When it is necessary He always comes, but as you may realize it is only in extreme cases that He does

not accomplish what He wills *mentally* through the
wonderful power of His Divine Wisdom and Love,
or through His Disciples and the many workers
under them, through Whom He principally works.

Study the Radio in connection with your own
thought processes in the light of the above, and
many illuminating explanations of mental phenomena will come to you and you may be able consciously to send and receive messages and to see
their senders and those who receive them.

Speaking the Word

In the 16th chapter we gave you suggestions to
try out in Group Work, and urged that you learn
the words on the card "Speaking the Word" and
practice using them so that you can speak them
freely and with full conviction of their Spiritual
power.

Some have reported using them with most bene-
ficial results, and we wish now to impress upon you
the importance of studying and perfectly acquaint-
ing yourselves with all that was stated about their
use in the first article of the 16th chapter. In fact
all should study carefully the whole article, for
these instructions when learned and proven are the
basis of all future work, and will establish you in
the consciousness necessary for real work in the
Cause of Brotherhood.

The truly in earnest ones will find, when speaking
these words in this consciousness, because of their
being pure Truth they have a magical power and
do bring about a definite change in the conscious-

ness of those for whom they are spoken. A healing results, or a happy change in conditions, or a freeing from mental bondage—whatever was the relief sought, convincing you that you are being used to help and bless others.

The question will arise, for just whom should one speak the Word—for anyone that asks, or for anyone who needs and who has not asked for help?

In the first place try always to be guided by the strong, loving urge in your heart, and always speak them with your heart filled with a loving desire to help. And then whenever called upon to help, turn within for guidance, and obey whatever you are led to do. If you always follow these suggestions you will never make any mistake.

Because the words given are the Truth about every human soul—for they are about the Higher Self of every soul—when spoken in the full consciousness of that Truth, only good and a blessing can result. But your mind must be cleansed of all doubt and hesitation, and only a confident knowing must accompany the words as they go forth on their mission.

When you have accustomed yourself thus to see and know Truth and to speak powerfully from that knowing, then you are ready for definite work.

Let each Group, when sufficiently established in this knowing, choose for itself how it can best serve in its community. Let them at a meeting selected ahead for this purpose, after meditation and prayer

decide on some regular active service, each one dedicating him or herself to the Master, Christ Jesus,
asking to be used to further in every way possible
the Work the Father is doing through the Brotherhood. Ask that you may become a conscious and
integral part of the Brotherhood, so that you may
work as one with Them.

Along with the service you have chosen to do—
whether it be a simple healing service held at a
stated hour each day, or if it be a more comprehen-
sive work that may be given to you from the Spirit
—we now suggest the following:

Each noon at 12 o'clock, whether a member of a
Group or not, train yourself to let nothing interfere with your dropping whatever you are doing,
preferably going into a room where you may be
alone—the same room each day—if possible, and
to "Speak the Word" according to the card, preceded by the following (adding whatever you may
be led to say):

*"Beloved Father, I come again this day to offer
myself as a channel through which Thou canst pour
the Light of Thy Love and Truth into the world of
men's consciousness.*

*"Through Thy power vested in me, I now speak
these words of Truth and direct the Light of Thy
Love especially to—(naming those you would help);
also to all the dear ones who are similarly consciously serving Thee; to all who are seeking the
Light, but whose human selves are still wandering*

*in darkness; to the President of our Country, and
to all representatives of Thy people who are holding
high places and who have pledged to do their duty
worthily in Thy sight; and finally to all souls, dear
Father, whom Thou wish quickened, awakened by
these Words and by them recalled to that which
they came into the world to do,—*

*"Beloved of God, in your true being, etc. (then
proceed with the words on the card.—see Appendix)."*

The faithful, regular and zealous following of
these instructions will accustom your mind and all
its faculties to actual service, and will train you into
being a capable instrument for the Master's use.
More than all it will be instilling into your mind
the consciousness of actually being used by the
Brotherhood; for definite evidence of such use will
soon be noted, from the blessed results that will
follow.

True workers, that is, conscious workers, those
fully conscious of the power and authority vested in
them as actual members of the Brotherhood of the
Spirit, are only too few; and the need is so great
that when any are found who give themselves sincerely and selflessly to the Master anxious to serve,
let no one doubt that they will be quickly put to
work; opportunities will soon be brought to them
and they will be shown clearly how they can serve.

However it is earnestly hoped by this time that
everyone anxious to serve will have so disciplined
the mind that it has become an obedient servant of

the will. An excellent aid to such discipline is in your daily meditation to arrange with the other members of your Group to meditate each day at the same hour and to meet in spirit at the same place— the one where you hold your weekly meetings. Try to see each one sitting in his or her regular chair and to *know* if they are actually there and check up afterwards to prove if you were correct in determining if they were or were not present meditating with you. For those who "feel" and "see" themselves in their places at such times are actually there in their soul bodies, and will be seen or sensed by the others who are sensitive enough.

This is a most valuable practice, for it may develop clairvoyant and other powers that will prove most useful in many ways, as you will soon learn.

Thus you will find yourself coming into that which your Higher Self intended from the beginning—the power to serve and to be a selfless instrument for His use. May it speedily manifest for each one who reads these words, is our earnest prayer.

CHAPTER 20

"THE COMFORTER"

IN THE last three chapters we have studied the various aspects of our Lord Jesus Christ that relate intimately to us, and we have found Him to be so vitally a part of ourselves that our nature and our consciousness would not be what they are without Him.

We have learned how He is both our Divine Teacher and the Way-Shower sent us by the Father, and that He is always available and will unfailingly come to us when we have need of Him. As a proof of this hear these His words:

"Let not your heart be troubled. Ye believe in God, believe also in me. . . . I go to prepare a place for you.

"And if I go to prepare a place for you, I will come again and receive you unto myself; that where I am, there ye may be also."—John 14:1-3.

"I will not leave you comfortless; I will come to you.

"Yet a little while and the world seeth me no more; but ye see me: because I live, ye shall live also.

"At that day ye shall know that I am in my Father, and ye in me, and I in you.

"He that hath my commandments, and keepeth them, he it is that loveth me; and he that loveth me shall be loved of my Father, and I will love him, and will manifest myself to him."—John 14:18–21.

If you will remember, these words were spoken to His disciples on that last night before His betrayal, and show that He knew what was before Him; His earthly work was finished—the part He had to do, and there remained now only the final act of the fulfillment of the prophecies—the yielding up of His life that the world could be saved.

He had given to the world the teaching. He had shown humanity the way all must live if they would come unto the Father and have eternal life. He had taught His disciples many deep truths, and they recognized His divinity and loved Him as their Teacher and Elder Brother, and believed Him to be the Christ, the Messiah sent of God.

But Jesus knew that because of their great love for Him—the man—they were as yet unable to grasp in its fullness the spirit of what He had been teaching. So in that last talk with them, after washing their feet, following His statements above quoted, He voiced these memorable words:

"These things have I spoken unto you, being yet present with you.

"But the Comforter, which is the Holy Ghost, whom the Father will send in my name, he shall teach you all things, and bring all things to your

remembrance whatsoever I have said unto you."—
John 14:25–26.

*"These things have I told you, that when the time
shall come, ye may remember that I told you of
them. And these things I said not unto you at
the beginning, because I was with you.*

*"But now I go my way to him that sent me;
. . . but because I have said these things unto you,
sorrow hath filled your heart.*

*"Nevertheless I tell you the truth; It is expedient
for you that I go away; for if I go not away, the
Comforter will not come unto you; but if I depart,
I will send him unto you."*—John 16:4–7.

*"I have yet many things to say unto you, but ye
cannot bear them now.*

*"Howbeit when he, the Spirit of truth, is come,
he will guide you unto all truth."*—John 16:12–13.

Who is the Comforter? Has he come to you, dear
friend?

You who are a follower and disciple of Jesus
Christ, and who love Him even as His disciples
loved Him when He lived among them, do you
realize that it is expedient that He, the *man* Jesus,
go away that the Comforter may come *to you.*

What do we mean? Is this not inconsistent with
what we have previously written?

No, it only emphasizes what He, our blessed Master and Teacher, Himself, would have you realize.
He, the Man and Teacher, has taught you all these

wonderful truths and has shown you the way unto
the Father, but now *He* must go away and *you*
must *apply* these truths, must follow in the way
He pointed and where He has gone; you must
turn within and seek Him *in the Kingdom,* where
He now is and where He has prepared a place
for you.

And as surely as you truly love Him and prove
it, as He said—by keeping His commandments, He
will not leave you comfortless. He will send the
Comforter, and on that day you will know that He
is in the Father, You in Him, and *He in you—that
you are all* ONE.

From all this you will see how imperative it is
that you seek *first* the Kingdom, seek and find the
Comforter *within you;* that you turn from the
Teacher *without,* even from your worship of Jesus
the Teacher, and seek to obey fully His teachings,
*so that the Comforter can come and guide you unto
all Truth.*

Do you grasp what we mean?

Try to realize that Jesus was not really a man,
but that He was *and is* the Spirit of God taken form
and living in a human body. He was *and is* the
Christ, the Logos, the actual LOVE of God, our
Father, made manifest.

In that last talk with His disciples He tried hard
to have them understand this, and it was what He
meant when He said that they could not "bear"

what He had to tell them then, and that He, the man, must go, so that He *as Love, the Comforter,* could come and guide them to all truth; and that *through Love He could again manifest to them.*

And it was Love, the Spirit of God, that the Father would send *in His Name,* or *as representing Him,* to teach them all things, the things He could not teach them while He was with them, because they would not understand so long as they worshipped and looked only to Him, Jesus the Man. But in that day, when Love, the Comforter, came and was established and *living in their hearts,* then they would know the *real* Christ, the Christ which was the real Jesus; and they would then know that they too were *in* the Father, and that the Father was *in* them.

From this you may now understand what Jesus meant when He said, *"If I go to prepare a place for you, I will come again and receive you unto myself; that where I am, ye may be also."* And, *"At that day ye shall know that I am in the Father, and ye in me, and I in you."* Also read the 19th and 21st verses of John 14.

Thus you see how Christ Jesus becomes the Comforter, the Holy Ghost, the Spirit of Truth, who will teach us all things and guide us unto all truth.

In the light received from these remarkable words, we earnestly urge that everyone study most carefully the 13th, 14th, 15th, and 16th chapters of St. John, trying to grasp all of the wondrous meaning therein. A glorious reward awaits all who persist until they get what the Master intends for them.

From what has been stated it should be clear that in these chapters Jesus sought to impress upon His disciples what was the crux—the vital essence of His Message and Mission upon Earth, so that they might carry it unto all the World and thus finally bring about the redemption of humanity.

The Christ, the Holy Spirit of the Father, is *within every Man,* is the Real Self of every man, even as it was the Real Self of Jesus. That was the essence of His Message, and must be the essence of the teaching of every one of His disciples, in order that all men may seek and find the Christ as the Comforter within themselves. And when they have found Him there, they become His true followers, and ever afterwards seek to have all of their brothers also find Him there.

Think you that Jesus has changed? He wants not your worship now, no more than He wanted it then. His work is as much now as it was then—if not more so—to have all men find the Christ within, that all may become a part of the One Consciousness where Divine Love rules; for only by seeking and finding that can humanity be redeemed and be led back into the Father's Kingdom, which Jesus tried so hard to explain and to have all understand is the great goal of humanity.

Now we would apply this truth in some very important ways.

First, to those who perhaps feel because they have never been blessed with a vision of the Master that they are not worthy enough or are not as Spiritual as others so privileged. Just know that if you are conscious of a Great Love in your heart and your soul yearns to serve wherever you can, you are surely known to the Master and are beloved and blessed by Him and by the Father. And also know that many of the world's greatest servers have not known conscious illumination and have never seen the Master's face.

Secondly, to those who are more or less conscious on the inner planes, and who believe they are being guided and taught by intelligences there. Let all such know that if such teachers are doing everything possible to help you find the Christ within, constantly pointing out to you that Christ as your Higher Self is the Greatest Teacher and God's Spirit within you, to whom you must always turn for confirmation of what they teach as your final authority, —then they are truly disciples of the Master sent to aid you to find the Kingdom. All others, no matter who they claim to be or who you assume them to be; no matter how much knowledge they may be teaching or how marvelous seem the things they say and do for you,—are leading you on to disappointment, disillusionment and discouragement; for they are not the Divine Ones your mind believes them to be. (Reread in this connection the chapter on Masters in *"The Impersonal Life."*) Think long and carefully on this, and seek positive confirmation of it from the Comforter *within your heart*.

Thirdly, to those who are receiving teachings from some earthly teacher, society, order, or religion, and whose teachings at present satisfy you and seem to be of the highest type. If they are teaching as above, ever pointing you within to Christ as the one source and authority for you; and not attracting and holding your interest by the promise of powers to be gained by purchasing and studying their teachings, subtly drawing your attention to themselves or to their leaders and to the powers and wonders accomplished by them,—then they too are beloved disciples and centers of Light and are bringing many souls to the harvest.

Those who are charging for their teachings, requiring students to pay a set price, while they may be helping many to gain the first principles of the truth, yet you may know they have no real Spiritual knowledge to impart; for Spiritual teachings are not given through such channels. Those who are drawn to such teachers and who pay the prices asked, however, get value received; for in time they learn what such teachers do not and cannot teach, and if they are real seekers they will later be brought to the consciousness where they can receive the true teachings of the Spirit.

Always remember then that within you is your Higher Self, the Comforter, the Christ of God, Who knows all things, and Who, when you turn in loving faith and trust to Him, will guide you unto all

Truth; that your **Higher** Self, as a Son of God, is superior to any **Master,** Guide or Teacher, for they likewise are guided and taught by their Higher Selves, Who are one with yours in Christ. Therefore there is sure guidance and the highest authority for you always *within you,* no matter how far you climb the Spiritual heights. And also remember that what any teacher, regardless of his name, wisdom or authority, teaches you, must always be confirmed by your Higher Self, before you can accept it and make it your own.

Think very earnestly on all of the above and see if any of it affects seriously any of your previous beliefs. If so, seek within for guidance—not from any outside teacher, and from outside we mean from any entity other than your Higher Self; for the time is here when you must decide whom you will serve—the Master within, or the one without.

Occult Teachings

Many are being attracted these days by teachings about the hidden or occult side of life, because of being stirred by forces within themselves causing strange dreams and inner experiences and for which they naturally seek explanations.

Many, without understanding what is taking place, are unfolding psychic or spiritual faculties as a natural growth, due largely to the powerful new spiritual force now active and affecting the whole earth and all upon it, and symbolized by the sign of Aquarius, a man walking across the skies pouring water from a pitcher; for we are now passing out from under the sign of Pisces, the fishes, and entering the Aquarian Age, which means that we are at the close of one Dispensation and that a new one is beginning.

We have been trying in preceding articles to prepare the minds of those who are accompanying us by telling them of their complex natures; teaching what is the soul, its life and its home, its relation to the human mind, and the necessary control of the personality the soul must obtain, through the mind, before the soul can accomplish what it came into physical embodiment to do.

Most of the earnest ones now realize that the outer man—the personality—is nothing but an instrument which the soul, under the direction of the Higher Self, is training to that end; and therefore it is not strange that many such are becoming more or less conscious of the inner man, the soul, and are being given glimpses of the inner life, the life of the soul.

And so we strongly feel that the time is come when much of the mystery that previously surrounded this inner life, due principally to ignorance of the definite part this life plays in man's spiritual growth, be entirely cleared away. And so we are making this a phase of our work.

The so-called "occultist" in the past has had much to do with creating so much mystery about this inner life. Occult means "covered from sight, con-

cealed, hidden," and an occultist in its true sense
would be one who studies and acquaints himself in
practical and useful ways with the hidden or invisible side of life. So that everyone who is studying
these teachings then is really an occultist.

But so much stigma has attached to the word
"occult," because of its being applied to teachings
and practices of a questionable character, which are
not serving and enlightening mankind, but are instead making the information gained serve selfish
ends by giving it out in a perverted or veiled form,
that many sincere students are repelled by anything
bearing the name "occult."

Another reason is that otherwise worthy students
who have gained a certain amount of knowledge of
the inner life and its laws and the accompanying
power such knowledge gives, and who pride themselves on being "occultists," look down upon other
students, those of the mystic and devotional type,
and particularly those who are declared followers
of Christ's teachings, deeming such as still on the
emotional plane and not yet progressed to the stage
the occultist has reached, where mind is supreme.

We will not enlarge upon this peculiarity of "occultists," for those who read probably have had personal experience with such. But we would caution
those who are convinced by an inner knowing of
Spiritual realities and who perhaps repudiate the
claims of such occultists, believing them to be not
of Christ, not to let pride enter and affect them in

any way. For all the knowledge and power that the occultist has gained through mental study and proven logic must later be gained—if not in this lifetime, in a succeeding one—by those who have found God and Christ within themselves, so that the Master within may use such knowledge and power for the purpose for which alone they are given; while the occultist must "come back" with all his intellectual knowledge and power and devote it solely to the use of the Loving One *within,* if and when he awakens to His Presence and consciously waits upon Him there.

And hearken! Both these stages are of equal importance—neither is higher than the other; for both will be superseded by a stage that will succeed them —when they are both given over wholly to the Master's use.

We mean just that; for not until all knowledge, all power, all consciousness of self and separation is merged into the Consciousness of the Master, the I AM, the Christ Self, so that there are no longer two—the higher and the lower self, but only One— the Master Self, neither the occultist or the mystic has found what his soul is seeking and what eventually he will find.

And here is another great truth that all must realize: all faculties and all powers given to man are *good*—when developed and used unselfishly and for the good of others. This includes all psychic gifts that have unfolded *naturally* in one who is earnestly trying to live the higher life. When they unfold in such it is for a good purpose, which all should strive unceasingly to learn by dedicating them to Christ and asking that He teach and guide them in their proper use.

We will again state that the inner life is just as real and just as natural a manifestation of the human consciousness as is the physical life, for in reality they are *one*—they are but the inner and outer phases of the one life of the soul; in fact the outer could not be if the inner soul phase did not exist.

This means that the astral phase of the inner life is just as natural as the mental or the physical phase, for just as long as the human soul has in its nature any emotions and any desires, good or bad, they must express on the astral plane, and the astral plane will be just as real a place to the soul as is the physical plane, to one whose inner senses are open to the astral—that is, to the emotional or desire world.

We tell you this that all may know that what is unfolding in them is a result of the spiritual quickening taking place in everyone, and that they may view it in a common sense way. And it *is* a spiritual quickening, for all is spirit, because all is God, and there is nothing that is not a part of Him and is not taking place in His Consciousness.

Never forget that, and therefore seek to learn His purpose in everything that is coming to you. He permits or sends it only for good. When you find that good you will learn its purpose, and will begin to co-operate with God and good, and that good then actually becomes yours.

APPENDIX

MEDITATION No. 1

I ALONE AM

DEAR FRIEND:

Do you truly want to come speedily and eternally into your own—that which you came here into manifestation to express?

Then meditate earnestly and persistently day after day on the below—ten minutes or more on the first part, until you realize its Truth:

In the ONE MIND there is the consciousness only of wholeness, completion, and perfection. In it there are no ideas of lack or limitation of supply of any kind.

To every center of that Mind—and every human mind is such a center—there flows naturally every needed idea, even as air rushes into a vacuum, or as the blood carries to every cell of the body everything needed for their growth and sustenance.

Remember, that One Mind is in You—Is YOUR MIND—as there is only One Mind.

Also remember, by your realization of this great Truth, and making it the dominant fact in your consciousness, are you and your Father truly One. For it unites your consciousness with His Consciousness, He who is your REAL SELF, and Whose Mind is the ONLY Mind (of course it does for you are then *in* His Consciousness); and therefore YOU ARE all that He is, and ALL THAT HE HAS IS YOURS.

Once believe this—once KNOW it, and you will be free from ALL lack and limitation FOREVER.

*　　*　　*　　*　　*

Then after trying to realize intensely the Truth of the above by thus meditating and letting it soak into your subconsciousness, let the following flood your consciousness for ten minutes more:

Be still, my child, and know *I* am your Life, your Health, your Strength, your Understanding, your Supply, your Power, your Love.

I am all these things—all these ideals you are seeking to be and to have.

Oh, my child, can you not see you can have none of these apart from Me—can get none without getting Me,—can get them nowhere else but from Me, your Real, your ONLY Self, who am all these things Now—and therefore YOU also are these things Now, AND FOREVER MORE.

SEE this, beloved, and know the Truth of your Self.

Come unto Me all ye who are weary and heavy laden, and I will give you rest.

Can you not realize that this life in you, any portion of health or strength or power or love or

APPENDIX 337

understanding that you have, is not of yourself, but is of ME, who am all these things IN you.

Then why not have done with your foolish, anxious striving to be that which you are now, always were, and always will be, in supreme fullness and perfection? Why not then let go completely and let Me, your Real and Perfect Self, have full sway in your consciousness, *letting no thoughts therein you know are not My thoughts?*

That is all YOU need to do—*I* will do the rest.

Beloved, if you abide thus in Me, and let this My Word abide in you, everything your heart seeketh will surely come to pass, in blessed richness and abundance.

A PRAYER

BELOVED Father; Thou, Oh blessed Christ Jesus; and Thou, our dear Brothers of the Kingdom,—hear this our earnest prayer.

Draw us in Consciousness deep within where Thou art, where self exists not, and where we may be one with and abide with Thee in Christ.

Help us to open wide our hearts and let out the Great Love, that It may possess us utterly, may rule, motivate and inspire our every thought, word and act, merging us completely into Love, thereby enabling us to love as Thou lovest, to see as Thou seest, to hear as Thou hearest; lifting the consciousness of our human minds into complete oneness with

our Christ Consciousness—Thy Consciousness; so
that henceforth we can consciously, at will, be with
Thee, work with Thee, commune with Thee, face
to face, at all times and on all planes, when the need
is in the Father's service; and may know with Thy
Understanding all things we seek and need to
know.

Cleanse us of all consciousness of self and of
separation from Thee, so that our Lord Christ henceforth may live His Life in us, do His Will in us,
be His Self in us, without let or hindrance of any
kind, for evermore.

BELOVED Father, make us to abide always in Thy
Consciousness, and Thy Word to abide in us, giving
us ever of Thy Wisdom to light and direct our
way; Thy Will to strengthen and sustain us; and
Thy Love to surround, protect and fill us; so that
we may see Thee, dear Christ, may feel Thee, may
know Thee, may be truly One with Thee, everywhere, in everything, and in every one of our
brothers.

We thank and glorify Thee, Beloved Father, for
Thy many blessings. Take us wholly unto Thyself,
so that we may be selfless and perfect instruments
for Thy use.

In Christ Jesus' Name, we ask it. AMEN.

MEDITATION No. 2

The following exercises are given for the development of mental power within yourself.

Seat yourself in a chair, in your own room if possible, or in one in which you will be undisturbed. Take a positive position, sitting upright, but comfortably, so that you will be as unconscious of your body as possible.

Now close your eyes and try to visualize the room as a mental room, or one within your mind in which you are going to fill full of and confine the mental qualities of Discrimination, Strength, the Power to Concentrate, and Truth, for your future and continuous use.

Then try to realize that you are actually a center of God's consciousness, for in His consciousness we all live, move and have our being; and that this mind which you call your mind is a center or focal point of His Mind—just as the consciousness of each cell of your body is a center or focal point of your mind—and that therefore deep within your mind there must be always present and ever available God's Love, Intelligence and Power; in fact, all that God Is in His Consciousness.

Now try to "see" this Consciousness—the Holy Love or Spirit of God—pouring forth from deep within and flowing through and radiating from you to all other centers of His Consciousness as a brilliant White Light; which Light in very truth is the Spiritual Self to one who has the inner sight, for It is the Light which lighteth every man that cometh into the world. Therefore realize that *you are that Light*, and that your mind being a part of God's Mind, you can consciously and actually call forth from within that Mind—if motivated and accompanied only by unselfish Love—any needed quality, for in It of course exist all God qualities.

Therefore "see" your Light ever shining and going thus *before* you, lighting fully your path and making everything so clear that no possible shadow can intrude to deceive or hinder your perfect spiritual sight and hence your fullest understanding. This gives true *Discrimination*.

Likewise, to your *right* see this Light radiating and pouring forth from you into the mental atmosphere of that part of your room as the *Strength* of Divine Mind, ever ready to support and sustain you in any need, and to enable you to do anything you wish to do.

While on your *left* see the great Light of *Truth* likewise flowing forth to fill that part of your mentality, so that whenever you need to know anything, no matter what, it is ever ready to flood your consciousness and to make all clear to you.

And then *back* of you, see this great Light from within pouring forth and filling that part of your mentality with the *Power to concentrate and focus it*, whenever you want to direct your mind upon any given idea or to any desired end.

Just see this Light as a mighty Power ever back of you, waiting to pour through your consciousness (as through a funnel) in which is held the idea you wish clearly to understand or the picture that you wish to outmanifest—whenever you call upon this Power to direct the Light of Divine Mind upon it. See your intellect or visioning faculty (located in the front of your mind back of center of forehead) serving as a lens to focus the Light and reflect the perfect picture in the outer realms of consciousness or of physical manifestation.

Just as the light pours through the small lens of a magic lantern, when you turn on the electric power, and throws the picture on the plate upon the screen, so will this Power, when you thus consciously direct it with intense purpose, cause the Light, Life and Substance of Divine Mind to pour into and through the idea or picture *you are holding in your mind* and will outmanifest it either as a perfect knowing or as the fulfillment of your desire.

Study this last carefully and *prove* it, for it can be used to acquire any needed wisdom, power or ability, or to create and make manifest any righteous thing or condition. But *be very sure you have the approval of your Higher Self* of that which you wish manifested; for it should never be attempted unless inspired by a loving desire to help someone or to fit yourself for the Father's use.

This rounds out your mentality, filling it full of those qualities that you want ever available for use. Any other qualities can be similarly brought forth and made available. The practice of actually calling forth these qualities from within you and "seeing" them surrounding you and filling your mental room, thereby creates an aura that will always surround and protect you. For it will be of such high vibration, because of the brilliancy of its Light and the Power of Love radiating from it, that none of the forces of darkness can penetrate or even approach. The powers of Discrimination and Truth thus built into your aura will instantly detect any inimical or inharmonious vibrations and enable you to know how to deal with them.

This practice also will gradually, if you do it faithfully day after day, make you conscious of the mighty Power *you* are, and of the wonderful instrument you have in this mind of yours, as you learn to make it obey your slightest command. This is what is meant above where it said that these exercises are for the development of mental power within yourself; they are that you may not only develop power, but that you may *become* Power, may learn to know *Who* you are and of *What* you are a part. But always remember that Power and Knowledge avail nothing unless Love inspires and directs their use.

Speaking the Word

For the Soul-quickening of those you would help.

.... (Repeat the name), dear one, in your true being you are one with the Father and with the Son, and in the Oneness of Consciousness of the Holy Spirit, your eternal abode, you walk and commune with and *know* with Them—

know that *you are Spirit*, holy, harmonious, pure, powerful, perfect; that all that the Father hath is yours, and that for you an abundance of riches is waiting to outmanifest. (Or for healing,—that all that the Father Is, *you are*, and that perfect health, strength and happiness is yours to express.)

Then let there be perfect Peace and Understanding, and truest Love and Trust between you and Them at all times and on all planes; that you may positively and continually manifest and be, may know and see, may think and speak and do, that only which the Father wills for you.

.....................(Repeat the given name), you are *not* bound by any claims of the flesh, or of the world, or of Mammon, or of the separate, selfish mind; for *these have no existence in Spirit.*

Then let the perfection of your True Self, and all of your Divine powers and understanding, all of your soul riches (or of your true health or happiness, which you would proclaim for such), and your own Good, which the Father hath waiting for you, *come forth* Now, and fully manifest—that the Father may be glorified in the Son that you are.

Say this slowly and powerfully, trying to put all the meaning and love into the words that you can. Then try to realize that these words go forth—as would a beam of powerful Light into the darkness —straight to the soul consciousness of the one addressed; that the soul will surely receive them, will be awakened by them, and will be reminded by them of its Divine nature and heritage.

Then know that as soon as the brain mind gets quiet the Truth will push through from the soul into the brain consciousness as an illumined thought from the Higher Self, and the one addressed will awaken from his dream of lack, disease or limitation of whatsoever nature, and will know the Truth, when all such false claims will dissolve in his consciousness to nothingness and their outer manifestation will disappear.

After fully realizing this, sing from the heart:

"We thank Thee, beloved Father, and praise Thy Holy Word, which is Spirit, which is Truth, which is Life, which is Power to accomplish that whereunto it is sent; for we send them in the Name of Christ Jesus, our Saviour and Redeemer. AMEN."

Books for Supplemental Reading

The Impersonal Life
The Teacher**
Wealth**
Brotherhood*
The Way Out
The Way Beyond**
Good and Evil*
Receiving and Giving*
The Great White Brotherhood*
Light on the Path, by Mabel Collins
As a Flower Grows,* by Mabel Collins
Talks to Students* by Manly P. Hall
Hunches,* by Anna W. Eldridge
Light of the Soul, by Alice Bailey

CPSIA information can be obtained at www.ICGtesting.com
Printed in the USA
BVOW08s0130150715

408622BV00002B/390/P